The Twentieth Century:
1914 to the Present

The Structure of European History
studies and interpretations

NORMAN F. CANTOR *and*
MICHAEL S. WERTHMAN, *Editors*

The Twentieth Century: 1914 to the Present

edited by NORMAN F. CANTOR

University of Illinois, Chicago Circle

and MICHAEL S. WERTHMAN

AHM PUBLISHING CORPORATION
ARLINGTON HEIGHTS, ILLINOIS 60004

ISBN: 0-88295-715-5 (Formerly 0-690-78138-5)
Library of Congress Card Number: 67-16644

Printed in the United States of America
738
Sixth Printing

ACKNOWLEDGMENTS: The editors wish to express their gratitude to the following publishers and individuals for permission to quote selections from the works designated:

Raymond Aron, *The Century of Total War*. Copyright 1954 by Raymond Aron. Reprinted by permission of the author and Doubleday & Company, Inc.

Geoffrey Barraclough, *An Introduction to Contemporary History*. Copyright © 1964 by Geoffrey Barraclough. Reprinted by permission of C. A. Watts & Co. Ltd., the original publisher, and Basic Books, Inc.

Alan Bullock, *Hitler: A Study in Tyranny*. Completely Revised Edition. Copyright © 1962 by Alan Bullock. Reprinted by permission of Harper and Row, Publishers, Incorporated and Odhams Books Ltd.

E. H. Carr, *The Bolshevik Revolution, 1917–1923*, Vol. I. Copyright 1950 by Edward H. Carr. Reprinted with permission of The Macmillan Company and Macmillan & Co. Ltd.

A. J. P. Taylor, *The Struggle for Mastery in Europe, 1848–1918*. Reprinted by permission of The Clarendon Press, Oxford.

Preface

The Structure of European History is an anthology series whose purpose is to present to the undergraduate and lay reader leading interpretations of fundamental political, economic, social, and intellectual change in European history from the advent of civilization to the present day. The series is devoted to the following eras of European history:

Ancient Civilization: 4000 B.C.–400 A.D., Second Edition

Medieval Society: 400–1450, Second Edition

Renaissance, Reformation, and Absolutism: 1450–1650,
    Second Edition

The Making of the Modern World: 1815–1914

The Twentieth Century: 1914 to the Present

Every volume consists of five relatively long selections each of which is preceded by an editors' introduction that outlines the problem, identifies the author, defines his methods and assumptions, and establishes his interpretation within the historiography of the subject. A brief list of additional important books on the same subject or on related subjects follows each selection. Each volume contains a brief introduction to the period as a whole that delineates the leading themes by which modern scholarship has illuminated the era.

All but one of the twenty-five selections in the series were written in the past forty years and the majority since 1940. In recent decades

Preface

historians of Europe have sought to extrapolate broad movements of historical change from the vast amount of data that modern research has built up. There has been a general tendency in modern scholarship to bridge the conventional compartmentalization of political, economic, social, and intellectual history and to analyze a movement or event which falls primarily in one of these categories within the context of a total view of social and cultural change. Historians more and more attempt to present a picture of the past as rich, as complex, and as full as human experience itself. The intertwining and mutual involvement of many kinds of aspirations and achievements are now seen to be the basic existential facts shaping previous societies just as they shape social conditions in our own time.

We have sought in these volumes to present to the student and lay reader examples of this comprehensive and total approach to the understanding of European history. In making our selections we have been governed by the criterion of choosing interpretations which view critical movements and trends in the history of Western civilization in as broad and as many-faceted a context as possible. We have also aimed to make selections which are distinguished by a clear and forceful style and which can be easily comprehended by students in a freshman survey course and by the college-educated reader.

Most of the selections in each of the volumes of this series are the original, seminal theses presented by distinguished scholars after many years of research and reflection. In a few instances the criterion of comprehension by the novice student and lay reader has led us to take an extract from a work of synthesis and high vulgarization which in turn is based on very important monographic studies.

N.F.C.
M.S.W.

Contents

vii

Introduction

There are historians still at work who were high school students during the First World War, and for all the senior members of the historical profession the events of the 1920's and 30's were among the great experiences that determined their lives and conditioned their outlooks. Until the 1950's it was fashionable for historians to look upon the most modern and contemporary era of history as beyond the limits of their subject. It used to be thought that the history of an era could be written only when it lay half a century or so in the past, when, so to speak, the historical dust had settled and the historian could take an "objective" view of what had happened, free from the passions and concerns of the present. The study of the contemporary era was something to be left to political scientists, sociologists, and journalists, all of whom were supposedly lacking in the austere dignity of the historian.

In the past two decades academic historians have abandoned this attitude, and the history of the contemporary world of the past half century has received careful and critical analysis. The line between past and present has grown less distinct. Historians have come more and more to agree with Benedetto Croce's view that in a sense they are studying "an eternal present" and that the world of the past is largely understood in terms of current experience. The feudal world of the twelfth century is illuminated by our knowledge of changes in underdeveloped societies today; the pattern of the industrial revolution of the eighteenth century has been repeated in many twentieth-century societies; the experience of contemporary revolutions enables us to understand more clearly the course of the French Revolution and the attitudes of its leaders. There is a growing consensus that historians, sociologists, political scientists, and cultural anthropologists are all studying the same subject, the nature of social change, and the examination of this problem with reference to the recent and contemporary era is as valid an undertaking for the historian as the study of any period before 1914.

Nevertheless the study of the twentieth century does offer special problems for the historian. The closer to the present the events that are being considered, the harder it is for the historian to get a firm perspective and to distinguish the important from the peripheral. There are, furthermore, some peculiar problems for the contemporary historian. Although the scholar who investigates the last fifty years of European history has a wealth of data, he encounters frustrating obstacles when he wants to examine the papers of important leaders. If the leader himself is not still alive and reluctant to be subjected to the scrutiny of academic scholarship, then his family and disciples are frequently determined to protect his reputation. Thus the papers of David Lloyd George, British prime minister during the First World War, are still not open to the public and many diplomatic records of the 1930's are still closed to general inquiry. A peculiar problem that the political historian of the contemporary era encounters is the fugitive nature of a great deal of twentieth-century communications as a result of telephone conversations and face-to-face conferences greatly facilitated by airplane travel. It may turn out that historians will

Introduction

know more about the motivations of nineteenth-century statesmen who left behind vast personal and official correspondence than of many comparably important twentieth-century leaders.

The shape of twentieth-century European history as it now appears in historical literature is an ambiguous and paradoxical combination of the themes of progress and achievement on the one hand, and disappointment and retrogression on the other. The last half century has seen the resolution, by and large, of the social problems caused by the industrial revolution in the Western world and the achievement of a generally high standard of living by the working classes as a result of the coming of the welfare state. The two decades since the Second World War have also witnessed the emancipation of the non-European peoples from direct Western imperialist exploitation and control. The last half century has been an era of unprecedented advance in theoretical and applied science and the understanding and control of nature by mankind to a degree scarcely dreamed of in 1914. On the other hand, the dangerous boom in world population, the colossal devastation and degradation of human life by authoritarian regimes, and the threat to the survival of the human race imposed by nuclear and biological weapons have made the twentieth century not only an era of progress and prosperity, but also one of hitherto unimaginable desperation, terror, and violence.

The five selections in this volume, from the work of five distinguished contemporary historians, illustrate the themes and subjects which have been most carefully investigated by academic scholars: the causes of the outbreak of the First World War; the way in which the Bolsheviks gained control of the Russian government and began a worldwide Communist revolutionary movement; the circumstances which allowed the Nazi seizure of power in Germany in the 1930's; the rise of American and Soviet hegemony in the world; and the emergence of a new world-consciousness.

The Outbreak of the First World War[*]

A. J. P. TAYLOR

The further in time we get from the events of the summer of 1914, the greater appears their significance and the more total loom the dimensions of the cataclysm that overtook European civilization in those few weeks. It is easy enough to say that European power and culture had reached its apogee and that western Europe was bound in any case slowly to lose its hegemony in the world in the succeeding decades. One can point to new doctrines of irrationalism, individualism, and nihilism which during the previous four decades had been undermining the cardinal doctrines of middle-class liberalism (see Volume V, Selection 5 in this series). One can point to a sharply intensified class conflict in England, France, and Germany after 1900. One can also point to the growing industrial and military power of the United States, Russia, and even of Japan and claim that the western European states in the twentieth century would have slowly and in-

[*] From A. J. P. Taylor, *The Struggle for Mastery in Europe, 1848-1918* (Oxford: The Clarendon Press, 1954), pp. 511-531.

4

evitably lost their world leadership to the powers on the periphery of the West. One can even venture to say that although in the half century before 1914 the European powers had selfishly carved colonies and spheres of influence out of Africa and Asia, the very penetration of Western technology into these primitive or slumbering civilizations would sooner or later have led to their partial westernization and rebellion against their European conquerors.

All these claims are plausible, and yet the fact remains that what happens in history is in the final analysis determined not by impersonal forces but by the free choice of individuals and societies. And in August of 1914, after avoiding a major conflagration for ninety-nine years, the leaders of the European states chose to become involved in a general war.

Of course these statesmen made a terrible miscalculation. As politicians and generals almost invariably do, they believed that the present war would follow the pattern and the military techniques of the previous one in their experience. It was thought that the Great War of 1914 would be decided in one campaign over two or three months and by one or two big battles, as had been the case with the Franco-Prussian War in 1870. They did not realize that because of the enormously increased firepower of artillery and the perfection of the machine gun, one of those moments had been reached in the history of warfare in which the defense catches up with the offense and only a long war of attrition can produce a victory. The one way out of the four years of unprecedented and still unmatched military slaughter (unmatched, that is, except for the German-Russian front of 1941–45) was the introduction of a new offensive weapon. Although this lay at hand in the technique of tank attack, which was in fact known to the British as early as 1915, the generals still believed in the glorious triumphs to be gained by cavalry and massed infantry attacks and refused to use the tank attack through four years of slaughter, while the world fell down around their ears.

If the First World War was not the irrevocable suicide of Europe —and a highly plausible argument can be made out that it was—

it inflicted such a severe wound on Western society that Europe and mankind in general entered a new era of violence, disorder, revolution, terror, and social transformation, an era in which we are still living and whose destiny is uncertain. Historians have taken great pains to list the consequences of the First World War, but they are so profound and far-reaching as to lie asymptotic to historical understanding. During the four years of mortal attrition, Europe lost a higher proportion of its population than at any other comparably short period since the Black Death of the mid-fourteenth century. And in some ways the impact of the loss of life in this case was even greater than that caused by the bubonic plague in late medieval society. The ten million killed in the First World War on the battlefield represented the best men out of a whole generation of European society, its potential leaders in every aspect of life. Is it any wonder that in the following quarter of a century the leaders of the European states should be singular in either their viciousness or their decrepitude? Only the old men or the bad men were left; hardly any men of high character and fine ideals survived the holocaust and those few who did were so shaken by the unspeakable magnitude of the cataclysm as to be impotent in the face of the forces of chaos and evil.

The First World War decimated the European aristocracy and destroyed what little credit remained to it. It bewildered and demoralized the bourgeoisie and greatly accelerated the decline in liberal idealism which had begun in the 1870's and 80's. The war also destroyed the three empires of central and eastern Europe. The extinction of the Austro-Hungarian empire left the Balkans in a power vacuum; the extinction of the Hohenzollern empire plunged Germany into an economic and political chaos and moral malaise that opened the way for the triumph of nazism. Most important of all, perhaps, the war almost inevitably brought down the already tottering tsarist regime in Russia and this in turn allowed for the Bolshevik triumph, which, except for the outbreak of the Great War, is the single most important political event of the twentieth century, for better or for worse. The catastrophic

*consequences of the war allowed the subjugated peoples of Africa
and Asia to raise their heads against their Western imperial masters and inaugurated the nationalist and independence movements
that expelled the Western rulers in the decade after 1945. These
Oriental and African peoples were therefore beneficiaries of the
First World War. The other beneficiaries of its terrible legacy were
the Russians, who under the new Communist regime began their
march to world leadership, and on the other flank the Americans,
who similarly found the way open for them, but who were reluctant
to take advantage of their opportunity until the 1940's. The struggle for power which in 1914 was still largely a European matter
became a conflict of worldwide proportions after 1918.*

*There are still yet other consequences that follow from the
First World War. After the first two years of conflict all the states
involved, but particularly England and Germany, had to undertake
unprecedented national control and direction of their domestic
economies. The experience thus gained in economic planning and
control was more influential in effecting the extinction of laissez
faire and bringing on the modern welfare state than all the passionate pronouncements of socialist theorists. The war also greatly
accelerated the discrediting and undermining of nineteenth-century
bourgeois culture that had been slowly going on for four decades.
The war separated the generation that controlled the instruments
of power from the one that was sent to die in the trenches or
would soon have died if the war had not finally come to an
end. The young did neither forgive nor forget the old men who
had told them that it was a good thing to be slaughtered in the
trenches; and everything that the old men stood for—their politics, their morals, their art, their literature, even their mode of at-
tire—was tainted forever with rottenness and corruption in the eyes
of the new generation. The First World War greatly diminished
the international solidarity of the working-class movement, but it
created a new international freemasonry of the young. A new
cult of rebellious youth emerged that has been one of the prime
faiths of twentieth-century civilization, all the way from the 1920's*

postwar "lost generation" to the Hitler Jugend *to the cult of the American adolescent and the Chinese Red Guards.*

Almost immediately after the seemingly endless agony was terminated in 1918, the states involved in the conflict sought to lay the blame at each other's door, or in the case of the Bolsheviks to add yet another listing in the litany of tsarist crimes. The governments published documents purporting to demonstrate their own innocence and the complicity and guilt of other parties. The historians of the 1920's, who in any case had a bizarre, insatiable appetite for diplomatic documents, studied these records and came up with a variety of "causes" of the First World War. These ranged from the balance of power system, through imperialist greed, to Germany's drive for world mastery, to the English liberal government's hesitancy and confusion, to France's desire for revenge, to Russia's Pan-Slav dreams of Balkan domination, and finally to the Austrian imperial government's desperate gamble to hold together its disintegrating empire.

After 1945 there was another round of historical inquiry into the causes for the outbreak of war in August 1914. The following analysis by the brilliant and prolific Oxford historian A. J. P. Taylor, published in 1954, pretty well sums up the consensus that has been widely assented to by scholars, including some of the younger generation of German historians. Taylor's thesis, from his very close study of the sources, is that if blame is to fall on any country for undertaking steps which made inevitable a general war in Europe, it is Germany who, much as the Allies claimed in 1914 and again at the peace conference in 1919, bears the brunt of the guilt. But of course it is not possible to indict a whole society, particularly one like that in Germany, in which the king, with the advice of his ministers and a few generals, still had autocratic control of foreign policy. As Taylor defines it, the cause of this literally inconceivable catastrophe and upheaval is something that sounds like a very sick joke, the blackest of black humor: the emperor and his little band of sycophants simply decided that the time was propitious for a German victory and pursued a series

8

of actions which made war inevitable. In Taylor's account Wilhelm II's Germany resembles a crazy truck driver who insists on driving his machine into a crowded department store. Everybody looks on in mesmerized horror, dumbly realizing that what could happen, but which seemed most improbable, has finally happened.

Taylor's well-informed and shrewd analysis raises certain additional questions. Granted that the German imperial government set Europe on a collision course to a war which was inevitable if all the other states pursued their self-interest and followed their customary policies, why did no statesman place the interests of civilization before his country's "commitments" and "interests"? Why was there no passionate, desperate idealism, some last-minute appeal to the conscience of mankind to avert the final outbreak? Taylor suggests the answer to this question; he points out that once all the other governments had been aroused by Germany's reckless policy, they calculated along the same lines as the emperor. Each state believed that it would be on the winning side in what was going to be a short war and that they stood to gain from the conflict. In other words, among all the leading parties there was insatiable greed and impotence of moral will which inhibited any statesman from making any last-minute sincere and bold effort to preserve the peace. All states and all leaders were corrupted by greed and a lust for power; they were willing to sacrifice the best instincts and highest ideals of European culture for military glory and strategic triumph. The ultimate cause of the war was the moral bankruptcy of Western civilization.

The new antagonism between Germany and Russia . . . dominated European relations in the spring of 1914. Both sought to strengthen their diplomatic position. But there was a basic difference of aim. The Russians wanted to create an alliance with Great Britain and France so strong that Germany would shrink from war; the Germans wanted to challenge Russia before the opposing alliance was consolidated and while they still had a military lead. Sazonov wrote to Benckendorff on 19 February: 'The peace of the world will be secure only when the Triple Entente . . . is transformed into a defensive alliance without secret clauses. Then the danger of a German hegemony will be finally ended, and each of us can devote himself to his own affairs: the English can seek a solution of their social problems, the French can get rich, protected from any external threat, and we can consolidate ourselves and work on our economic reorganization.' Benckendorff replied, 'If Grey could, he would do it to-morrow.' This was an exaggeration. Though the permanent officials at the foreign office advocated an alliance with Russia—as much to keep her favour as to restrain Germany—Grey would have none of it. He sheltered behind the excuse of public opinion; and any proposal for alliance with Russia would certainly have broken up the liberal government. But the policy of keeping a free hand represented Grey's own outlook. He wished to be on good terms with Russia; and he would undoubtedly urge support of France if she were attacked by Germany. Beyond this he would not go. He could not understand an alliance as a security for peace; like most Englishmen, he regarded all alliances as a commitment to war. Besides, though he welcomed Russia's weight in the Balance of Power, he was not convinced that her interests in the Near East were a vital concern for Great Britain—perhaps it would be better if Russia and Germany fought things out there and exhausted each other. In April he accompanied George V to Paris—his first visit to the Continent as foreign secretary—and, while there, defined his attitude to the French:

If there were a really aggressive and menacing attack made by Germany upon France, it was possible that public feeling in Great Britain would justify the Government in helping France. But it was not likely that Germany would make an aggressive and menacing attack upon Russia; and, even if she did, people in Great Britain would be inclined to say that, though Germany might have successes at first, Russia's resources were so great that, in the long run, Germany would be exhausted without our helping Russia.

The French did not welcome this reply. They felt themselves to be a hostage towards Germany for both Great Britain and Russia; and were more anxious to bring the two together than at any time since Delcassé first launched the project of a Triple Entente in the days before the Russo-Japanese war.

Grey made some concession, more to please the French than the Russians: he agreed to Anglo-Russian naval talks on the model of the 1912 discussions with France. This was not a serious project: the two fleets could not co-operate anywhere. As Grey wrote later, it was useful 'for the purpose of keeping Russia in good disposition, and of not offending her by refusing'. The British cabinet held that they were not committed by the naval agreement with France; therefore they authorized similar talks with the Russians. These, on the other hand, exaggerated the extent to which Great Britain was committed to France; and therefore supposed that they were getting something of value. Grey exacted a price even for this concession. He repeated his old demand that Russia must behave better in Persia if she wanted the entente to become more effective; and this time the Russians did something to meet him. Sazonov tried to restrain his agents in Persia. Moreover, he offered to surrender the neutral zone to the British and even to give them a guarantee of India, for what that was worth, if only the naval agreement could be settled. These negotiations were still hanging fire at the end of June: there was no Anglo-Russian alliance, nor even any certainty that their disputes in Persia would be smoothed over.

Russia had not improved her diplomatic position against Germany. On the contrary, the Germans learnt of the proposed naval talks through the treachery of a member of the Russian embassy in London, who kept them regularly supplied with Benckendorff's correspondence; and they published the story in a German newspaper. The outcry which followed in England made it impossible for Grey to go on with the talks for the moment. What is more, radical members of the government still believed that relations with Germany were improving. Churchill imagined that a meeting between himself and Tirpitz 'might do good, and could not possibly do any harm'. Lloyd George went further. On 23 July he spoke in the house of commons and said of Germany: 'Our relations are very much better than they were a few years ago. . . . The two great Empires begin to realize they can co-operate for common ends, and that the points of co-operation are greater and more numerous and more important than the points of possible controversy.' A general election was now approaching in Great Britain; and, though a historian should never deal in speculations about what did not happen, it is difficult to resist the surmise that Lloyd George was planning to fight this election as leader of a radical-labour coalition. Reconciliation with Germany, and resistance to Russia in Persia, must have been part of the coalition's programme. In France, too, opinion was changing. There a general election in April returned a majority against the three-year service; and in June Poincaré had to appoint a left-wing government under Viviani, much against his will. Only a sordid private scandal enabled him to escape Caillaux, supported by Jaurès and the socialists, with a programme of full Franco-German reconciliation. In fact, a coalition of the three advanced western Powers against the Russian colossus seemed just round the corner.

Bethmann, at least, recognized that the situation was changing in Germany's favour. He wrote on 16 June: 'Whether a European conflagration comes depends solely on the attitude of Germany and England. If we both stand together as guarantors of European peace which is not prevented by the engagements of either the Triple Alliance or the entente, *provided we pursue this aim on a common plan from the start,* war can be avoided.' Nor had the Germans any illusion about Austria-Hungary. Tschirschky, the ambassador at Vienna, wrote in May: 'How often do I consider whether it is really worth while to unite ourselves so closely to this state-structure which is cracking at every joint and to continue the laborious task of dragging her along.' The Germans could have escaped this task, if security was their only object, by accepting the friendship of British and French pacific radicalism; but a genuine alliance for peace was not to their taste. The Germans were bent on going forward in the world; and Austria-Hungary was essential to them if they were to gain control of the Near East. The Austro-Hungarian ambassador at Constantinople posed the choice before the Germans with bitter satisfaction: 'Either the abandonment of the Bosphorus and of Germany's position in the Near East or marching on the side of Austria through thick and thin.' As often happens, Germany's ambitions made her the captive of her weaker partner. The Germans set out to refloat Austria-Hungary as a Great Power; her ambitions had to be encouraged, her resources bolstered up for the conflict. On 12 May Conrad met Moltke at Karlsbad (Kárlovy Vary). Previously Moltke had urged Conrad to keep the peace until a more favourable opportunity. Now he declared that it was hopeless to wait for a promise of neutrality from Great Britain which she would never give: 'Any delay means a lessening of our chances; we cannot compete with Russia in man-power.' The conclusion was obvious: Germany and Austria-Hungary must strike before the expansion of the Russian army got under way.

The two central Powers were still far from an agreed programme. The Germans had neither sympathy nor understanding for the national problems of the Habsburg monarchy. Certainly they wanted to preserve it as a Great Power; and they even recognized that Hungary was its core. William II said to Tisza in March: 'a *German* Austria and a *Hungarian* Hungary were the two firm pillars of the Monarchy.' But they thought that this was compatible with a policy which would win both Serbia and Rumania to their side. They never considered how this could be done with Serbia, except for vague talk 'of the dependence of the lesser upon the greater as in the planetary system'. Rumania seemed to them to hold the key to the Balkans: if she were loyal to her alliance of 1883 she could force Serbia on the same course. This policy was antiquated. Rumania had once sought security against Russia; now, as a great wheat-exporting country, she had a common interest with her in the free passage of the Straits. Even more decisive, her national aspirations had been stirred by the victory of the Balkan states. Unlike theirs, these could not be achieved against Turkey. They could succeed only by liberating the 2,000,000 Rumanians of Transylvania who were under Hungarian rule. This was a more dangerous challenge to the Habsburg monarchy than even the South Slav movement. A South Slav, or at any rate a Croat, kingdom might have been set up if Francis Ferdinand had come to the throne. The rulers of Hungary would never surrender Transylvania, where lay their richest estates and where lived nearly a million Magyars.

William II preached 'a *Hungarian* Hungary'; yet he also advocated a conciliation of the Rumanians, which must have caused a head-on struggle with the Magyars. Only Francis Ferdinand was ready for this; and even he dared not air it to William II. The party of the heir-apparent made some feeble efforts to achieve their policy. In the autumn of 1913 Czernin, one of this group, went as minister to Bucharest. He soon reported: 'the treaty of alliance is not worth the paper and ink with which it is written.' He proposed that Berchtold should put matters right by offering Rumania and Serbia a 'guarantee'—as though this would have satisfied either of them. The guarantee could have operated only against Bulgaria; and Berchtold was always dreaming of an alliance with her, so far as he had a policy at all. Czernin also urged some concessions to the Rumanians in Transylvania. Tisza, the Hungarian prime minister, brushed these aside; the German alliance should be used to force Rumania back into line. The Germans wanted Hungary to make concessions to Rumania and Serbia in order to strengthen the Austro-German alliance; Tisza answered that this alliance made concessions unnecessary. He got his way. No one in Vienna could control him; and the Germans were dazzled by his resoluteness. William II found him 'a truly great statesman'.

On 13 June Francis Ferdinand met William II, for the last time, at Konopischt. He nerved himself to denounce Tisza as the cause of all their troubles. William II only replied that he would instruct his ambassador to repeat to Tisza: 'Lord, remember the Rumanians.' The Magyars were free to continue on their intransigent course; in the last resort, they dominated the Habsburg monarchy and so Germany, and could drag both Powers along with them. On

24 June Berchtold completed a memorandum on Austro-Hungarian policy, which had originated with Tisza. It advocated alliance with Bulgaria against both Serbia and Rumania. This was nothing new —it had been urged ineffectively by Berchtold since the beginning of the Balkan wars. But the Russian spectre was now brought in to make the proposal more attractive to the Germans: 'the open endeavours of Russia to encircle the Monarchy have the ultimate aim of making it impossible for the German Empire to oppose Russia's distant aims of gaining political and economic supremacy.'

The Austrians had been raising the cry for thirty years that Russia was aiming directly at their destruction. The Germans had always been able to reply that Austria-Hungary was in no danger, so long as she kept clear of aggressive action in the Balkans; and this reply was often given. It was truer now than it had ever been. The Russians had no interest in the aggrandizement of either Serbia or Rumania; they merely wanted to keep these two countries as independent barriers between Germany and the Straits. But the Austrians could now argue that the real Russian challenge was to Germany and that she must therefore support Austria-Hungary's Balkan plans for her own sake. The Germans, like the Russians, had no Balkan interests. Their route to Constantinople was predominantly by sea through the Channel to the Mediterranean. They, too, wanted to keep Serbia and Rumania independent, though, of course, they hoped to keep them friendly by concessions at Austria-Hungary's expense. Instead they were dragged into these Balkan disputes in order to keep their only reliable ally afloat. The greater includes the less, as William II said on another occasion. The Germans anticipated a struggle for the mastery of Europe and the Middle East; the Austrians merely wished to end the nationalist agitation of two Balkan states with whom Germany had no quarrel. The only point of agreement between them was in believing that both problems could be settled by war.

The Austrians were right on the question of fact: both Serbia and Rumania were lost to the central Powers. That had been obvious with Serbia for long enough; though the Austrians exaggerated the

Serb danger in order to excuse their own helpless incompetence in dealing with the South Slavs. The defection of Rumania was a more dramatic blow; it symbolized the ending of the precarious balance which had existed on the lower Danube since the Crimean war. On 14 June Nicholas II and Sazonov visited the king of Rumania, at Constantsa. Sazonov, on a motor-tour, crossed the Hungarian frontier into Transylvania. This somewhat tactless sign of approval for Rumanian irredentism was rewarded by assurances of neutrality, though not of armed support, in an Austro-Russian war. Sazonov noted: 'Rumania will try to go with the side that turns out to be the stronger and can offer her the greater gains.' Sazonov had no serious intention of offering these gains unless war actually broke out. His policy was encirclement, not aggression, so far as the Balkans were concerned; or, to use a more respectable modern term, it was containment. Exactly the same was true of Great Britain in the west. No Power of the Triple Entente wanted a European upheaval; all three would have liked to turn their backs on Europe and to pursue their imperial expansion in Asia and Africa. Germany, on the other hand, had come to feel that she could expand her overseas empire only after she had destroyed the European Balance of Power; and Austria-Hungary wanted a Balkan war in order to survive at all.

Yet it would be wrong to exaggerate the rigidity of the system of alliances or to regard the European war as inevitable. No war is inevitable until it breaks out. The existing alliances were all precarious. Italy was only the extreme example—renewing the Triple Alliance and making exaggerated promises of military support to Germany on one side; seeking to negotiate a Mediterranean agreement with France and Great Britain on the other. In France the Russian alliance was increasingly unpopular; it was threatened by a coalition between Caillaux the radical and Jaurès the socialist, which in the summer of 1914 seemed inevitable. Both men were anti-Russian, or at least anti-tsarist; both were friendly to Germany. In England the crisis over Home Rule was reaching its height. If it had exploded, there must have followed either a radical government, which would have been friendly to Germany, or—less likely—a conservative government, so weak as to be debarred from having a foreign policy. Moreover, in June 1914, the British government at last reached agreement with Germany over the Bagdad railway; and the French had already done so in February. Both seemed to be taking sides with Germany against Russia in the great question of Turkey-in-Asia. The Russians had every reason to be dissatisfied with their position. The conservatives at court disliked both the estrangement from Germany and the demagogic patronage of Serbia. Imperialists were offended by British policy in Persia, especially its pursuit of oil-concessions. They would gladly have swung on to an anti-British course, if Germany had given them security at the Straits. Some Russians, more daring still, thought of an alliance with Turkey against the three western 'capitalist' Powers; and in May 1914 a Turkish delegation visited Nicholas II at Livadia. If this revival of Unkiar Skelessi had been achieved, a diplomatic revolution must certainly have followed. As it was, alliance between Russia and Turkey had to wait until 1921.

Plenty of Germans knew that the ring round them was not solid. Bethmann and the foreign ministry counted rightly that Great Britain would turn away from Russia and towards them, if France were left alone. The great capitalists were winning the mastery of Europe without war: the industries of southern Russia, the iron fields of Lorraine and Normandy were already largely under their control. Each group in Germany had a single enemy and would have liked to make peace with the others. But Germany lacked a directing hand to insist on priorities. It was easier to acquiesce in all the aggressive impulses and to drift with events. Germany lay in the centre of Europe. She could use this position to play off her neighbours against each other, as Bismarck had done and as Hitler was to do; or she could abuse her position to unite her neighbours against her, not from policy, but by having none. Tirpitz and his capitalist supporters wanted a naval conflict with Great Britain and deplored the hostility to France and Russia; the professional soldiers and their capitalist supporters wanted a continental war, especially against France, and deplored the naval rivalry with Great Britain; the mass parties—the social democrats and the Roman Catholic Centre—were friendly to both Great Britain and France and could be won only for the old radical programme of war against Russia. It is futile to discuss whether the great navy, the Bagdad railway, or the bid for continental supremacy was the decisive factor in German policy. But the bid for continental supremacy was certainly decisive in bringing on the European war. If Germany destroyed France as an independent Power, she could then pursue her imperial rivalries against Russia and Great Britain with some chance of success. Both Powers had recognized this by supporting the independence of France long before either the German navy or the Bagdad railway existed. Nevertheless, they would not have been so ready to co-operate with France, and not ready at all to co-operate with each other, if Germany had not also challenged them directly. German policy, or rather lack of it, made the Triple Entente a reality. The feeble rulers of Germany, William II and Bethmann, preferred a ring of foreign enemies to trouble at home.

It has been strongly argued that the Germans deliberately timed war for August 1914. There is little evidence for this, and a decisive argument against it. Bethmann and William II were incapable of consistent policy; Moltke, the chief-of-staff, could not conduct a campaign, let alone make a war. The Germans were involved in war by Austria-Hungary, but they went with her willingly. It was easy to co-operate with her; it would have needed a statesman to refuse. On 28 June Francis Ferdinand was assassinated at Sarajevo, the capital of Bosnia, by a Bosnian Serb. Berchtold was weary of being jeered at by Conrad as irresolute and feeble. Moreover, when Turkey-in-Asia took the place of the Balkans as the centre of international rivalry, Austria-Hungary was pushed aside too; and the Germans had rejected with impatience Berchtold's claim to be allotted a 'sphere' in Asia Minor. The murder at Sarajevo revived the Balkan question and enabled Austria-Hungary to reappear misleadingly as a Great Power. This time she could only hold the centre of the stage if she actually provoked a war. The German talk of writing off Austria-Hungary and of somehow restoring good relation with Russia at her expense had not escaped Austrian attention: and the Habsburg monarchy brought on its mortal crisis to prove that it was still alive.

Berchtold determined to force war on Serbia, though he had no proofs of Serbian complicity and never found any. Tisza, the Hungarian prime minister, opposed him. Berchtold wanted to restore the prestige of the monarchy; Tisza cared only for great Hungary. Like Kossuth before him, he looked to Germany, not to Vienna, as Hungary's ally and would not have much regretted the collapse of the Dual Monarchy, so long as great Hungary survived. Berchtold turned Tisza's opposition by appealing to Germany for support; Tisza could not hold out if Berlin, not Vienna, urged war. Berchtold took out his memorandum of 24 June, which had urged alliance with Bulgaria; added a postscript blaming Serbia for the assassination; and accompanied this with a letter from Francis Joseph to William II, which managed to blame Russian Panslavism as well. The conclusion: 'Serbia must be eliminated as a political factor in the Balkans . . . friendly settlement is no longer to be thought of.' These two documents were presented to William II on 5 July.

At Berlin there was no serious consultation. William II invited the Austro-Hungarian ambassador to lunch at Potsdam. At first he said that he must wait for Bethmann's opinion; them changed his mind after lunch and committed himself. Szögyény, the Austrian ambassador, reported: 'Action against Serbia should not be delayed. . . . Even if it should come to a war between Austria and Russia, we could be convinced that Germany would stand by our side with her accustomed faithfulness as an ally.' Bethmann arrived in the afternoon, went for a walk in the park with William II, and approved of what he had said. The next day he gave Szögyény official confirmation: 'Austria must judge what is to be done to clear up her relations with Serbia; but whatever Austria's decision, she could count with certainty upon it, that Germany will stand behind her as an ally.' Berchtold's plan of partitioning Serbia with Bulgaria was explained to Bethmann. He approved of it and added: 'If war must break out, better now than in one or two years' time when the Entente will be stronger.'

William II and Bethmann did more than give Austria-Hungary a free hand; they encouraged her to start a war against Serbia and to risk the greater consequences. They had grown used to Berchtold's irresolution during the Balkan wars and were determined not to be blamed for it. The most probable outcome of all the stir, they expected, would be an Austro-Hungarian alliance with Bulgaria. Further, both of them thought that Russia was not ready for war and that she would allow the humiliation of Serbia after some ineffective protest; then their position would be all the stronger to strike a bargain with Russia later. On the other hand, if it came to war, they were confident of winning it now and less confident of winning it later. They did not decide on war; but they did decide on 5 July to use their superior power either to win a war or to achieve a striking success. Bethmann had always said that Germany and Great Britain should cooperate to keep the peace. If he had wanted a peaceful solution of the present crisis, he would have approached the British at once. Instead he did nothing. He did not wish to alarm them. His aim, so far as he had one, was to keep them neutral in a continental war, not to enlist their support for a general peace.

The German reply gave Berchtold what he wanted: it enabled him to convert Tisza. He could now argue that Germany was urging them to war. On 14 July Tisza gave way: great Hungary had to keep German favour. He laid down one condition: Austria-Hungary should not acquire any Serbian territory. Though Berchtold accepted this condition, he meant to cheat Tisza, once Serbia had been crushed: her southern territories would be partitioned between Albania and Bulgaria, and the rest would become a dependency of the monarchy, even if it were not directly annexed. The one chance of success for Austria-Hungary would have been rapid action. Instead Berchtold dawdled, in the usual Viennese fashion. The ultimatum to Serbia was sent on 23 July, when all Europe had forgotten its first indignation at the archduke's murder. The Serbs replied on 25 July, accepting Berchtold's conditions much more nearly than had been expected. It made no difference. The Austrians were determined on war; and the Germans encouraged them to action. On 28 July Austria-Hungary declared war on Serbia. Military reasons were not the motive: the Austro-Hungarian army could not be ready even against Serbia until 12 August. But, as Berchtold said: 'the diplomatic situation will not last as long as that'. He needed a declaration of war in order to reject all attempts at mediation or a peaceful solution: they had now been 'outstripped by events'.

The Austro-Hungarian declaration of war on Serbia was the decisive act; everything else followed from it. Diplomacy had been silent between the assassination of Francis Ferdinand on 28 June and the Austro-Hungarian note of 23 July; there was nothing it could do until the Austro-Hungarian demands were known. Then the statesmen tried to avert the crisis. The Russians advised Serbia not to resist, but to trust to the Great Powers; Grey offered to mediate between Serbia and Austria-Hungary. But the Russians had repeatedly declared that they would not allow Serbia to be crushed; they could do no other if they were to maintain the buffer of independent Balkan states. Poincaré and Viviani were in St. Petersburg just before the Austro-Hungarian note to Serbia was sent off. They emphasized again French loyalty to the alliance; but there is no evidence that they encouraged Russia to provoke a war, if a peaceful settlement could be found. When Austria-Hungary declared war on Serbia, the Russians attempted to mobilize against her alone, although they had no plans except for total mobilization. They were, in fact, still acting in terms of diplomacy; they were raising their bid, not preparing for war. The Germans now entered the field. They had assured the Austrians that they would keep Russia out of things, and they set out to do so. On 29 July they warned Sazonov that 'further continuation of Russian mobilization would force us to mobilize also'.

This time the Russians were determined not to retreat; they raised their bid still higher. On 30 July they resolved on general mobilization. This, too, was a diplomatic move; the Russian armies could not be ready for many weeks. But, in Jagow's words, 'the German asset was speed'. Their only military plan was to defeat France in six weeks and then to turn against Russia before she was fully prepared. Therefore they had to precipitate events and to force a rupture on both Russia and France. William II might still carry on a private telegraphic correspondence with Nicholas II, which was prolonged even after the declaration of war; Bethmann might still seek an impossible diplomatic success. They were both swept aside by the generals; and they had no answer to the military argument that immediate war was necessary for Germany's security. Yet even the generals did not want war; they wanted victory. When Bethmann urged caution at Vienna and Moltke at the same time urged speedier action, Berchtold exclaimed: 'What a joke! Who rules at Berlin?' The answer was: nobody. German statesmen and generals alike succumbed to the demands of technique.

On 31 July the Germans took the preliminary step towards general mobilization on their side. From this moment, diplomacy ceased so far as the continental Powers were concerned. The only German concern was to get the war going as soon as possible. On 31 July they demanded from Russia the arrest of all war measures; when this was refused, a declaration of war followed on 1 August. The French were asked for a promise of neutrality in a Russo-German war; if they had agreed, they would also have been told to surrender their principal fortresses on the frontier, Toul and Verdun, as pledge of their neutrality. Viviani merely replied: "France will act in accordance with her interests.' The Germans had no plausible excuse for war against France. They therefore trumped up some false stories of French violation of German territory; and with these decked out a declaration of war on 3 August.

Negotiations between Germany and Great Britain were more prolonged. Their object, on the German side, was to secure British neutrality, not to avert a continental war. All along, Bethmann had urged Berchtold to appear conciliatory in order to impress the British, not in order to find a compromise. On 29 July he offered not to annex any French territory if Great Britain remained neutral; the offer did not extend to the French colonies. As well, Germany would respect the integrity of Belgium after the war, provided that 'she did not take sides against Germany'. Grey stuck to his line of policy to the end. He made repeated attempts to settle the original Austro-Serb dispute by negotiation; later he tried to assemble a conference of the Great Powers. He warned the Germans not to count on British neutrality; equally he warned the French and Russians not to count on her support.

It is sometimes said that Grey could have averted the war if he had defined his policy one way or the other. This is not so. The German general staff had long planned to invade France through Belgium and would not have been deterred by any British threat. Indeed they had always assumed that Great Britain would enter the war; they did not take her military weight seriously, and naval questions did not interest them. Bethmann had wanted a British declaration of neutrality in order to discourage France and Russia; once it was clear that they would go to war in any case, British policy ceased to interest him. Emotionally he deplored the breach with Great Britain; but he did nothing to avert it and, in any case, was impotent to influence the German generals. On the other side, France and Russia decided on war without counting firmly on British support; the French believed that they could defeat Germany, and the Russians could not risk their own diplomatic defeat. A British declaration of neutrality would not have influenced their policy. Besides, Grey was resolved that they should decide their policy without encouragement from him; war must spring from their independent resolve.

Those who urged a clear British line did so from contradictory motives. Nicolson feared that Russia and France would win a complete victory and that the British empire would then be at their mercy. Eyre Crowe, more representative of official opinion, feared that France would be defeated and that Great Britain would then be at the mercy of Germany. In any case it was impossible for Grey to make any clear declaration; public opinion would not have allowed it. If there is a criticism of Grey, it must be that he had not educated the British public enough in the previous years. No doubt he had shrunk from increasing the tension in Europe; but, as well, the unity of the liberal party and the survival of the liberal government had ranked higher in his mind than a decisive foreign policy. It was common form to regret discussion of foreign issues. Eyre Crowe, for instance, 'deplored all public speeches on foreign affairs'; and Grey agreed with him. As a result, in July 1914, the cabinet overruled any commitment. On 27 July Lloyd George said: 'there could be no question of our taking part in any war in the first instance. He knew of no Minister who would be in favour of it.'

Moreover, Grey supposed that British intervention would not carry much weight. He thought solely of naval action; it seemed impossible to him to send even an expeditionary force to France, and he certainly never imagined military intervention on a continental scale. On 2 August the cabinet authorized him to warn the Germans that their fleet would not be allowed to attack France in the Channel. Even this condition was not decisive; the Germans would have gladly agreed to it, in exchange for British neutrality. But on 3 August they sent an ultimatum to Belgium, demanding free passage to invade France; the British answered on 4 August demanding that Belgian neutrality be respected. Here again Grey has been criticised for not acting earlier; he should, it is said, have made British neutrality conditional on respect for Belgium. It would have made no difference. The German ultimatum to Belgium was drafted on 26 July, that is, even before the Austro-Hungarian declaration of war on Serbia; invasion of Belgium was an essential, indeed the essential, part of their plans. Only a French surrender could have held them from it. If Grey had acted earlier he would have achieved nothing, except perhaps the break-up of the liberal government; if he had delayed longer he would not have saved Belgium and he would have lost the inestimable value of moral superiority.

On 4 August the long Bismarckian peace ended. It had lasted

more than a generation. Men had come to regard peace as normal; when it ended, they looked for some profound cause. Yet the immediate cause was a good deal simpler than on other occasions. Where, for instance, lay the precise responsibility for the Crimean war, and when did that war become inevitable? In 1914 there could be no doubt. Austria-Hungary had failed to solve her national problems. She blamed Serbia for the South Slav discontent; it would be far truer to say that this discontent involved Serbia, against her will, in Habsburg affairs. In July 1914 the Habsburg statesmen took the easy course of violence against Serbia, as their predecessors had taken it (though with more justification) against Sardinia in 1859. Berchtold launched war in 1914, as consciously as Buol launched it in 1859 or Gramont in 1870. There was this difference. Buol counted on support from Prussia and Great Britain; Gramont on support from Austria-Hungary. They were wrong. Berchtold counted rightly on support from Germany; he would not have persisted in a resolute line if it had not been for the repeated encouragements which came from Berlin. The Germans did not fix on war for August 1914, but they welcomed it when the occasion offered. They could win it now; they were more doubtful later. Hence they surrendered easily to the dictates of a military time-table. Austria-Hungary was growing weaker; Germany believed herself at the height of her strength. They decided on war from opposite motives; and the two decisions together caused a general European war.

The Powers of the Triple Entente all entered the war to defend themselves. The Russians fought to preserve the free passage of the Straits, on which their economic life depended; France for the sake of the Triple Entente, which she believed, rightly, alone guaranteed her survival as a Great Power. The British fought for the independence of sovereign states and, more remotely, to prevent a German domination of the Continent. It is sometimes said that the war was caused by the system of alliances or, more vaguely, by the Balance of Power. This is a generalization without reality. None of the Powers acted according to the letter of their commitments, though no doubt they might have done so if they had not anticipated them. Germany was pledged to go to war if Russia attacked Austria-Hungary. Instead, she declared war before Russia took any action; and Austria-Hungary only broke with Russia, grudgingly enough, a week afterwards. France was pledged to attack Germany, if the latter attacked Russia. Instead she was faced with a German demand for unconditional neutrality and would have had to accept war even had there been no Franco-Russian alliance, unless she was prepared to abdicate as a Great Power. Great Britain had a moral obligation to stand by France and a rather stronger one to defend her Channel coast. But she went to war for the sake of Belgium and would have done so, even if there had been no Anglo-French entente and no exchange of letters between Grey and Cambon in November 1912. Only then, the British intervention would have been even less effective than it was.

As to the Balance of Power, it would be truer to say that the war was caused by its breakdown rather than by its existence. There had been a real European Balance in the first decade of the Franco-Russian alliance; and peace had followed from it. The Balance broke down when Russia was weakened by the war with Japan; and Germany got in the habit of trying to get her way by threats. This ended with the Agadir crisis. Russia began to recover her strength, France her nerve. Both insisted on being treated as equals, as they had been in Bismarck's time. The Germans resented this and resolved to end it by war, if they could end it no other way. They feared that the Balance was being re-created. Their fears were exaggerated. Certainly, Russia would have been a more formidable Power by 1917, if her military plans had been carried through and if she had escaped internal disturbance—two formidable hypotheses. But it is unlikely that the three-year service would have been maintained in France; and, in any case, the Russians might well have used their strength against Great Britain in Asia rather than to attack Germany, if they had been left alone. In fact, peace must have brought Germany the mastery of Europe within a few years. This was prevented by the habit of her diplomacy and, still more, by the mental outlook of her people. They had trained themselves psychologically for aggression.

The German military plans played a vital part. The other Great Powers thought in terms of defending themselves. No Frenchman thought seriously of recovering Alsace and Lorraine; and the struggle of Slav and Teuton in the Balkans was very great nonsense so far as most Russians were concerned. The German generals wanted a decisive victory for its own sake. Though they complained of 'encirclement', it was German policy that had created this encirclement. Absurdly enough, the Germans created their own problem when they annexed Alsace and Lorraine in 1871. They wanted an impregnable frontier; and they got one, as was shown in August 1914, when a small German force held its own there against the bulk of the French army. After 1871 the Germans could easily have fought Russia and stood on the defensive in the west; this was indeed the strategical plan of the elder Moltke. It was not a strategy which guaranteed final, decisive vistory; and Schlieffen therefore rejected it. In 1892 he insisted that France must be defeated first; ten years later he drew the further inevitable conclusion that the German armies must go through Belgium. If the strategy of the elder Moltke had been adhered to with all its political consequences, it would have been very difficult to persuade French and British opinion to go to the assistance of Russia; instead, it appeared in 1914 that Russia was coming to the assistance of France and even of Great Britain. Schlieffen first created the Franco-Russian alliance; and then ensured that Great Britain would enter the war as well. The Germans complained that the war could not be 'localized' in 1914; Schlieffen's strategy prevented it. He would be content with nothing less than total victory; therefore he exposed Germany to total defeat.

There is a deeper explanation still. No one in 1914 took the dangers of war seriously except on a purely military plane. Though all, except a few fighting men, abhorred its bloodshed, none expected a social catastrophe. In the days of Metternich, and even afterwards, statesmen had feared that war would produce 'revolution'—and revolutionaries had sometimes advocated it for that very reason. Now they were inclined to think that war would stave off their social and political problems. In France it produced the 'sacred union'; in Germany William II was able to say: 'I do not see parties any more; I see only Germans.' All thought that war could be fitted into the existing framework of civilization, as the wars of 1866 and 1870 had been. Indeed, these wars had been followed by stabler currencies, freer trade, and more constitutional governments. War was expected to interrupt the even tenor of civilian life only while it lasted. Grey expressed this outlook in extreme form, when he said in the house of commons on 3 August: "if we are engaged in war, we shall suffer but little more than we shall suffer if we stand aside'; and by suffering he meant only the interruption of British trade with the continent of Europe. No country made serious economic preparations for war. In England the cry was raised of 'business as usual' to mitigate the unemployment which war was expected to cause. The Germans so little understood the implications of total war that they abstained from invading Holland in August 1914, so as to be able to trade freely with the rest of the world.

The Balkan wars had taught a deceptive lesson. Everyone supposed that decisive battles would be fought at once, and a dictated peace would follow. The Germans expected to take Paris; the French expected to break through in Lorraine. The Russian 'steam-roller' would reach Berlin; more important, from the Russian point of view, their armies would cross the Carpathians and take Budapest. Even the Austrians expected to 'crush' Serbia. The British expected to destroy the German fleet in an immediate naval engagement and then to establish a close blockade of the German coast; apart from that, they had no military plans, except to applaud the victories of their allies and perhaps to profit from them.

None of these things happened. The French armies failed to make headway in Lorraine and suffered enormous casualties. The Germans marched through Belgium and saw from afar the Eiffel

Tower. On 6 September they were halted on the Marne and driven back in defeat. But though the French won the battle of the Marne, they could not exploit their victory; the Germans were neither destroyed nor even expelled from French soil. By November there was a line of trenches running from Switzerland to the sea. The Russians invaded east Prussia; they were catastrophically defeated at Tannenberg on 27 August, and their armies in Galicia failed to reach the Carpathians. The Austrians occupied Belgrade, from which the Serbs had withdrawn; they were driven out again in November, and Serbian forces entered southern Hungary. The German fleet remained in harbour; and the British fleet was similarly imprisoned in order to balance it. Everywhere siege warfare superseded decisive battles. The machine-gun and the spade changed the course of European history. Policy had been silenced by the first great clash; but in the autumn of 1914 diplomacy was renewed. All the Powers sought to consolidate their alliances; to enlist new allies; and, more feebly, to shake the opposing coalition.

Suggestions for Further Reading

ALBERTINI, LUIGI, *The Origins of the War of 1914.* 3 vols. London and New York: Oxford University Press, 1952–57.

FALLS, CYRIL, *The Great War: 1914–1918.* New York: Capricorn Books, 1961.

HORNE, ALISTAIR, *The Price of Glory: Verdun, 1916.* New York: St. Martin's Press, 1962.

MANSERGH, NICHOLAS, *The Coming of the First World War.* London and New York: Longmans, Green and Co., 1949.

TUCHMAN, BARBARA W., *The Guns of August.* New York: The Macmillan Company, 1962.

The Bolshevik Revolution*

E. H. CARR

The Bolshevık seizure of supreme power in Russia in the autumn of 1917 was indeed "ten days that shook the world," in the famous phrase of the American left-wing observer of the revolution, John Reed. The world is still shaking. After the cataclysm of August 1914 the October Days in Leningrad in 1917 are the most decisive moments in twentieth-century history. If the First World War was the suicide of bourgeois European society, the Bolshevik revolution opened the way to power for the most influential anti-liberal philosophy of the twentieth century. It is this social theory, this view of man and society, which has proved to be more appealing than any other to the millions of Latin Americans, Asians, and Africans who were ruthlessly subjugated and exploited by those European imperial powers whose nadir was inaugurated by the First World War.

Just as the non-Europeans absorbed from the West the science

* From E. H. Carr, *The Bolshevik Revolution 1917-1923*, Vol. I (London: Macmillan & Company, Ltd., 1950), pp. 71-123.

and technology that eventually gave them the military and economic power to turn against their European masters, likewise the ideology of revolution against European hegemony in the twentieth century—Marxism—was very much a product of nineteenth-century European culture. If we designate the decline of European hegemony as one of the main themes of modern and contemporary history, then we must also emphasize that both the theoretical and physical instruments for the non-European attack on the West were the products of European civilization. Those who believe in the continued vitality of Oriental civilization in the twentieth century have to overlook the fact that the emancipation of the Eastern civilizations was effected with European weapons— economic, military, and intellectual.

Karl Marx's intellectual development was a long and complex one and particularly in the early phase of his philosophical career he seems to have been deeply committed to the ideals of middle-class liberalism, as the neo-Marxian critics of the last decade have claimed (see Volume V, Number 4 in this series). But the Marxist philosophy that became the faith of Lenin and the Bolsheviks and then of the other Communist movements in Europe and the rest of the world was the work of Marx's mature years and represents his profound alienation from the middle-class humanist tradition. The Marxist-Leninism that came to power in Russia in 1917 was a distillation and synthesis of several currents in nineteenth-century thought, all of them for one reason or another deterministic, collectivistic, and hostile to the freedom of the individual personality. From the extremely influential German philosopher Hegel, Marx borrowed the idea that history is the working out of an immanent dialectical force which the individual cannot control or resist. The individual must support the absolute authority of the historical dialectic or be submerged by it. From English classical economics (which in a superficial sense was anticollectivist in its advocacy of laissez faire and the exclusion of government economic regulation), Marx adopted the idea that the economic world is an autonomous mechanism which determines social change by iron laws that the individual is powerless to breach. From romanticism Marx borrowed the idea of group struggle and conflict as the creative force in social life. And the result is a social philosophy which makes the individual powerless to decide the course of social change. Our lives are determined by membership in social classes; the form of the means of production determines the ascendancy of a particular social class; economic change undermines the position of a previously dominant class and gives power to a new class. History is advanced by inevitable climactic struggles, each of which inaugurates a new order and a new era. Thus the bourgeoisie, which had replaced the feudal aristocracy as the dominant class in European society, would find its position undermined by growing dislocation in the capitalist economy, and the proletarian revolution would inaugurate a new socialist era under the dictatorship of the proletariat, i.e., the Communist party.

Even in his later years Marx, in spite of his claim to dispassionate economic science, could never divest himself entirely of his early utopian humanism and belief in the freedom and dignity of the individual. He therefore posited an ultimate final stage in social development in which humanity would finally escape from the determinism of the historical dialectic and the authoritarianism of the dictatorship of the proletariat. This vaguely defined golden age of the distant future would be characterized by the withering away of the state, and the coming of a true communism would allow the spontaneous exercise of the liberated human personality.

Many commentators have noted how much Marx's philosophy appears to be a secularization of the old Christian providential view of history, in which God's determination of historical events, the impotence of the human will to achieve peace and happiness, and the terror and fire of the last judgment are contrasted with the glorious felicity and angelic freedom enjoyed by those souls who finally attain the kingdom of God.

Like all good nineteenth-century Europeans, Marx and his associate Frederick Engels detested Russia, which appeared to them to be the most backward society in Europe, feudal and prebour-

geois in its stage of development, and controlled by the tsarist government, the most reactionary in Europe. Marx and Engels believed that England and Germany, as the states furthest advanced in industrialization, were the most probable foci of the proletarian revolution and Russia was the least likely of any of the major European countries to be the earliest scene of the climactic stage of history.

It is of course one of the great ironies of modern history that the backward Russians had the first Communist regime and this is sometimes taken by itself as the discrediting of Marxist doctrine. Perhaps in a strict sense it is, but on the other hand Marxism preached the control of society by an authoritarian government and Russia already had the most despotic ruler in Europe. In 1917 the despotism of the Romanovs, who ruled by divine right in their dynastic interests, was simply replaced by the despotism of the Bolsheviks, who ruled by right of historical determinism and the interests supposedly of all Russian society, but in fact, if not in theory, in the interests of a narrow oligarchy. If Marxist-Leninism is seen as an elaborate historical myth and social theory to justify authoritarian rule by a clique of professional revolutionaries, the Bolshevik triumph is not a surprising or paradoxical event; it represents the continuity of Russian civilization.

The Menshevik opponents of Lenin and some members of his own party were opposed to the establishment of a Soviet "proletarian" dictatorship on the grounds that the previous historical stage in Marxist theory, bourgeois liberal democracy, had not yet been reached in Russia. All the more does Lenin's insistence on immediately establishing a Communist dictatorship and bypassing the bourgeois era in history exhibit a profound historical intuition. A discredited authoritarian regime finally collapsed at a point in Russian history when the economy was just beginning to move from a preindustrial to an industrial stage. The vast majority of the population was still an illiterate peasantry who could comprehend no other form of government than the most rigid autocracy. It is difficult to see how in 1917 democratic liberalism could have

33

succeeded in Russia. The only viable government was another kind of ideologically based authoritarianism. Lenin triumphed because he understood the reality of the Russian situation better than any of the other socialist leaders of his time. And he was one of the prophets of the twentieth century, because all other societies which in the succeeding half century tried to make a quick jump from feudalism to industrialism decided that this foreshortening of history was possible only under the aegis of an authoritarian regime. This is, of course, the prime reason that Marxist-Leninism has had such a wide appeal in the underdeveloped countries of the twentieth century, whether in Latin America, Asia, or Africa. In 1945 these societies found their economic conditions no further along, and in some cases much further behind, than that of Russia in 1917. Is it to be wondered at, that they found Russian communism such an attractive ideology and that they tried to imitate the governmental structure and policies that Lenin inaugurated in Russia?

The most distinguished authority on the history of the Russian revolution is the Cambridge University scholar E. H. Carr, from whose multivolume history of the Soviet Union the following selection is taken. Carr is a dedicated Marxist and a sympathizer with the revolution, but he is by no means blind to its paradoxical problems and limitations, nor does he approach his subject with any preconceived aim either to glorify or to condemn any of its leading characters. By carefully fitting together the evidence and writing with an easy and modulated narrative style, Carr has given us a continually absorbing and convincing picture of the motives, decisions, and happenstances that brought the Bolsheviks to power.

In reading the speeches and letters of the leaders of the Russian revolution we are immediately struck by the prominence of the rhetoric that has been so common in the last quarter of a century: it is the rhetoric of permanent revolution. Nineteenth-century socialism's great expectations and noble vision of a renaissance of human dignity were in 1917 already institutionalized into vague slogans: "All power to the Soviets"; "Hail the worldwide socialist revolution." These were the testaments of a new faith that gained the adherence of hundreds of millions of people in the following half century. But how far has modern civilization really come from the dehumanized slogans of the old regime? Men no longer respond to anxieties and conflicts by asserting the primacy of "the great chain of being" or the authority of "the powers that be that are ordained of God." They mouth new slogans and appeal not to God and the hierarchy but to "history" and "the people." But is the freedom of the individual and the realization of the potential of the human mind any more likely to be achieved in societies that respond with the new clichés rather than the older ones? In both cases there is the same deadening of the spirit, the same arbitrary and abstract authoritarianism, the same kind of one-dimensional collectivist approach to the problems of individual human lives, the same depersonalization of mankind. New left is old absolutism writ large.

The February revolution of 1917 which overthrew the Romanov dynasty was the spontaneous outbreak of a multitude exasperated by the privations of the war and by manifest inequality in the distribution of burdens. It was welcomed and utilized by a broad stratum of the bourgeoisie and of the official class, which had lost confidence in the autocratic system of government and especially in the persons of the Tsar and of his advisers; it was from this section of the population that the first Provisional Government was drawn. The revolutionary parties played no direct part in the making of the revolution. They did not expect it, and were at first somewhat nonplussed by it. The creation at the moment of the revolution of a Petrograd Soviet of Workers' Deputies was a spontaneous act of groups of workers without central direction. It was a revival of the Petersburg Soviet which had played a brief but glorious rôle in the revolution of 1905, and was, like its predecessor, a non-party organization elected by factory workers, Social-

Revolutionaries, Mensheviks and Bolsheviks being all represented in it. It did not at first aspire to governmental power, partly because its leaders took the hitherto accepted view that Russia was ripe only for a bourgeois, and not yet for a socialist, revolution, and partly because it had no sense of its own competence or preparedness to govern. The attitude of the Soviet was afterwards described by Lenin as a *"voluntary* surrender of state power to the bourgeoisie and *its* Provisional Government". The fact, however, that the writ of the Soviet was recognized by an ever-increasing number of workers and soldiers gave it, in spite of itself, a position of authority which could not be ignored; and this was the practical and almost accidental basis of the so-called "dual power" set up by the February revolution, when public authority was in some sort exercised by two bodies whose attitude to each other swung uneasily between rivalry and cooperation: the Provisional Government, which was the legal successor of the Tsarist government and recognized as such by the outside world, and the self-constituted and therefore revolutionary Soviets of Workers' Deputies. The example of Petrograd was followed by the setting up of Soviets in Moscow and other large cities and, somewhat later, in country districts; and this, in turn, led to the summoning of a first "all-Russian conference" of Soviets at the end of March 1917.

Of the two factions of the Russian Social-Democratic Workers' Party it was the Mensheviks who at first profited most by the February revolution. As in 1905, the promise of constitutional government seemed to justify their programme and gave them the advantage of the Bolsheviks. A bourgeois revolutionary régime, enjoying the critical support of good Marxists until such time as bourgeois capitalism had exhausted its potentialities and the way was open for the socialist revolution—this was precisely the Menshevik picture of the first stage in the revolutionary process. Indeed the "dual power", considered as a constitutional partnership between bourgeois government and proletarian "legal opposition", was essentially Menshevik in conception. The main point of embarrassment for the Mensheviks was their attitude to the war, on which they were not agreed among themselves. But a policy of pressing the bourgeois government to end the war on a democratic programme without entering into precise details of the ways and means of ending it seemed for the moment to meet all requirements. The Mensheviks quickly emerged into a predominant position in the Petrograd Soviet: its first president was the Georgian Menshevik Chkheidze. The principal rivals of the Mensheviks were the Social-Revolutionaries. It was not long before the Soviets of Workers' Deputies became Soviets of Workers' and Soldiers' Deputies; and, as the armies dissolved into struggling masses of peasants crying out for peace and land and counting on the Social-Revolutionaries, the traditional party of the peasant revolution, to fulfil their ambitions, the star of the Social-Revolutionaries (or SRs, as they were commonly called) continued to ascend.

The Bolsheviks seemed to have gained least. The suddenness of the revolution had left the determination of Bolshevik policy in the hands of three men (two of them young and without experience) cut off not only from the party centre in Switzerland, but from the other experienced party leaders marooned in Siberia. The position was embarrassing. On the one hand, they were committed by Lenin's theses of 1914 and by everything he had since written to the sensational policy, known to be distasteful even to many Bolsheviks, of advocating civil war and national defeatism. On the other hand, the party resolution of 1905 had contemplated the establishment of a provisional revolutionary government as the result of a democratic revolution and had admitted that Bolshevik cooperation in such a government might be desirable "for the purposes of a ruthless struggle against all counter-revolutionary attempts and of the defence of the independent interests of the working class". With so much guidance and no more, Shlyapnikov, Zalutsky and Molotov, constituting the Russian bureau of the central committee, drafted a party manifesto which was issued as a broadsheet on February 26, 1917, and appeared two days later as a supplement to the first issue of the *Izvestiya* of the Petrograd Soviet.

All things considered, it was a creditable effort. Since no provisional government had yet been proclaimed, the question of defining relations to it did not arise. The manifesto called on the working class and the revolutionary army to create a "provisional revolutionary government", which would establish a republic, introduce democratic reforms such as the eight-hour day, the confiscation of estates and the creation of a constituent assembly on a basis of universal suffrage and secret ballot, confiscate and distribute stocks of food, and "enter into negotiations with the proletariat of the belligerent countries for a revolutionary struggle of the peoples of all countries against their oppressors and enslavers . . . and for the termination of the bloody human slaughter which has been imposed on the enslaved peoples". Factory workers and insurgent armies were urged to elect their representatives to this provisional revolutionary government. The appeal ended with salutes to "the red banner of revolution", "the democratic republic", "the revolutionary working class" and "the revolutionary people and insurgent army". Lenin, who read extracts from this manifesto in the German press while he was still in Switzerland struggling to arrange for his journey to Russia, noted as "especially important and especially topical" the "perfectly correct idea of our central committee that the indispensable thing for peace is relations with the proletarians of all the belligerent countries".

The February revolution had removed all obstacles other than the shortage of man-power to a revival of the party journal. The publication of *Pravda* was resumed on March 5, 1917, under an editorial board consisting of Molotov, who as member of the bureau of the central committee bore the chief responsibility, Kalinin, valued perhaps, then as later, less for his intellectual qualities than for his prestige as a usable party member of peasant origin, and Eremeev, of whom little is known except that he had been a contributor to the *Pravda* of 1912. The first issue was distributed free, the second sold 100,000 copies. The views expressed in the first seven numbers of the new *Pravda* were broadly those of the party manifesto. It denounced the existing Provisional Government as "a government of capitalists and landowners", and thought that the Soviet should convene a constituent assembly to establish a "democratic republic". On the issue of the war, it published on March 10, 1917, a resolution of the bureau advocating a transformation of the imperialist war into a civil war for the liberation of the peoples from the yoke of the ruling classes, though it still refrained from the explicit advocacy of national defeatism. But it was not immune from backslidings. The same issue which printed this resolution printed an article by Olminsky which concluded:

> The [bourgeois] revolution is not yet completed. We live under the slogan of "striking together". In party affairs, each party for itself; but all as one man for the common cause.

The position was complicated by the revival of the local Petrograd party committee, which, having for the first time acquired legal status, had attracted a large number of new recruits and exhibited a disconcerting variety of opinions. In general, the Petrograd committee stood further to the Right than the bureau. When on March 5, 1917, young Molotov appeared at one of its sessions as delegate of the bureau and proposed a resolution attacking the Provisional Government as counter-revolutionary and demanding its replacement by a government capable of carrying out a programme of democratic revolution, he failed to convince the majority of the committee, which adopted a text promising not to oppose the Provisional Government so long as "its actions correspond to the interests of the proletariat and of the broad democratic masses of the people".

This confused situation was worse confounded by the arrival in Petrograd from Siberia on March 13, 1917—the day on which the seventh issue of *Pravda* appeared—of Kamenev, Stalin and Muranov. Kamenev was an experienced writer and had been appointed editor of the central party organ—at that time the *Rabochaya Gazeta*—by the Prague conference of 1912; Stalin, having been a member of the central committee of the party since 1912, replaced Shlyapnikov as senior party organizer in Petrograd;

Muranov was one of the Bolshevik deputies of the fourth Duma. All three had formerly worked on the old *Pravda*. They at once took over the reins of authority from Shlyapnikov and his young colleagues; and *Pravda* of March 15, 1917, carried an announcement that Muranov had assumed the direction of the journal and that Stalin and Kamenev had joined the editorial board. The former members of the board presumably remained, though with diminished influence and prerogatives.

These proceedings, however distasteful to the stop-gap leaders who had acquitted themselves well in a difficult situation, were natural enough, and would have excited little interest but for the fact that the newcomers carried out a contentious change of policy. A brief article by Stalin in *Pravda* of March 14, 1917, was less remarkable for what was said than for what was omitted. It urged workers, peasants and soldiers to rally to the Soviets "as organs of the union and the power of the revolutionary forces of Russia". But it did not mention either the Provisional Government or the war; and the cautious appeal to "maintain the rights that have been won in order finally to beat down the old powers and to move the Russian revolution forward" approached more nearly to the Menshevik formula of pressing the bourgeoisie forward from behind than to the Bolshevik formula of taking the lead. The issue of the following day, which contained the announcement of the changes in the editorial board, carried on its front page a proclamation issued by the Petrograd Soviet "To the Peoples of the Whole World", announcing that "we shall stoutly defend our own liberty" and that "the Russian revolution will not flinch before the bayonets of the aggressors". This was followed by a signed article from Kamenev:

When army faces army, it would be the most inane policy to suggest to one of these armies to lay down its arms and go home. This would not be a policy of peace but a policy of slavery, which would be rejected with disgust by a free people.

A free people could only "answer bullet with bullet, shell with shell". This whole-hearted endorsement of national defence signally confirmed Kamenev's statement in court over two years earlier that he did not share Lenin's position.

According to Shlyapnikov, who at this point becomes our sole authority, *Pravda*'s change of front excited dismay among the Bolshevik factory workers, and a meeting was held at which the bureau, the Petrograd committee and the exiles from Siberia were all represented. In the course of the discussion, Stalin and Muranov disowned the views of Kamenev, who "submitted to the general decision and took up in the organization a 'moderate position' ". What resulted from the discussion seems to have been less a compromise than a deadlock; for while *Pravda* published no more articles so outspokenly in favour of national defence as that of Kamenev, it equally refrained from any fundamental attack on the Provisional Government or on its war policy. An older and more cautious editorial board had repressed the rash ardour displayed in the earlier issues and retired to a more comfortable position on the fence. When a party conference was held to decide the line to be taken at the first all-Russian conference of Soviets at the end of March 1917, the proposal put forward by Stalin to "support the Provisional Government in its activity only in so far as it moves along the path of satisfying the working class and the revolutionary peasantry" scarcely differed in substance from the formula approved by the Menshevik majority at the conference of Soviets; and most Bolsheviks shared the view expressed by Stalin that unification was possible "on a Zimmerwald-Kienthal line" with those Mensheviks who were against national "defencism".

More than seven years later, at the height of his controversy with Trotsky, Stalin confessed his error at this time. After arguing that the party could neither seek the overthrow of the Provisional Government, since it was bound up with the Soviets, nor support it, since it was an imperialist government, Stalin continued:

The party—its majority— . . . adopted a policy of pressure by the Soviets on the Provisional Government in the question of peace, and did not decide at once to take the step forward from the old slogan of the dictatorship of the proletariat and peasantry to the new slogan of power for the Soviets. This half-and-half policy was intended to give the Soviets a chance to detect in the concrete questions of peace the imperialist nature of the Provisional Government and so to detach them from it. But it was a profoundly mistaken position since it bred pacifist illusions, added fuel to the flame of defencism and hindered the revolutionary uprising of the masses. This mistaken position I shared with other party comrades, and renounced it completely only in the middle of April when I adhered to Lenin's theses.

The argument is not particularly convincing and attributes to subtlety of intention what was due to mere confusion. But sympathy may be felt with those who sought to hammer out a consistent Bolshevik policy in Petrograd in the March days of 1917. Nobody had yet contested the view that the Russian revolution was not, and could not be, other than a bourgeois revolution. This was the solid and accepted framework of doctrine into which policy had to fit. Yet it was difficult to discover within this framework any cogent reason to reject out of hand the Provisional Government, which was indubitably bourgeois, or to demand a transfer of power to the Soviets, which were essentially proletarian, or—least of all—to denounce the quest for a "democratic" peace and preach civil war and national defeat. The circle could not be squared. It was left to Lenin, before the eyes of his astonished followers, to smash the framework.

The scene of Lenin's arrival at the Finland station in Petrograd on the evening of April 3, 1917, has been recorded by at least four eye-witnesses. He had been met at Beloostrov, the last station outside Petrograd, by a group representing the Russian bureau of the central committee and headed by Shlyapnikov. In the train Lenin plied Shlyapnikov with questions "about the position of things in the party . . . about the causes of the turnover in *Pravda* towards 'defencism', about the position of individual colleagues". On arrival in Petrograd he was greeted by members of the central committee and the Petrograd committee of the party and of the staff of *Pravda*. Among them was Kamenev, whom he at once began good-humouredly to chide: "What is this you are writing in *Pravda*? We saw some of your articles and roundly abused you." Alexandra Kollontai produced a bouquet which Lenin carried awkwardly; and the party proceeded to the former imperial waiting-room. Here Lenin was officially welcomed by Chkheidze, the president of the Petrograd Soviet, who, in a few carefully chosen words, expressed his hopes for "a closing of the ranks of democracy" in defence of "our revolution". Lenin, turning vaguely away from the official party towards the assembled crowds outside, addressed them as "dear comrades, soldiers, sailors and workers", greeted in their persons "the victorious Russian revolution", declared that the "robber imperialist war" was the beginning of civil war all over Europe, and concluded:

Any day, if not today or tomorrow, the crash of the whole of European imperialism may come. The Russian revolution, made by you, has begun it and opened a new epoch. Hail the world-wide socialist revolution.

As Sukhanov notes, it was not a reply to Chkheidze. It did not even fit "the 'context' of the Russian revolution as understood by all without exception who had witnessed it or taken part in it". Lenin had spoken; and his first words had been not of the bourgeois, but of the socialist, revolution.

On the square outside the station there was a mass demonstration of Bolsheviks headed by an armoured car carrying the banner of the party. Lenin, standing on the armoured car, addressed the cheering crowds in similar terms and, later on the same evening, spoke for two hours to a party audience at party headquarters. The slowly mounting astonishment with which his words were received by the other party leaders was described by an eye-witness ten years later:

It had been expected that Vladimir Ilich would arrive and call to order the Russian bureau of the central committee and especially comrade Molotov, who occupied a particularly irreconcilable position in regard to the Provisional Government. It turned out, however, that it was Molotov who was nearest of all to Ilich.

On the following day there were more discussions at his sister's flat and at the editorial offices of *Pravda*; and in the afternoon he spoke before a gathering of social-democrats—Bolshevik, Menshevik and independent—at the Tauride palace, where the Soviet held its sessions. It was on this last occasion that Lenin for the first time read the famous "April theses" which summarized his views; that Bogdanov interrupted with cries of "Delirium, the delirium of a madman"; that Goldenberg, another former Bolshevik, declared that "Lenin had proposed himself as candidate for a European throne vacant for 30 years, the throne of Bakunin"; and that Steklov, the editor of *Izvestiya* and soon to join the Bolsheviks, added that Lenin's speech consisted of "abstract constructions" which he would soon abandon when he had acquainted himself with the Russian situation. Lenin's speech was attacked from all sides, only Kollontai speaking in support of it; and he left the hall without exercising his right of reply. On the same evening he re-read the theses to a gathering of Bolshevik leaders, and once more found himself completely isolated. The theses *On the Tasks of the Proletariat in the Present Revolution* were published in *Pravda* of April 7, 1917.

The key to Lenin's position was in the second of his theses:

> The peculiarity of the current moment in Russia consists in the *transition* from the first stage of the revolution, which gave power to the bourgeoisie as a result of the insufficient consciousness and organization of the proletariat, *to its second* stage, which should give the power into the hands of the proletariat and poorest strata of the peasantry.

The negative conclusion of this was to reject the Provisional Government and its support of the war, and to abandon the folly of demanding that "this government, a government of capitalists, should *cease* to be imperialist". The positive conclusion was to explain to the masses that "the Soviet of Workers' Deputies is the *one possible* form of revolutionary government". So long as the Soviet was "subject to the influence of the bourgeoisie", that is to

44

say, so long as it contained a non-Bolshevik majority, this work of education was the main task of the party. But the goal was clear:

> Not a parliamentary republic—a return to that from the Soviet of Workers' Deputies would be a step backwards—but a republic of Soviets of Workers', Poor Peasants' and Peasants' Deputies throughout the country, growing from below upwards.

Lenin thus implied that the moment when the Bolsheviks, by means of mass education, secured a majority in the Soviet would be the moment of the passing of the revolution into its second, or socialist, phase. This implication was carried into the economic theses, which proposed the nationalization of all land and the transformation of large estates into model farms under the control of the Soviet, the fusion of existing banks into a national bank (a milder periphrasis for the nationalization of banks), and added as the third point:

> Not the "introduction" of socialism as our *immediate* task, but immediate transition merely to *control* by the Soviet of Workers' Deputies over the social production and distribution of products.

The theses ended with a proposal to revise the party programme and to change the name of the party from "social-democratic" to "communist", and with a demand for the creation of a revolutionary International.

Lenin's cautious phraseology left room for a certain practical vagueness about the precise moment of the transition to socialism, but none for doubt about this transition as the main goal; and it was on this point that the battle was at once joined. On the day after the publication of the theses, *Pravda* carried what appeared to be an editorial note signed by Kamenev emphasizing that they represented only Lenin's "*personal* opinion" and concluding:

> In so far as concerns Lenin's general scheme it appears to us unacceptable, since it starts from the assumption that the bourgeois revolution is *finished* and counts on the immediate transformation of this revolution into a socialist revolution.

On the same day the Petrograd committee of the party discussed Lenin's theses and rejected them by 13 votes to 2, with 1 abstention. The challenge had still to be taken up at the Petrograd "all-city" party conference on April 14, 1917, and at the all-Russian conference which was to follow ten days later. Meanwhile Lenin developed his views in a further article in *Pravda* and in two pamphlets, though the second of these was not published till some months later.

In Lenin's analysis the "dual power" consisted of two distinct governments. The Provisional Government was the government of the *bourgeoisie*; the Soviets were a dictatorship formed by "the proletariat and the peasantry (dressed in soldiers' uniforms)". Since the transfer of power to this dual authority had taken place, it was "to this extent" true that "the bourgeois or bourgeois-democratic revolution is *finished*", even though all the necessary bourgeois-democratic reforms had not yet been carried out; "the revolutionary-democratic dictatorship of the proletariat and the peasantry has been realised" ("in a certain form and to a certain degree", added Lenin cautiously in a footnote). The peculiarity of the situation was the "interweaving" (Lenin used this word several times) of the bourgeois power of the Provisional Government and the (potential, if not actual) revolutionary dictatorship of the Soviets. The future turned on the struggle between the bourgeoisie and the proletariat for the peasant masses. For the moment "the fact of *class* cooperation between the bourgeoisie and the peasantry" was decisive; the Soviets were still, in accordance with the Menshevik view, "an annex of the bourgeois government". But if and when the peasantry seized the land for itself (meaning, in class terms, that the peasantry would split away from the bourgeoisie and ally itself with the revolutionary proletariat, and, in political terms, that the Bolsheviks would win a majority in the Soviets), "then this will be a new stage of the bourgeois-democratic revolution". Lenin's powerful argument once more implied the transition to socialism, though it stopped short of explicitly proclaiming it. He still regarded it as premature to demand the overthrow of the Provisional Government. But he emphasized that the "dual power" could be no more than a transitional phase of struggle which must end in a victory for one side or the other. *"There cannot be* two powers in the state." The Menshevik conception of partnership would not work. Sooner or later the Soviets must overthrow the Provisional Government or themselves be destroyed.

The Petrograd party conference proved to be a sort of rehearsal for the all-Russian party conference, so that the issues were debated twice over by the same protagonists and with the same results in the smaller and in the larger assembly. The proceedings again demonstrated Lenin's immense power over the party, a power resting not on rhetoric, but on clear-headed and incisive argument conveying an irresistible impression of a unique mastery of the situation. "Before Lenin arrived", said a delegate at the Petrograd conference, "all the comrades were wandering in the dark." Now only Kamenev presented a coherent defence of the policies accepted by all the leading Bolsheviks in Petrograd before the presentation of the April theses. The main issue was narrowed down to the question whether, as Lenin proposed, the party should work for the transfer of power to the Soviets, or whether, as Kamenev desired, it should be content with "the most watchful control" over the Provisional Government by the Soviets, Kamenev being particularly severe on anything that could be construed as incitement to overthrow the government. In the decisive vote Kamenev's amendment was defeated by 20 votes to 6, with 9 abstentions.

The all-Russian party conference (known in party history as the "April conference") met ten days later under the shadow of a ministerial crisis. Milyukov's note of April 18, 1917, promising fidelity to the undertakings given to the allies by the Tsarist government, had raised a storm of protest which led to his enforced resignation. At the conference the tide flowed still more strongly in Lenin's favour. Stalin briefly, and Zinoviev at greater length, supported him against Kamenev. Lenin at one moment held out an olive branch to Kamenev by saying that, though the Provisional Government must be overthrown, it could not be overthrown "at once or in the ordinary way". The main resolutions were passed by overwhelming majorities of the 150 delegates. With only seven abstentions, the conference declared that the advent of the Provisional Government "did not change and could not change" the imperialist character of Russia's participation in the war, and undertook to assist "the transfer of all state power in all belligerent countries into the hands of the revolutionary proletariat". This was followed by a resolution, carried with only three dissentients and eight abstentions, condemning the Provisional Government for its "open collaboration" with the "bourgeois and landowners' counter-revolution", and demanding active preparations among the "proletarians of town and country" to bring about "the rapid transfer of all state power into the hands of the Soviets of workers' and soldiers' deputies or of other organs directly expressing the will of the majority of the people (organs of local self-government, constituent assembly, etc.)". The most substantial opposition was manifested to the resolution containing an analysis of the "current situation"; for, even after it had accepted Lenin's policy, the party, long attuned to the conception of a bourgeois revolution as the proximate goal, still had its hesitations about proclaiming the transition to the socialist stage of the revolution. This resolution declared that "the objective conditions of the socialist revolution, which were undoubtedly present before the war in the most advanced countries, have ripened further and continue to ripen in consequence of the war with extreme rapidity"; that "the Russian revolution is only the first stage in the first of the proletarian revolutions inevitably resulting from the war"; and that common action by the workers of different countries was the only way to guarantee "the most regular development and surest success of the world socialist revolution". It then reverted to the old argument that, while the immediate realization of "the socialist transformation" was not possible in Russia, the proletariat should none the less refuse to support the bourgeoisie and should itself take the lead in carrying out the practical reforms requisite to complete the bourgeois revolution. This resolution was carried only by a majority of 71 to 39, with 8 abstentions. Nor did anyone answer the question which only Rykov seems to have raised:

Whence will arise the sun of the socialist revolution? I think that with all existing conditions, with our standard of living, the initiation of the socialist revolution does not belong to us. We have not the strength, nor the objective conditions, for it.

The adoption at the April conference of the slogan "all power to the Soviets", though it did not betoken immediate revolutionary action, for the first time gave concrete shape and a constitutional mould to the Bolshevik scheme of revolution. Lenin's somewhat lukewarm attitude towards the Soviets in 1905 had been modified by their vigour and success in mobilizing popular support, and by the prestige which attached to them even after their downfall. In the spring of 1906 he referred to them as "new organs of *revolutionary power*":

These organs were founded exclusively by the *revolutionary* strata of the population, they were founded outside all laws and regulations in an entirely revolutionary way as a product of primitive popular creativeness, as an exhibition of the independent action of the people.

They could thus be regarded as an approximation to Lenin's conception of a revolutionary-democratic dictatorship of the proletariat and the peasantry, and as the "*de facto* beginnings of a provisional government". But in the ensuing period of reaction and discouragement the memory of the Soviets faded and little was heard of them in party discussions. When Lenin delivered a long lecture on the 1905 revolution to a Swiss audience in January 1917, the Soviets were dismissed in three or four sentences, though it was still claimed for them that in some places they had "really functioned in the capacity of a new state power".

It was therefore understandable that the revival of the Petrograd Soviet in February 1917 should not at first, in view of Menshevik predominance in its ranks, have greatly excited the Bolshevik group

49

in the capital: it was not mentioned in the first Bolshevik proclamation of February 26. But here a curious parallel occurs between
Marx and Lenin. Marx's "dictatorship of the proletariat" remained,
for twenty years after he first enunciated it, an abstract and disem-
bodied conception, till Marx eventually discovered its embodiment
in an institution created by men who were for the most part not
his disciples, and regarded at the outset by Marx himself with thinly
veiled suspicion: the Paris commune. Lenin had evolved all the
essentials of his theory of revolution before Soviets had been heard
of; and his attitude to the first Petersburg Soviet—a non-party or,
worse still, a Menshevik affair—was as hesitant as that of Marx to
the commune. Yet the Soviets, raised to a pinnacle by their challenge to autocracy in 1905, became in the spring of 1917 the predestined repositories of the revolutionary power of which Lenin
dreamed. The first of his *Letters from Afar* written from Switzerland in March 1917, and the only one of them to be published before his arrival in Petrograd, hailed the Petrograd Soviet as a "new,
unofficial, undeveloped, still comparatively weak *workers' government* expressing the interests of the proletariat and of all the
poorest part of the town and country population"; and this view
implied, as Lenin saw, that the situation was already "in transition
from the first to the second stage of the revolution". The way
was thus prepared for the April theses, in which recognition of
this transition was clearly connected with the new slogan "all
power to the Soviets". It was at this time that Lenin proclaimed
the Soviets to be "a power *of the same type* as the Paris commune
of 1871"—a power whose source was "not a law previously discussed and passed by a parliament, but a direct initiative of the popular masses from below and on the spot, a direct 'usurpation', to
employ the current expression". Lenin thus triumphantly linked
himself with Marx and the Soviets with the commune. The Soviets
were not only a realization of the "revolutionary-democratic dictatorship"; they were, like the commune, a foretaste of the Marxist
dictatorship of the proletariat.

But the party line remained fluid on one point. The concluding words of the party programme adopted in 1903 and still unaltered in 1917 demanded "a constituent assembly elected by the whole people"; and the third all-Bolshevik party congress of 1905 had once more called for "the convening by way of revolution of a constituent assembly on the basis of universal equal and direct suffrage and with secrecy of the ballot". It is true that Lenin at the same time poked fun at those who believed in the "immediate birth" of a constituent assembly, and declared that "without armed insurrection a constituent assembly is a phantom, a phrase, a lie, a Frankfort talking-shop". But this essentially bourgeois-democratic institution continued none the less to occupy a cardinal place in Lenin's scheme of revolution. In April 1917 it would have been possible to argue that this plank in the party platform belonged to a period when the bourgeois revolution lay in the future and had been rendered obsolete by the advent of the February revolution. But this argument was never used, no doubt because neither Lenin himself nor—still less—his followers were prepared to commit themselves to the view that the bourgeois revolution had been completed. The resolution of the April conference had named both the Soviets and the constituent assembly as potential recipients of power, without apparently choosing between them; and throughout the period from February to October 1917 the Bolsheviks, in common with all other Left groups, continued to voice the demand for the constituent assembly and to censure the Provisional Government for dilatoriness in convening it, unconscious of any inconsistency between this demand and the concurrent slogan "all power to the Soviets". If this inconsistency—or this inability to choose—had been probed to the source, it might have thrown light on the initial dissensions in the party over the April theses. But for the present it reflected, not a division of opinion, but an uncertainty and lack of definition in the mind of the party leaders, including Lenin, on the character of the current revolutionary process. Events were left to prepare the eventual clarification.

From the moment of the April conference every move on the political chessboard seemed to play into the hands of the Bolsheviks and to justify Lenin's boldest calculations. Milyukov's note of April 18 had been a slap in the face not so much for the Bolsheviks as for those moderate elements in the Soviet which, while rejecting the Bolshevik policy of peace through civil war and national defeat, were none the less insistent on a renunciation of "imperialist" designs and on immediate efforts to secure a "democratic" peace. Milyukov's resignation brought about the downfall of the government. In the first Provisional Government Kerensky had been the only socialist minister; and his equivocal position had been marked by his frequent attempts to disown responsibility for acts of other ministers. Early in May a new government was formed in which, though Lvov remained premier, six socialist ministers were included as representatives of the Soviet: two portfolios were held by SRs, two by Mensheviks and two by independent socialists.

This rearrangement was designed ostensibly to increase the power and prestige of the Soviet by strengthening its control of the government. The results were quite different. The new government, still the prisoner of an administrative machine run by the bourgeoisie and by the old official class, hard pressed by the allies and faced by the quite insoluble problem of a democratic peace, could do little to satisfy the soldiers and workers who more and more clamoured for some token that an end to the war was at hand. The Soviet had hitherto been a coalition of socialist parties for the defence of the interests of the workers against the bourgeoisie. Now it could no longer win credit in their eyes by harassing a bourgeois government in which it was strongly represented. Splits developed in the SR and Menshevik parties between those who supported and those who attacked the socialist ministers. Most important of all, the Bolsheviks were now the only party uncompromised by participation in a feeble bourgeois-socialist coalition and offering a clear-cut policy of peace at any price. The process by which they eventually won the confidence of the vast majority of soldiers and workers, and became the dominant power in the Soviets, had begun.

Early in May another significant event had occurred. Among the exiles now flocking back in large numbers, Trotsky reached Petrograd from the United States, having been delayed for five weeks by the British authorities. On the day after his arrival he spoke in the Petrograd Soviet; and his prestige as the outstanding figure of the original Soviet of 1905 at once made him a potential leader. He joined a small social-democratic group called the "united social-democrats" (more commonly known as the *Mezhraiontsy*), which had existed in Petrograd since 1913 and claimed independence both of Bolsheviks and of Mensheviks. In the past his restless intellect and temperament had led him to quarrel with every party leadership. But now he thirsted for action, and saw in Lenin the only man of action on the scene, despising alike the SRs, the Mensheviks and those weak-kneed Bolsheviks who had hesitated to answer Lenin's call. Almost from the moment of his arrival it was clear that an alliance would be struck. The April conference itself had recognized the importance of "rapprochement and union with groups and movements which really stand on the ground of internationalism". On May 10, 1917, Lenin in person attended a meeting of the *Mezhraiontsy* and offered them a seat on the editorial board of *Pravda* and on the organizing committee of the forthcoming party congress, proposing also to extend the offer to Martov's group of "internationalist" Mensheviks. According to notes taken by Lenin at the time, Trotsky replied that he was in agreement "in so far as Bolshevism internationalizes itself", but added proudly: "The Bolsheviks have de-bolshevized themselves, and I cannot call myself a Bolshevik. It is impossible to demand of us a recognition of Bolshevism." The meeting led to no result. In effect, Trotsky, faithful to his old policy of reconciliation all round, wanted an amalgamation of the groups on equal terms and under a new name. Lenin had no intention of weakening or diluting the instrument which he had created; the party must remain supreme and intact. He could afford to wait.

The summer of 1917 in Petrograd was a period of incessant conferences. An all-Russian peasant congress in May was dominated by the SRs and voted firmly for support of the Provisional Government. On the other hand, a conference of Petrograd factory workers at the end of the same month was the first representative body to yield a Bolshevik majority—a foretaste of what was to come. The beginning of June brought the first All-Russian Congress of Soviets. Of its 822 delegates with voting rights, the SRs accounted for 285, the Mensheviks for 248 and the Bolsheviks for 105. Nearly 150 delegates belonged to various minor groups, and 45 declared no party allegiance—an indication that the political affiliations of many outlying Soviets were still fluid. The Bolshevik leaders attended in full force; Trotsky and Lunacharsky were among the 10 delegates of the "united social-democrats", who solidly supported the Bolsheviks throughout the three weeks of the congress.

The most dramatic moment of the congress occurred on its second day during the speech of the Menshevik Minister of Posts and Telegraphs, Tsereteli, and was thus reported in the official records:

At the present moment there is no political party which would say: "Give the power into our hands, go away, we will take your place". There is no such party in Russia. (Lenin from his seat: "There is.")

The claim, or the threat, was not taken very seriously. The Bolsheviks were in a small minority at the congress, and Lenin's principal speech was frequently interrupted. The congress passed a vote of confidence in the Provisional Government, rejecting a Bolshevik resolution which demanded "the transfer of all state power into the hands of the All-Russian Soviet of Workers', Soldiers' and Peasants' Deputies". Not the least important decision of the congress was to give itself a regular constitution. The congress itself was to meet every three months, and created for current action a "central organ" in the form of an "All-Russian Central Executive Committee" (Vserossiiskii Tsentral'nyi Ispolnitel'nyi Komitet or, from its initials, VTsIK) whose decisions would be binding on all Soviets in the intervals between congresses. VTsIK was elected forthwith on a proportional basis: of its 250 members 35 were Bolsheviks.

Lenin's assertion of the Bolshevik willingness to take power was

a declaration of war on the Provisional Government and was intended as such. The authority of the coalition was wilting: it was
the period of what Trotsky called "the dual powerlessness". The
next step was to test the state of mind of workers and soldiers in
Petrograd. The Bolsheviks summoned their supporters to a street
demonstration on June 9, 1917, but called it off in face of opposition in the congress. The congress itself then arranged a monster street demonstration in support of the Soviets on June 18,
1917. But not more than a handful of the banners carried expressed confidence in the Provisional Government, and it was
said that the slogans inscribed on 90 per cent of them were Bolshevik. A more serious popular rising began on July 3, 1917, at
the moment when the government, hard pressed by the allies, had
ordered a large-scale military offensive in Galicia. The demonstrations lasted for four days and became seriously menacing. It was
freely believed that this was the beginning of a serious Bolshevik
attempt to seize power, though the party leaders insisted that it was
a spontaneous demonstration which they themselves struggled to
keep within bounds; and Lenin himself argued that it was impossible to act so long as a majority still believed in "the petty bourgeois capitalist-controlled policy of the Mensheviks and SRs".
This time, however, the government took up the challenge. Loyal
troops were drafted into the capital; *Pravda* was suppressed; and
orders were issued for the arrest of the three chief Bolshevik leaders. Kamenev was taken; Lenin and Zinoviev went into hiding,
and escaped to Finland.

Within the next few days the Galician offensive failed, with
heavy losses; another ministerial crisis led to the resignation of
Lvov and the appointment of Kerensky as premier; Trotsky and
the *Mezhraiontsy,* some 4000 strong, at length joined the Bolsheviks; and there was a flood of further arrests, including Trotsky,
Lunacharsky and Kollontai. At the end of July, 1917, with Lenin
and other leaders still in hiding or in prison, the sixth party congress—the first since the London congress of 1907—was held in
Petrograd. Sverdlov presided; and it fell to Stalin and Bukharin

to make the main political reports. Lenin had furnished guidance in a small pamphlet written since his retirement into hiding *On the Slogans,* in which he argued for the withdrawal of the slogan "all power to the Soviets". This had been devised in the days when a peaceful transfer to Soviets representing the proletariat and the peasantry still seemed possible. Since the July troubles it was clear that the bourgeoisie had declared for counter-revolution, and that it would fight: the existing Soviets were tools of the bourgeoisie. The congress, skilfully led by Stalin in face of some opposition on this point, declared that "all power to the Soviets" was "the slogan of the peaceful development of the revolution, of the painless transfer of power from the bourgeoisie to the workers and peasants", and that nothing would now avail short of the complete liquidation of the counter-revolutionary bourgeoisie. When Nogin, echoing the doubt expressed by Rykov at the April conference, asked whether the country had "really made such a leap in two months that it is already prepared for socialism", Stalin boldly replied that "it would be unworthy pedantry to ask that Russia should 'wait' with her socialist transformation till Europe 'begins' ", and that "the possibility is not excluded that Russia may be the country which points the way to socialism"—an acceptance of Trotsky's thesis of 1906. At the same time there was a warning against being provoked into "premature fighting". With the leaders dispersed, and the party itself threatened at any moment with official persecution, the congress could do little but mark time.

The principal event of August 1917 was an all-party "state conference" convened in Moscow by Kerensky to advise on the state of the nation. Composed of more than 2000 delegates drawn from a variety of public bodies and organizations, it proved a wordy fiasco. It was followed at the end of August by the one attempt of this period at a military *coup* from the Right—the Kornilov insurrection. Though the plot miscarried ignominiously without a blow being struck, it caused a flurry of alarm in all the Left parties and groups. Even Lenin offered a compromise to the Mensheviks and SRs: the Bolsheviks would resume their support of the Soviets if they in their turn would finally break with the bourgeois parties. But this led to nothing. The Mensheviks and SRs convened a "democratic conference" to match the "state conference" in Moscow; and this created a "council of the republic" (the so-called "pre-parliament") designed to fill the gap until the constituent assembly should meet. By this time the Bolshevik star was rising rapidly. After the Kornilov affair the Bolsheviks secured majorities in the Petrograd and Moscow Soviets, though the SRs and Mensheviks still dominated VTsIK. In the country, as the self-demobilized soldiers returned to their homes, land-hunger grew more acute and peasant disorders and the ransacking of estates more frequent; and with this went a discrediting of the SRs, who had done nothing, and a shift of sympathy towards the Bolsheviks, who promised everything. The conditions which Lenin had foreseen in his April theses as justifying the transition to the second stage of the revolution were maturing fast.

Lenin's first reaction was to revive the slogan "all power to the Soviets". This was done in an article written in the first part of September and published on September 14, 1917, in *Rabochii Put'*. Then on September 12, 13 and 14, growing more and more impatient in his enforced retreat, Lenin wrote two secret letters in succession to the party central committee declaring the time ripe for the Bolsheviks to seize power by armed force. Trotsky, released from prison in the middle of September, was elected president of the Petrograd Soviet, which became the principal focus of Bolshevik militancy. Throughout the next month the battle over the April theses was repeated in a new context. The first clash in the central committee occurred over participation in the "democratic conference", Kamenev and Rykov supporting it and Trotsky and Stalin demanding a boycott. The decision went in favour of participation and was severely blamed by Lenin who applauded Trotsky's stand. Towards the end of September, 1917, Lenin, more and more excited and determined, moved up from Helsingfors to Viborg to be nearer the scene of action. A short article in

Rabochii Put' entitled *The Crisis Is Ripe* repeated previous arguments and added a new one: growing disorders in the belligerent countries and the beginning of mutinies in the German army and fleet made it clear that "we stand on the threshold of a world-wide proletarian revolution". But the most significant part of the article was a postscript not for publication, but for communication to members of the central committee. He accused them of ignoring his previous communications and offered his resignation from the central committee in order to regain his freedom to agitate among the rank and file of the party; "for it is my profound conviction that if we 'wait' for the congress of Soviets and let slip the present moment, we shall ruin the revolution".

Lenin's threat seems to have once more reduced the central committee to an embarrassed silence: there is no record of any answer. The personal touch was required to shake the prevailing inertia or scepticism. On October 9, 1917, Lenin came in disguise to Petrograd, and on the following day appeared at a meeting of the committee which was destined to become historic. His presence and reproaches of "indifference to the question of insurrection" sufficed to turn the scale. By a majority of 10 votes (Lenin, Trotsky, Stalin, Sverdlov, Uritsky, Dzerzhinsky, Kollontai, Bubnov, Sokolnikov, Lomov) to 2 (Kamenev and Zinoviev, now for the first time united in an inglorious partnership) the committee decided to prepare for armed insurrection and to appoint a "political bureau" to carry out the decision. This "politburo" (the first germ of what later became a permanent institution) consisted of seven persons: Lenin, Zinoviev, Kamenev, Trotsky, Stalin, Sokolnikov and Bubnov. It is significant of the sense of solidarity among the party leaders at this time and of the requirements of party discipline that the two who had voted against the decision were none the less included as a matter of course in the executive organ. Six days later the Petrograd Soviet created a "military-revolutionary committee" under the presidency of Trotsky as president of the Soviet, with Podvoisky as his effective deputy; and it was this body rather than the party "politburo" which made the military preparations for the revolution.

The battle was, however, still not finally won. On October 11, 1917, Kamenev and Zinoviev circulated a letter to all the principal Bolshevik organizations protesting against the decision for "armed insurrection". On October 16, Lenin once more stated the case for the immediate seizure of power to an enlarged meeting of the central committee attended by Bolsheviks from the Petrograd party committee, from the military organization of the Petrograd Soviet and from the trade unions and factory committees. Since the Kornilov affair, he argued, the masses had been behind the party. But the question was not one of a formal majority:

The position is clear. Either a Kornilov dictatorship or a dictatorship of the proletariat and the poorest strata of the peasantry. We cannot be guided by the mood of the masses: that is changeable and unaccountable. We must be guided by an objective analysis and estimate of the revolution. The masses have given their confidence to the Bolsheviks and ask from them not words, but deeds.

Lenin reverted to the international, especially the German, situation which justified the conclusion that "if we come out now, we shall have on our side all proletarian Europe". The discussion showed that, though the central committee might have been haltingly won over by Lenin's magnetism, the doubts of Kamenev and Zinoviev were still shared in wider party circles. Zinoviev and Kamenev repeated their objections. Stalin and other members of the central committee supported Lenin.

Here are two lines [said Stalin]: one is headed for the victory of the revolution and leans on Europe: the other does not believe in the revolution and counts only on being an opposition. The Petrograd Soviet has already taken its stand on the road to insurrection by refusing to sanction the removal of the armies.

The debate was somewhat unreal. Active preparations were being pressed forward by the Petrograd Soviet and its military-revolutionary committee. But military preparations could not be discussed at such a gathering; and neither Trotsky nor Podvoisky spoke, if indeed they were present. The meeting reaffirmed by 19 votes to 2 the decision to proceed with the preparations for an immediate insurrection, though a proposal of Zinoviev to await the meeting of the second All-Russian Congress of Soviets, convened for October 20 (but afterwards postponed to October 25), obtained 6 votes against 15. At the conclusion of the meeting the central committee met alone, and appointed a "military-revolutionary centre" consisting of Sverdlov, Stalin, Bubnov, Uritsky and Dzerzhinsky which was to form part of the military-revolutionary committee of the Petrograd Soviet. This was a curious early instance of the fusion of party and Soviet institutions. Contemporary records make no further mention of the centre: it was evidently intended as a contact group rather than as a separate organ, and, like the "politburo" appointed a week earlier, never seems to have come into existence.

At the end of the meeting of October 16, 1917, Kamenev resigned his membership of the central committee. Two days later he published in *Novaya Zhizn'*, a non-party journal of the Left, a letter once more protesting, in his own name and that of Zinoviev, against the decision. The letter was not only a breach of party discipline (since Kamenev was still a member of the party), but a betrayal to the world of the party decision—though in the state of disorganization and impotence into which the Provisional Government had now fallen the disclosure of preparations for an insurrection against it was perhaps as likely to intensify panic as to provoke effective counter-measures. The party, on the eve of the decisive action which was to put its fortunes to the supreme test, was threatened with a grave domestic crisis. Lenin, after the meeting of October 16, had retired once more into hiding. But on October 18—the day of the publication in *Novaya Zhizn'*—he wrote a letter to members of the party describing the act of Kamenev and Zinoviev as "strike-breaking" and "a crime", and declaring that he no longer regarded them as comrades and would demand their exclusion from the party. This was followed on the next day by a more detailed letter in the same sense to the central committee. Trotsky, in an attempt to cover up Kamenev's indiscretion, publicly denied in the Petrograd Soviet that any decision had been taken for armed insurrection. Kamenev, believing or pretending to believe that Trotsky had been converted to his view, declared that he agreed with every word Trotsky had said; and Zinoviev wrote in the same sense to the party journal *Rabochii Put'*. His letter was published on the morning of October 20, 1917, in the same issue which carried the last installment of an article by Lenin vigorously attacking the views of Kamenev and Zinoviev, though without naming them. Stalin tried to pour oil on the waters by appending an editorial note in the following terms:

We in our turn express the hope that the declaration of comrade Zinoviev (as well as the declaration of comrade Kamenev in the Soviet) may be considered to close the question. The sharp tone of comrade Lenin's article does not alter the fact that in fundamentals we remain of one mind.

Feelings therefore ran high when, in the absence of Lenin, the central committee met on October 20, 1917. Sverdlov read Lenin's letter to the committee. After a debate Kamenev's resignation was accepted by a majority of five to three; and a specific injunction was issued to Kamenev and Zinoviev to make no further public pronouncements against decisions of the central committee or of the party. Lenin's demand for their expulsion from the party was not taken up. Meanwhile Trotsky protested not only against the declarations of Kamenev and Zinoviev, but against the editorial note in *Rabochii Put'* which appeared to exculpate them. Sokolnikov declared that, though a member of the editorial board, he had no responsibility for the note and did not approve of it; and Stalin offered his resignation from the board. The committee prudently decided not to discuss the matter or accept the resignation, and passed to other business. It was the first open clash between the future rivals.

The critical moment was now at hand, being fixed by the decision to strike the blow before the second All-Russian Congress of Soviets met on the evening of October 25. On the eve of the appointed day the central committee met to put the final touch to some practical arrangements; and Kamenev—the decision of four days earlier having been reversed or forgotten—resumed his seat. Trotsky asked that members of the committee should be attached to the military-revolutionary committee of the Petrograd Soviet to look after postal and telegraphic and railway communications and to keep watch on the Provisional Government. Dzerzhinsky was detailed for railways, Bubnov for posts and telegraphs, Sverdlov for the Provisional Government; and Milyutin was put in charge of food supplies. An embryonic administration was taking shape within the party committee. In the early morning of October 25, 1917, the Bolshevik forces went into action. The key-points in the city were occupied; the members of the Provisional Government were prisoners or fugitives; in the afternoon Lenin announced to a meeting of the Petrograd Soviet the triumph of "the workers' and peasants' revolution"; and in the evening the second All-Russian Congress of Soviets proclaimed the transfer of all power throughout Russia to Soviets of Workers', Soldiers' and Peasants' Deputies. On the evening of October 26, 1917, the second and last meeting of the congress adopted the decrees on peace and on the land, and approved the composition of the Council of People's Commissars, popularly known as Sovnarkom—the first Workers' and Peasants' Government.

For the organization of the almost bloodless victory of October 25/November 7, 1917, the Petrograd Soviet and its military-revolutionary committee were responsible. It was the military-revolutionary committee which took the power as it fell from the nerveless hands of the Provisional Government, and proclaimed to the world the achievement of the revolution. As Stalin afterwards said, the congress of Soviets "only received the power from the hands of the Petrograd Soviet". All contemporary witnesses pay tribute to the energy and ability displayed by Trotsky at this time and to his services to the revolutionary cause. But the higher strategy of the revolution had been directed by Lenin through his chosen instrument, the Bolshevik wing of the Russian Social-Democratic Workers' Party. The victory, though won under the slogan "all power to the Soviets", was a victory not only for the Soviets, but for Lenin and the Bolsheviks. Lenin and the party, the man and the instrument, were now indissolubly one. The triumph of the party seemed almost exclusively due to Lenin's consistent success in stamping his personal will upon it and in leading his often reluctant colleagues in his train. The prestige of Lenin's name had been firmly established; the foundations had been laid of the ascendancy in the party of the single leader.

The relation of Lenin's policy to the wider issues raised by the Russian revolution opens an endless debate. The decision foreshadowed in Lenin's April theses and carried out at his instigation six months later to seize power on a socialist programme and on the foundations of an unfinished bourgeois revolution has been the subject of volumes of commentary and controversy. It has been treated as a prolongation of the Marxist line consistently pursued by the party since 1903, though the Bolsheviks in Petrograd in the confusion of the February revolution and in the absence of their leader had momentarily deviated from the line: this remains the official view. It has been treated as a final abandonment by Lenin and the Bolsheviks of the Marxist line and a plunge, in defiance of Marx's teaching, into the adventure of a socialist revolution not resting on the foundations of a preceding bourgeois revolution: this was the Menshevik view. It has been treated as a last-minute correction by Lenin, based on true Marxist principles, of a long-standing party deviation due to excessive devotion to the formal aspects of Marx's scheme of revolution: this was Trotsky's view. Since these divergent views rested on different texts of Marx, on different interpretations of what Marx meant and on different estimates of what was required to apply Marx's meaning to Russian conditions, the argument proved inexhaustible and inconclusive. The question hotly debated in later years between Bolsheviks and Mensheviks whether the course adopted by Lenin could and did lead to the socialist goal also turned on a point of interpretation: what was meant by socialism.

But behind these arguments conducted in conventional Marxist terminology lay the real problem which the makers of the October revolution had to face. It may well have been true, as the rapid disintegration of the February revolution seemed to show, that bourgeois democracy and bourgeois capitalism on the western model, which was what the Mensheviks wanted and expected, could not be rooted in Russian soil, so that Lenin's policy was the only conceivable one in the empirical terms of current Russian politics. To reject it as premature was to repeat, as Lenin once said, "the argument of the serf-owners about the unpreparedness of the peasants for freedom". But what this policy committed its sponsors to was nothing less than to make a direct transition from the most backward to the most advanced forms of political and economic organization. Politically, the programme involved an attempt to bridge the gap between autocracy and socialist democracy without the long experience and training in citizenship which bourgeois democracy, with all its faults, had afforded in the west. Economically, it meant the creation of a socialist economy in a country which had never possessed the resources in capital equipment and trained workers proper to a developed capitalist order. These grave handicaps the victorious October revolution had still to overcome. Its history is the record of its successes and failures in this enterprise.

The October revolution had triumphed with the Bolsheviks still divided on the scope of the revolution, and uncertain whether to regard it as bourgeois-democratic or as proletarian-socialist. The revolution, by overthrowing the Provisional Government, had consecrated the Soviets as the supreme repositories of revolutionary power. But this did not imply rejection of the ultimate authority of a constituent assembly, which was the characteristic organ of bourgeois democracy, and to whose early convocation the Bolsheviks, equally with the Provisional Government, were committed. The decree of October 26/November 8, 1917, which established the Council of People's Commissars, described it as a "provisional workers' and peasants' government" exercising authority "until the convocation of the Constituent Assembly"; and the decree on land opened with the statement that "the land question in all its magnitude can be settled only by the nation-wide Constituent Assembly". It is true that a laconic decree of the same date proclaiming that "all power belongs to the Soviets" added no such reservations; and the Declaration of Rights of the Peoples of Russia promulgated a few days later announced the principles of a future "voluntary and honourable union of the peoples", and promised the prompt elaboration of "concrete decrees" to give effect to them, without referring at all to the powers of the Constituent Assembly. But in the heat of revolution such formal inconsistencies were not likely to be noticed. The Provisional Government, far more pedantic than its successor about constitutional properties, had itself flagrantly forestalled the functions of the constituent assembly by its decree of September 1, 1917, proclaiming Russia a republic.

The student of the documentary records of the October revolution will at once be struck by the infrequent and inconspicuous appearance of the words "socialism" and "socialist" in its earliest pronouncements. To defend "the revolution" or "the revolution of the workers and peasants" is a sufficient definition of purpose; "revolutionary" is by itself an adjective of commendation ("revolutionary order", "revolutionary justice"), "counter-revolutionary" the quintessence of evil. Derivatives of the neutral word "democracy", equally acceptable to supporters of the bourgeois and of the socialist revolution, appear four times in the initial proclamation of the second All-Russian Congress of Soviets of October 25/November 7, 1917 ("a democratic peace", "democratization of the army"), and over and over again in the peace decree of the following day. "As a democratic government", said Lenin in introducing the land decree to the same session of the congress, "we cannot evade the decision of the popular masses, even if we were not in agreement with it." The vital first steps of the régime were thus taken under the banner not of socialism, but of democracy. A little later the epithet "democratic" was used to commend the system of election to the Soviets and to the Constituent Assembly and especially the "right of recall", as well as the principle of the election of judges.

This emphasis on democracy was accompanied by a proclamation of socialism as the ultimate goal. The most revealing evidence of Lenin's attitude at the moment of the revolution is his speech at the Petrograd Soviet on the afternoon of October 25/November 7, 1917, announcing the triumph of the "workers' and peasants' revolution". Having declared that "this third Russian revolution must lead in its final result to the victory of socialism", he reverted in his concluding words to the two conditions which he had laid down long ago for the transition to socialism—the support of the peasants and the support of world revolution:

We shall win the confidence of the peasants by a single decree abolishing the property of the landowners. The peasants will understand that the salvation of the peasantry lies only in union with the workers. . . . We have the mass strength of organization which will conquer all and lead the proletariat to world revolution.

In Russia we must at once occupy ourselves with the building of the proletarian socialist state.

Hail the world-wide socialist revolution.

The international aspect of the revolution was present to Lenin's mind with peculiar vividness at the moment of its victory in Russia. Ten days later he declared in his capacity as president of Sovnarkom:

We shall march firmly and unswervingly to the victory of socialism which will be sealed by the leading workers of the most civilized countries and give to the peoples solid peace and deliverance from all oppression and all exploitation.

And the Declaration of Rights of the Toiling and Exploited People drafted by Lenin at the beginning of January 1918 proclaimed "the socialist organization of society and the victory of socialism in all countries" as part of the "fundamental task" of the Soviet order. The achievement of socialism was still thought of by Lenin at this time primarily in terms of world revolution.

These hesitations about the scope and character of the October revolution are reflected in early constitutional terminology. The word "Russia" having been abandoned, there were difficulties in finding an appropriate name for the new authority. It called itself the "Provisional Workers' and Peasants' Government" or simply the "revolutionary government", resting on "Soviet power" and on the triumph of the slogan "all power to the Soviets". Only once in a particular context did it refer to itself as the "socialist government of Russia". The first fundamental constitutional declaration in Soviet history is contained in the Declaration of Rights of the Toiling and Exploited People, which opens with the words:

> Russia is declared a republic of Soviets of workers', soldiers' and peasants' deputies. All power in the centre and locally belongs to the Soviets.

And the following clause for the first time names the country the "Soviet Russian Republic". It might be dangerous to draw conclusions from a terminology so fluctuating and uncertain. But whatever Lenin himself may have thought, the word "socialist" was still a bugbear to many of his supporters and allies. A substantial minority, if not a majority, of the party at this time seems clearly to have clung to the view, fervently held by Mensheviks and SRs alike, that the revolution had not yet fully completed its bourgeois stage and was consequently still unripe for its transition to socialism. On this view the October revolution was merely a continuation and deepening of the February revolution, and did not differ from it in principle or purpose. On this view it was legitimate to look forward to the Constituent Assembly as the crowning achievement of the democratic revolution.

Waverings within the party had not been ended by the victory of the revolution. At the moment of victory an all-Bolshevik government had been proclaimed. But in the first few days its authority was not established far outside Petrograd; and under pressure from the executive committee of the railwaymen's union (Vikzhel for short), which controlled communications and aspired for some weeks to act as an independent power dictating terms to the government, the central committee of the party agreed to open negotiations with the SRs and Mensheviks for a coalition government of all parties represented in the Soviets. For Lenin this was merely a tactical manœuvre; for Kamenev and Zinoviev it was an admission of the correctness of the view taken by them on the eve of October 25 that the time was not yet ripe for a specifically proletarian revolution. When, therefore, on November 1/14, 1917, Lenin proposed to abandon the negotiations as futile, he encountered strong opposition from Kamenev, Zinoviev and Rykov. In the debate in the party central committee he received unequivocal support only from Trotsky; but the majority voted solidly for a resolution laying down conditions which would of necessity lead to a breakdown of negotiations. Kamenev and Rykov, in their capacity as Bolshevik delegates to VTsIK, failed to act on the decision. In a declaration of November 3/16, 1917, Lenin carried the issue on to the plane of party discipline; and three days later a formal ultimatum was delivered by the central committee to its recalcitrant members. Five members of the committee, Kamenev, Zinoviev, Rykov, Milyutin and Nogin, at once resigned. The last three resigned their positions as People's Commissars, and several lesser members of the government also resigned. Of the recalcitrants only Zinoviev recanted forthwith and was reinstated in the central committee. A considerable split among the party leaders had once more occurred at a critical moment on an issue of tactics which was also an issue of doctrine.

Having surmounted this crisis and gradually extended its authority over the northern and central provinces of European Russia, the régime had now to face the elections to the Constituent Assembly, fixed by the Provisional Government before its downfall for November 12/25, 1917. What Lenin thought about them at this time is not certainly known. But the party was deeply committed to them by its repeated utterances between the February and October revolutions; the official machine was in motion and would have proved difficult to reverse at the last moment. One of the first acts of Sovnarkom had been to confirm the date set by the Provisional Government. Uritsky, one of the leading Bolsheviks, was appointed as commissar to supervise the work of the electoral commission appointed by the Provisional Government. The commission in its turn refused to cooperate with Uritsky and complained of having been placed under duress. But the elections went forward and seem to have been conducted without interference from any side, though in some outlying districts they were not held at all.

The results justified any apprehensions that may already have been felt in the Bolshevik ranks. Of the 707 elected members of the assembly (out of a total of 808 originally provided for) the SRs could claim a comfortable majority—410 in all. The Bolsheviks secured just under a quarter of the seats, i.e. 175. Most of the 86 members of the "national groups", of which the Ukrainians formed the largest, were strongly anti-Bolshevik. The Kadets, the only surviving bourgeois party, had 17 seats, the Mensheviks 16. If this could be read as a verdict on the government set up by the October revolution, it was a crushing vote of non-confidence.

The first effect of the defeat was to convince Lenin of the necessity of a compromise on the issue of a coalition. At the moment of the elections an All-Russian Congress of Peasants' Deputies was in session in Petrograd. At the first All-Russian Congress of Soviets in June 1917 a group of Left SRs had already rebelled against the party leadership and supported the Bolshevik minority, though this had little effect on the party as a whole. Now at the All-Russian Congress of Peasants' Deputies, Lenin and the other Bolshevik delegates were successful in bringing about a split in the ranks of the SRs. Agreement for a coalition was reached between the Bolsheviks and the Left wing, which secured a majority in the congress and whose most noteworthy figure was Spiridonova. It was an agreement, as Lenin emphatically remarked, "possible only on a socialist platform". On November 15/28, 1917, a joint meeting of VTsIK, of the Petrograd Soviet and of the executive committee of the peasants' congress was held to celebrate the act of union. VTsIK already consisted of 108 members elected by the second All-Russian Congress of Soviets of Workers' and Soldiers' Deputies. Its membership was now doubled by the addition of an equal number of delegates elected by the peasants' congress; and 100 delegates of the army and the fleet as well as 50 from the trade unions were added to its ranks, raising the numbers to something over 350. It now became "the All-Russian Central Executive Committee of the Soviets of Workers', Soldiers' and Peasants' Deputies". In order to complete the coalition, Left SRs were appointed to three People's commissariats—Agriculture, Justice, and Posts and Telegraphs—carrying membership of Sovnarkom, as well as to several minor government posts. About the same time the commissariats were transferred from party headquarters at Smolny to the premises of the old ministries; Bolshevik rule was rapidly fitting itself into the traditional framework of state power.

The agreement with the Left SRs not only reinforced the position of the Bolsheviks, but also provided them with their strongest argument to explain away the results of the elections to the Constituent Assembly—the potentially deceptive character of the SR vote. The SRs had gone to the polls as a single party presenting one list of candidates. Its election manifesto had been full of lofty principles and aims but, though published on the day after the October revolution, had been drafted before that event and failed to define the party attitude towards it. Now three days after the election the larger section of the party had made a coalition with the Bolsheviks, and formally split away from the other section which maintained its bitter feud against the Bolsheviks. The proportion between Right and Left SRs in the Constituent Assembly —370 to 40—was fortuitous. It was entirely different from the corresponding proportion in the membership of the peasants' congress, and did not necessarily represent the views of the electors on a vital point which had not been before them. "The people", said Lenin, "voted for a party which no longer existed." Reviewing the whole issue two years later Lenin found another argument which was more cogent than it appeared at first sight. He noted that in the large industrial cities the Bolsheviks had almost everywhere been ahead of the other parties. They secured an absolute majority in the two capitals taken together, the Kadets here being second and the SRs a poor third. But in matters of revolution the well-known principle applied: "the town inevitably leads the country after it; the country inevitably follows the town". The elections to the Constituent Assembly, if they did not register the victory of the Bolsheviks, had clearly pointed the way to it for those who had eyes to see.

The results of the elections made it certain that the Constituent Assembly would serve as a rallying-point for opposition to the Soviet régime from both wings—from the surviving bourgeois supporters of the Provisional Government and from the dissident socialists. The Bolsheviks, well versed in revolutionary history, were alive to the precedent of the French Constituent Assembly of May 1848 whose function, three months after the February revolution, had been, in a well-known phrase from Marx's *Eighteenth Brumaire,* "to cut down the results of the revolution to bourgeois standard" and to prepare the way for the massacre of the workers by Cavaignac. An attempt was made in the name of former ministers of the Provisional Government, and in defiance of the Soviet Government, to convene the assembly on November 28/December 11, 1917. This was resisted by force. Anti-Soviet forces under former Tsarist generals were beginning to mass in south Russia; and Sovnarkom, now thoroughly alarmed, issued a decree which accused the Kadets of providing "a 'legal' cover for the Kadet-Kaledin counter-revolutionary insurrection", declared the Kadet party "a party of enemies of the people", and announced that "the political leaders of the counter-revolutionary civil war" would be arrested. Though the Right SRs and many of the Mensheviks sided with the Kadets, the Bolsheviks did not as yet venture to apply measures of repression to other socialist parties.

From this time onwards the fate of the Constituent Assembly was the subject of constant preoccupation in party circles. What appears to have been the first warning of Bolshevik intentions was given by Lenin in a speech to VTsIK on December 1/14, 1917:

We are asked to call the Constituent Assembly as originally conceived. No, thank you! It was conceived against the people and we carried out the rising to make certain that it will not be used against the people. . . . When a revolutionary class is struggling against the propertied classes which offer resistance, that resistance has to be suppressed, and we shall suppress it by the same methods by which the propertied classes suppressed the proletariat. New methods have not been invented yet.

And he followed up this declaration with a set of *Theses on the Constituent Assembly,* which appeared anonymously in *Pravda* of December 13/26, 1917, and constituted the most important brief analysis from his pen of the character of the October revolution.

The *Theses on the Constituent Assembly* brought uncompromisingly into the open what had been implicit in everything Lenin had written since the famous April theses eight months earlier—the conviction that the bourgeois revolution in Russia was a spent force and that the right course was to turn one's back resolutely on it and pursue the road to socialism. He began by admitting that "in a bourgeois republic the constituent assembly is the highest form of the democratic principle", so that its appearance in past party programmes, drawn up before the achievement of the bourgeois revolution, was "fully legitimate". Ever since the February revolution of 1917, however, "revolutionary social-democracy" had been insisting that "a republic of Soviets is a higher form of the democratic principle than the customary bourgeois republic with its constituent assembly"; it was indeed "the only form capable of assuring the least painful transition to socialism". This process of transition had been assisted, first, by the re-grouping of "class forces" due to the permeation of the army and peasantry with revolutionary ideas, secondly, by the struggle between the Soviet power and the bourgeois régime in the Ukraine (and in part, also, in Finland, White Russia and the Caucasus), and thirdly, by the counter-revolutionary rising of Kaledin and the

Kadets which had "taken away all possibility of resolving the most acute questions in a formally democratic way". These developments had created an inevitable clash between the Constituent Assembly and "the will and interest of the toiling and exploited classes who began on October 25 the socialist revolution against the bourgeoisie". Thus "any attempt, direct or indirect, to look at the question of the Constituent Assembly from the formal, juridical standpoint, within the framework of bourgeois democracy" was treason to the proletariat, an error into which "a few of the Bolshevik leaders fall through failure to appraise the October rising and the tasks of the dictatorship of the proletariat". All that was left for the Constituent Assembly was "an unconditional declaration of acceptance of the Soviet power, of the Soviet revolution". Otherwise "a crisis in connexion with the Constituent Assembly can be solved only by revolutionary means".

There is no record of the discussion of Lenin's theses in the central committee of the party; but, whether or not formal discussion took place, they thenceforth became accepted party doctrine. For the Bolsheviks Lenin's *Theses on the Constituent Assembly* were a final tearing asunder of the veil of bourgeois constitutionalism. For the other socialist parties painful events were required to bring home to them what the proletarian revolution meant. The acceptance of the theses had two practical results. In the first place it made irrevocable the breach between the Bolsheviks and the socialist parties, which (except for the Left SRs) adhered to the view that the revolution was still in its democratic stage; once the proletarian character of the revolution was accepted, those who maintained the democratic view logically and inevitably became counter-revolutionaries, in intention if not in action. Secondly, it sealed the fate of the Constituent Assembly, the crown of the democratic revolution, but an anachronism once that stage had been superseded by the proletarian socialist revolution. The burning issue of the "dual power", the clash between the Soviets and the representative organs of bourgeois democracy which had raged since the February revolution, was resolved at last. The Constituent

Assembly had now only to surrender or be wiped out. Any suggestion that the action taken against the assembly was the result of a sudden or unpremeditated decision prompted by anything that happened after the assembly met must be dismissed as erroneous. The action of the Bolsheviks was the outcome of a considered policy and of a clear-cut view of the progressive development of the revolution from its bourgeois-democratic to its proletarian-socialist phase.

The publication of Lenin's *Theses on the Constituent Assembly* was in the nature of a declaration of war on the assembly and on the political parties which were likely to control it. The actions of the next three weeks were so many tactical steps in a campaign whose main strategy had been decided. On December 17/30, 1917, came the arrest of the Right SR leader, Avxentiev, together with some of his followers, not, as a leading article in *Izvestiya* explained, "in his quality as a member of the Constituent Assembly", but "for the organization of a counter-revolutionary conspiracy." It was the first occasion on which such measures had been applied to representatives of a socialist party. On December 20, 1917/January 2, 1918, a decree of Sovnarkom convened the Constituent Assembly for January 5/18, 1918, subject to the attainment of a quorum of 400 members; and two days later it was decided by a resolution of VTsIK to summon the third All-Russian Congress of Soviets for January 8/21, 1918, and an All-Russian Congress of Peasants' Deputies a few days later. Zinoviev, now once more Lenin's obedient henchman, pointed the decision by a clear enunciation of Leninist doctrine:

We see in the rivalry of the Constituent Assembly and the Soviets the historical dispute between two revolutions, the bourgeois revolution and the socialist revolution. The elections to the Constituent Assembly are an echo of the first bourgeois revolution in February, but certainly not of the people's, the socialist, revolution.

The terms of the resolution were an avowed challenge. It denounced the slogan "all power to the Constituent Assembly" as the rallying-point of "elements all without exception counter-revolutionary" and as a screen for the watchword "down with the Soviets"; the purpose of the resolution was "to support with all the organized force of the Soviets the Left half of the Constituent Assembly against the Right, bourgeois and compromisers', half". The Menshevik Sukhanov dryly put the logical dilemma. If current events were part of the bourgeois revolution, then the Constituent Assembly should be fully supported; if they were in fact the socialist revolution, then it should not be summoned at all. But the chosen tactics, though possibly the result of a compromise in the counsels of the party, were more dramatic. They were correctly diagnosed in a protest issued by the non-Bolshevik survivors of the first VTsIK appointed by the first All-Russian Congress of Soviets, which maintained a shadowy existence and still more shadowy claim to legitimacy: the third All-Russian Congress of Soviets was being summoned "in order to torpedo the Constituent Assembly".

The preparations for the campaign were completed at a meeting of VTsIK on January 3/16, 1918, when the Declaration of Rights of the Toiling and Exploited People was drafted for adoption by the Constituent Assembly. The declaration opened with the constitutional announcement already quoted:

1. Russia is declared a republic of Soviets of workers', soldiers' and peasants' deputies. All power in the centre and locally belongs to these Soviets.
2. The Russian Soviet Republic is established on the basis of a free union of free nations, as a federation of national Soviet republics.

Then, in a long enunciation of principles which was an endorsement, put into the mouth of the Constituent Assembly, of Soviet policy and legislation, it introduced two paragraphs which constituted an act of abdication on the part of the assembly:

Being elected on the basis of party lists compiled before the October revolution, when the people could not yet rise in its masses against the exploiters and, not having yet experienced the full force of the resistance of the exploiters in defence of their class privileges, had not yet undertaken in practical form the building of a socialist society, the Constituent Assembly would think it fundamentally incorrect, even from the formal standpoint, to set itself up against the Soviet power. . . .

Supporting the Soviet power and the decrees of the Council of People's Commissars, the Constituent Assembly recognises that its tasks are confined to the general working out of the fundamental principles of the socialist reconstruction of society.

And lest the moral of this should be overlooked, *Izvestiya* of January 4/17,1918, the day before the assembly met, carried the text of a resolution also emanating from VTsIK and couched in curt and unmistakable terms:

On the basis of all the achievements of the October revolution and in accordance with the Declaration of Rights of the Toiling and Exploited People adopted at the session of the Central Executive Committee on Januuary 3, 1918, all power in the Russian republic belongs to the Soviets and Soviet institutions. Therefore any attempt on the part of any person or institution whatever to usurp this or that function of state power will be regarded as a counter-revolutionary act. Any such attempt will be crushed by all means at the disposal of the Soviet power, including the use of armed force.

The outlawing of the Kadets and the arrest of several leading Right SRs had blunted the main potential offensive power of the Constituent Assembly. But a certain note of caution in the procedure adopted was due to the apprehension felt by some Bolsheviks, though not justified by the events, of the supposed prestige of the Constituent Assembly among the masses. When the assembly met on January 5/18,1918, Sverdlov ousted from the tribune the oldest member of the assembly, who in accordance with tradition was about to open the proceedings, and in the name of VTsIK declared the assembly open. The French revolution, he said, had issued its Declaration of the Rights of Man and of the Citizen which was "a declaration of rights to the free exploitation of those not possessing the tools and means of production"; the Russian revolution must issue its own declaration of rights. He then read the draft prepared two days earlier by VTsIK and briefly requested the assembly to adopt it.

The remainder of the proceedings served mainly to illustrate the unreality of the assembly and the fundamental differences of doctrine between those who composed it. Chernov, the Right SR leader, was elected president by a substantial majority over Spiridonova, the Left SR, who had Bolshevik support. Bukharin, for the Bolsheviks, spoke eloquently of the immediate issues of the socialist revolution:

> The watershed which at this moment divides this assembly into . . . two irreconcilable camps, camps of principle—this watershed runs along the line: for socialism or against socialism.

Chernov, in his speech from the chair, had proclaimed the "will to socialism":

> But of what socialism was citizen Chernov speaking? Of the socialism which will come in 200 years, which will be made by our grandchildren? Was he speaking of that socialism? We speak of a living, active, creative socialism, about which we do not only want to speak, but which we want to realize. And that, comrades, is what is called being an active socialist.

Steinberg, the spokesman of the Left SRs, who was People's Commissar for Justice in Sovnarkom, evaded the issue of principle, but argued that the time had passed for a discussion of policy (which was what the Right SRs proposed) and that the only function of the assembly, as the "child of the people", was to "submit to the will of the toiling people set forth in the programme of the Soviet of Workers' and Soldiers' Deputies". The speech of Tsereteli for the Mensheviks was on a high plane of theoretical cogency and consistency. He argued, at enormous length, as the Mensheviks had argued for fourteen years, against "anarchic attempts to introduce a socialist economy in a backward country", and protested that "the class struggle of the workers for their final liberation" could only be conducted under conditions of "popular sovereignty based on universal and equal suffrage". Speech-making went on unabated for nearly twelve hours. But little that was said had any relation to the world outside. The harsh challenge implicit in the Soviet declaration was ignored; so was the concentration of effective power in the hands of the proletariat and of the Soviet

Government. No alternative government capable of wielding power was suggested or could have been suggested. In these circumstances the debate could have no issue.

At midnight the Bolshevik declaration was rejected by a majority of 237 to 138 in favour of a motion of the Right SRs to discuss current questions of policy. The debate continued. Then, in the early hours of the morning, a Bolshevik, Raskolnikov, announced that in view of "the counter-revolutionary majority" in the assembly the Bolsheviks would leave it. An hour later the Left SRs also withdrew. Then the central committee of the Bolshevik party, which had remained in session elsewhere in the building, decided to act. The sailor in command of the military guard, Zheleznyakov by name, announced to the president of the assembly that he had received instructions to close the meeting "because the guard is tired". In the ensuing confusion a resolution on the agrarian question and an appeal to the allied Powers for peace were read to the assembly and declared carried. It was characteristic of the bankruptcy of the assembly that it could do nothing more than repeat in substance what the second All-Russian Congress of Soviets had done on the morrow of the revolution ten weeks earlier. Then shortly before 5 A.M. it adjourned for twelve hours. It never met again. Later in the same day VTsIK, having listened to a two-hour speech from Lenin, decreed its formal dissolution. Its reassembly was prevented by the simple method of placing a guard on the door of the Tauride palace.

Marx, in discussing Louis Bonaparte's *coup d'état* of December 2, 1851, commented in a famous passage on the procedure of his predecessors:

Cromwell, when he dissolved the Long Parliament, walked alone into its midst, pulled out his watch in order that the body should not continue to exist one minute beyond the term fixed for it by him, and drove out each individual member with gay and humorous invectives. Napoleon, smaller than his prototype, at least went into the legislative body on the 18th Brumaire and, though in a tremulous voice, read to it its sentence of death.

Every period of history has its own dramatic symbols. The dismissal of the All-Russian Constituent Assembly by an armed sailor "because the guard is tired" was one of these. The contemptuous gesture masked a certain nervousness in Bolshevik circles as to the possible consequences of their high-handed action. A demonstration in favour of the Constituent Assembly at the moment of its meeting had been dispersed by troops, and several persons variously described as "peaceful demonstrators" and "armed conspirators" were killed. But the act of dissolution passed almost without protest; and the verdict of a Right member of the Soviet, equally unsympathetic to the SRs and to the Bolsheviks, seems to reflect accurately the prevailing mood:

> The impression of the "injustice" committed by the Bolsheviks against the Constituent Assembly was attenuated to a considerable extent by dissatisfaction with the Constituent Assembly itself, by its (as was said) "undignified behaviour", and by the timidity and feebleness of its president Chernov. The Constituent Assembly was blamed more than the Bolsheviks who dispersed it.

It was one more demonstration of the lack of any solid basis, or any broad popular support, in Russia for the institutions and principles of bourgeois democracy.

When, therefore, the third All-Russian Congress of Soviets opened at the Tauride palace on January 10/23, 1918, it found itself the natural, though self-constituted, heir to the Constituent Assembly, whose formal dissolution it at once confirmed. After the singing of the "Internationale", the "Marseillaise" was also played "as a historical recollection of the path traversed". The symbolism is explained by the enthusiastic compiler of the official records of the congress: "The Internationale has conquered the Marseillaise as the proletarian revolution leaves behind it the bourgeois revolution". The business of the congress, as Sverdlov, its president, informed it in his opening speech, was "to build the new life of the future and to create an all-Russian power"; it had to "decide whether this power is to have any link with the bourgeois order or whether the dictatorship of workers and peasants will be finally and irrevocably constituted". Lenin was, as usual, cautious in diagnosis, but firm in conclusion:

He who has understood the meaning of the class struggle, the significance of the sabotage organized by the officials, knows that we cannot all at once make the leap to socialism. . . . I have no illusions about the fact that we have only begun the transitional period to socialism, that we have not yet arrived at socialism. But you will act correctly if you say that our state is a socialist republic of Soviets.

Martov repeated once again the Menshevik argument:

The full socialist transformation is possible only after prolonged work caused by the necessity to re-create a whole political organization of society, to strengthen the economic position of the country, and only after that to proceed to the realization of the slogans of socialism.

And Lenin in reply traced the course traversed in the past twelve years:

The Bolsheviks talked of the bourgeois-democratic revolution in 1905. But now when the Soviets are in power, when the workers, soldiers and peasants . . . have said, "We will take the whole power and will ourselves undertake the building of a new life", at such a time there can be no question of a bourgeois-democratic revolution. And this was already said by the Bolsheviks in congresses and meetings and conferences, in resolutions and decisions, in April last year.

Politically, Lenin's argument could hardly be refuted. The October revolution had settled the question for good or ill. Whether the bourgeois revolution had been completed or not, whether the time was or was not ripe for the proletarian revolution—and whatever the ultimate consequences if these questions had to be answered in the negative sense—the proletarian revolution had in fact occurred. After October 1917 nobody could undo what had been done or force the revolution back into a bourgeois-democratic mould. Political development seemed to have outrun economic development. This was indeed the assumption which Lenin made on the eve of October:

Owing to the revolution Russia in a few months has caught up the advanced countries in her *political* organization. But this is not enough. War is inexorable and puts the question with unsparing sharpness:

either perish, or catch up and overtake the advanced countries *economically* as well.

But the hypothesis of a suddenly acquired political maturity did some violence to the facts as well as to Marxist doctrine. Lenin himself was not unconscious of the embarrassment; for, in his retrospect on the situation in the autumn of 1918, he offered a substantially different analysis from that given at the third All-Russian Congress of Soviets in January of the same year:

> Yes, our revolution is a bourgeois revolution *so long as* we march *with* the peasantry *as a whole.* . . . *At first* with "all" the peasantry against the monarchy, against the landowners, against mediaevalism (and, so far, the revolution remains bourgeois, bourgeois-democratic). *Then,* with the poorest peasantry, with the semi-proletariat, with all the exploited *against capitalism,* meaning also against rich peasants, the *kulaks* and the speculators; and, so far, the revolution becomes *socialist.*

And Lenin continued, reviving after a long interval Marx's idea (though not the phrase itself) of "permanent" or "uninterrupted" revolution:

> To attempt to put up an artificial Chinese wall between one and the other, to separate one from the other by any other element *except* the degree of preparedness of the proletariat and the degree of its unity with the poor of the countryside, is the greatest perversion of Marxism, its vulgarization, its replacement by liberalism.

Nor were these difficulties of analysis purely scholastic. They reflected the persistent dilemma of a socialist revolution struggling retrospectively to fill the empty place of bourgeois democracy and bourgeois capitalism in the Marxist scheme.

Suggestions for Further Reading

REED, JOHN, *Ten Days That Shook the World.* New York: Random House, Inc., 1960.

TROTSKY, LEON, *The History of the Russian Revolution.* New York: Simon & Schuster, Inc., 1932.

ULAM, A. B., *The Bolsheviks: The Intellectual and Political History of the Triumph of Communism in Russia.* New York: The Macmillan Company, 1965.

WILSON, EDMUND, *To the Finland Station.* Garden City, N.Y.: Doubleday and Company, Inc., 1953.

WOLF, BERTRAM C., *Three Who Made a Revolution.* New York: Dial Press, 1948.

The Nazi Revolution[*]

ALAN BULLOCK

In the first half of the nineteenth century when English writers had occasion to typify Germans, they spoke of them as romantic, impractical dreamers. By 1900 the Germans were viewed as hard, realistic, and coldly efficient. These national stereotypes are significant because unfortunately there is a good deal of truth in both of them. By the first decade of the twentieth century the German character was a paradoxical and dangerous combination of highflown idealism and tremendous practical ability. There is no doubt that the inhabitants of Bismarck's and Wilhelm II's German empire were the ablest people in Europe. After several centuries of political disunity and economic stagnation, German power and wealth became the most important new factor in European history in the last three decades of the nineteenth century.

In 1900 Germany had by far the best army in Europe and her industrial growth was proceeding at a phenomenal rate, matched

* From Alan Bullock, *Hitler: A Study in Tyranny*, completely rev. ed. (New York: Harper and Row, Publishers, 1962), pp. 253-311.

only by that of the United States, while Britain's economic potential was leveling off. The German empire was preeminent in other fields as well. In order to forestall the advance of a strong working-class party, Bismarck had introduced the first comprehensive scheme of state-sponsored social welfare. In addition Germany had the best state-supported educational system in Europe and the German universities with their tremendous achievements in science and also in the humanities founded modern academic research and scholarship and established the model upon which the graduate schools of the United States and other countries were based. The Germans were an intensely competitive, hard-working, serious-minded people. Their streets were the cleanest in Europe, their schools and universities the most enterprising, their industries the most efficient and most skillful in the application of scientific discovery, and their armies the best equipped and best trained.

Many historians have pointed out that if the Germans had only stuck to their work and their studies, their labor and intelligence was bound to carry them to world hegemony in the twentieth century. If things had continued the way they were going in 1900, by the mid-twentieth century German industry and Kultur *would have enjoyed the preponderance that English industry and liberal civilization had enjoyed in the mid-nineteenth century. The Germans, however, could not let well enough alone. There was a fatal flaw in the German character, an overcompensation, perhaps, for the long centuries of failure and humiliation. The Germans were totally lacking in a sense of humor and they were noticeably deficient in common sense. They were compulsive, humorless extremists who could not enjoy the present because they were always intent on fulfilling a master plan for gaining some perfected future.*

It is highly significant that of all the European peoples in 1914 the Germans alone had no fondness for organized athletics and spectator sports. While English gentlemen and officers devoted weeks on end to playing cricket and golf, and shooting grouse on the moors, the German aristocrats pored over maps and railway

84

timetables and concocted military plans that were supposed to give them the mastery of Europe in a couple of weeks. What they would do with the mastery of Europe once they had gotten it is not a point that engaged their attention. Their major concern was the satisfaction of their insatiable ambition and arrogance. This was the outlook of the ruling class in German society, the Junker aristocrats, bureaucrats, and army officers, and the high bourgeoisie of industrial capitalists and university professors. The large working-class movement, led by the quasi-Marxist Social Democratic party, was supposed to have another outlook. It seemed to favor international peace and brotherhood and to be opposed to the industrial-military-academic complex. But when war broke out, the Social Democrats, like everybody else in Wilhelm II's empire, hailed the kaiser and enthusiastically sought the glory of the fatherland.

With that distinctive German mixture of sublime efficiency and maddening impracticality, the German general staff had developed the Schlieffen plan, according to which a quick victory over France was to be achieved by marching through Belgium. This would inevitably bring Britain as the protector of Belgian neutrality into the war, but the Germans were willing to take this risk because they believed they would be able to reach Paris before the British forces could engage themselves in the conflict. The German general staff thus offered itself a very narrow margin and by failing to take Paris in the summer of 1914 found itself committed to a long defensive war of attrition which in the end impoverished and demoralized German society and brought down the Hohenzollern dynasty.

In 1918 the second German empire was replaced by the Weimar Republic, a disastrous experiment in central-European liberal democracy. The only loyal supporters of the republic were middle-class liberals and trade union officials. All others—particularly Communists on the left and the old military-industrial clique on the right—from the beginning sought to undermine and destroy it. Economic chaos, social disorder, and governmental impotence

85

were then added to national defeat and humiliation. This was the dismal background for the rise and triumph of Hitler and the Nazis.

The roots of the Nazi ideology and the coming to power of Hitler are among the most carefully studied subjects in twentieth-century history. There was nothing new or original about the Nazi ideology. It was simply the garbage pail of nineteenth-century culture. All the antiliberal, antihumanist, authoritarian, hypernationalist, racist, nihilist, and paranoid delusions of late nineteenth-century society were drawn upon by Hitler and his gang. The second fact that is very clear about Nazism is that Hitler's triumph would have been impossible without the active alliance and cooperation of the old military-industrial ruling class of the imperial era that detested the liberal Weimar Republic and was eager to participate in its destruction. After 1945 the vestiges of this clique pointed to the conspiracy of army officers against Hitler in 1944 as proof of their hatred of the Führer. But these officers turned against Hitler only when he had failed to lead the German army to victory in its second twentieth-century drive for world power. From the 1930's until the defeat of the German army by the Russians in 1943, the German militarists were completely loyal to Hitler and satisfied with his policies. They in no way dissented from his program of mass murder and it was simply Hitler's strategic errors, not his policy as Führer, that in the end turned some of the army officers against him.

The most judicious and well-informed account of Hitler's incomparable career of evil and carnage is the biography written by the Oxford scholar Alan Bullock, Hitler: A Study in Tyranny, *from which the following selection is taken. Bullock was able to make extensive use of the voluminous German government and army records of the Nazi period captured by the Western Allies in 1945 and made available for academic historical study. He shows conclusively that Hitler's coming to power was the result neither of election by a majority of the German people nor of a coup d'état by the Nazi gang. The Nazis became the absolute mas-*

The Nazi Revolution

ters of Germany between 1932 and 1934 because of an alliance of infamy made between Hitler and the military-industrial clique. It was strictly a quid pro quo: the old autocratic group helped Hitler to destroy his left-wing opponents while at the same time he satisfied the generals by purging the group among his followers who were hostile to the old officer class. Of course the generals thought that once the Weimar Republic had been destroyed they could control this petty-bourgeois upstart and in due time get rid of Hitler and restore the empire. Instead Hitler and the Nazis proclaimed a Third Reich that would live for a thousand years and the generals and industrialists became its willing servants.

Nazi propaganda later built up a legend which represented Hitler's coming to power as the upsurge of a great national revival. The truth is more prosaic. Despite the mass support he had won, Hitler came to office in 1933 as the result, not of any irresistible revolutionary or national movement sweeping him into power, nor even of a popular victory at the polls, but as part of a shoddy political deal with the "Old Gang" whom he had been attacking for months past. Hitler did not seize power; he was jobbed into office by a backstairs intrigue.

Far from being inevitable, Hitler's success owed much to luck and even more to the bad judgment of his political opponents and rivals. While the curve of Communist success at the elections continued to rise, the Nazis had suffered their sharpest set-back in November, 1932, when they lost two million votes. As Hitler freely admitted afterwards, the Party's fortunes were at their lowest ebb when the unexpected intervention of Papen offered them a chance they could scarcely have foreseen.

Before he came to power Hitler never succeeded in winning more than thirty-seven per cent of the votes in a free election. Had the remaining sixty-three per cent of the German people been united in their opposition he could never have hoped to become

Chancellor by legal means; he would have been forced to choose between taking the risks of a seizure of power by force or the continued frustration of his ambitions. He was saved from this awkward dilemma by two factors: the divisions and ineffectiveness of those who opposed him, and the willingness of the German Right to accept him as a partner in government.

The inability of the German parties to combine in support of the Republic had bedevilled German politics since 1930 when Bruening had found it no longer possible to secure a stable majority in the Reichstag or at the elections. The Communists openly announced that they would prefer to see the Nazis in power rather than lift a finger to save the Republic. Despite the violence of the clashes on the streets, the Communist leaders followed a policy approved by Moscow which gave priority to the elimination of the Social Democrats as the rival working-class party.

Once the organization of the Social Democratic Party and the Trade Unions had been destroyed and the Nazis were in power the Communists believed that they would be within sight of establishing the dictatorship of the proletariat. Sectarian bitterness and dogmatic miscalculation continued to govern their actions even after Hitler became Chancellor, and they rejected any suggestion of a common front with the Social Democrats up to the dissolution of the Party by the new Government. The Social Democrats themselves, though more alive to the Nazi threat, had long since become a conservative trade-union party without a single leader capable of organizing a successful opposition to the Nazis. Though loyal to the Republic, since 1930 they had been on the defensive, had been badly shaken by the Depression and were hamstrung by the Communists' attacks.

The Catholic Centre, like the Social Democrats, maintained its voting strength to the end, but it was notoriously a Party which had never taken a strong independent line, a Party whose first concern was to make an accommodation with any government in power in order to secure the protection of its particular interests. In 1932–1933 the Centre Party was so far from recognizing the danger of a

88

Nazi dictatorship that it continued negotiations for a coalition with the Nazis and voted for the Enabling Law which conferred overriding powers on Hitler after he had become Chancellor.

In the 1930s there was no strong middle-class liberal Party in Germany—the lack of such a Party has more than once been one of the disasters of German political development. The middle-class parties which might have played such a role—the People's Party and the Democrats—had suffered a more severe loss of votes to the Nazis than any other German parties, and this is sufficient comment on the opposition they were likely to offer.

But the heaviest responsibility of all rests on the German Right, who not only failed to combine with the other parties in defence of the Republic but made Hitler their partner in a coalition government. The old ruling class of Imperial Germany had never reconciled itself to the loss of the war or to the overthrow of the monarchy in 1918. They were remarkably well treated by the republican régime which followed. Many of them were left in positions of power and influence; their wealth and estates remained untouched by expropriation or nationalization; the Army leaders were allowed to maintain their independent position; the industrialists and business men made big profits out of a weak and complaisant government, while the help given to the Junkers' estates was one of the financial scandals of the century. All this won neither their gratitude nor their loyalty. Whatever may be said of individuals, as a class they remained irreconcilable, contemptuous of and hostile to the régime they continued to exploit. The word "Nationalist," which was the pride of the biggest Party of the Right, became synonymous with disloyalty to the republic.

There was certainly a period after Hindenburg was elected President in 1925 when this attitude was modified, but it hardened again from 1929 onwards, and both Papen and Hugenberg shared it to the full. What the German Right wanted was to regain its old position in Germany as the ruling class; to destroy the hated republic and restore the monarchy; to put the working classes "in their places"; to rebuild the military power of Germany; to reverse the decision of 1918 and to restore Germany—their Germany—to a dominant position in Europe. Blinded by interest and prejudice, the Right forsook the role of a true conservatism, abandoned its own traditions and made the gross mistake of supposing that in Hitler they had found a man who would enable them to achieve their ends. A large section of the German middle class, powerfully attracted by Hitler's nationalism, and many of the German Officer Corps followed their lead.

This was the policy put into effect by the formation of the coalition between the Nazis and the Right at the end of January, 1933. The assumption on which it was based was the belief that Hilter and the Nazis, once they had been brought into the government, could be held in check and tamed. At first sight the terms to which Hitler had agreed appeared to confirm this belief.

He was not even a presidential chancellor; Hindenburg had been persuaded to accept "the Bohemian corporal," on the grounds that this time Hitler would be able to provide—what he had been unable to provide in November, 1932—a parliamentary majority. No sooner was the Cabinet formed than Hitler started negotiations to bring the Centre Party into the coalition. For this purpose the Ministry of Justice had been kept vacant, and when these negotiations did not lead to agreement it was Hitler who insisted, against Hugenberg's opposition, that new elections must be held in order to provide a parliamentary basis for the coalition in the form of an electoral majority.

Papen might well feel scepticism about Hitler's sincerity in looking so assiduously for a parliamentary majority; but he still saw nothing but cause for self-congratulation on his own astuteness. He had levelled scores with General von Schleicher, yet at the same time realized Schleicher's dream, the harnessing of the Nazis to the support of the State—and this, not on Hitler's, but on his own terms. For Hitler, Papen assured his friends, was his prisoner, tied hand and foot by the conditions he had accepted. True, Hitler had the Chancellorship, but the real power, in Papen's view, rested with the Vice-Chancellor, himself.

It was the Vice-Chancellor, not the Chancellor, who enjoyed the special confidence of the President; it was the Vice-Chancellor who held the key post of Minister-President of Prussia, with control of the Prussian administration and police; and the Vice-Chancellor who had the right, newly established, to be present on all occasions when the Chancellor made his report to the President.

Only three of the eleven Cabinet posts were held by Nazis, and apart from the Chancellorship both were second-rate positions. The Foreign Ministry and the Ministry of Defence—with control of the Army—had been reserved for men of the President's own choice—the first for Freiherr von Neurath, a career diplomat of conservative views, the second for General von Blomberg. The key economic ministries—the Ministry of Economy, and the Ministry of Food and Agriculture, both in the Reich and in Prussia—were in the hands of Hugenberg, while the Ministry of Labour had been given to Seldte, the leader of the *Stahlhelm*. This was highly reassuring to the industrialists and landowners. All that was left for Hitler's own Party was the Reich Ministry of the Interior (which did not control the States' police forces) for Frick, and a Ministry without Portfolio for Goering. In addition Goering was made Prussian Minister of the Interior, but, with Papen as head of the Prussian Government, Goering too would be pinned down.

It was with these arguments that Papen overcame Hindenburg's reluctance to make Hitler Chancellor. In this way they would obtain that mass support which the "Cabinet of Barons" had so notoriously lacked. Hitler was to play his old role of "Drummer," the barker for a circus-show in which he was now to have a place as partner and his name at the top of the bill, but in which the real decisions would be taken by those who outnumbered him by eight to three in the Cabinet. This was *realpolitik* as practised by Papen, a man who—as he prided himself—knew how to distinguish between the reality and the shows of power.

Rarely has disillusionment been so complete or so swift to follow. Those who, like Papen, believed they had seen through Hitler were to find they had badly underestimated both the leader and the movement. For Hitler's originality lay in his realization that effective revolutions, in modern conditions, are carried out with, and not against, the power of the State: the correct order of events was first to secure access to that power and then begin his revolution. Hitler never abandoned the cloak of legality; he recognized the enormous psychological value of having the law on his side. Instead he turned the law inside out and made illegality legal.

In the six months that followed the formation of the coalition government, Hitler and his supporters were to demonstrate a cynicism and lack of scruple—qualities on which his partners particularly prided themselves—which left Papen and Hugenberg gasping for breath. At the end of those six months they were to discover, like the young lady of Riga, the dangers of going for a ride on a tiger.[1] The first part of this chapter is the history of how the Nazis took their partners for a ride.

At five o'clock on the afternoon of Monday, 30 January, Hitler presided over his first Cabinet meeting, the minutes of which are among the German documents captured after the war. The Cabinet was still committed to seeking a parliamentary majority by securing the support of the Centre Party, and Goering duly reported on the progress of his talks with the leader of the Centre, Monsignor Kaas. If these failed, then, Hitler suggested, it would be necessary to dissolve the Reichstag and hold new elections. One at least of Hitler's partners, Hugenberg, saw the danger of letting Hitler conduct an election campaign with the power of the State at his command. On the other hand, it was Hugenberg who, more than anyone else, objected to the inclusion of the Centre in the coalition. Hugenberg's own solution was frankly to dispense with the Reichstag and set up an authoritarian régime. This, however, conflicted with the promise to Hindenburg that, if he agreed

---

1 "There was a young lady of Riga," it will be recalled,
   "Who smiled as she rode on a tiger.
    They returned from the ride
    With the lady inside,
   And a smile on the face of the tiger."

to Hitler as Chancellor, the new Ministry would relieve him of the heavy responsibility of governing by the use of the President's emergency powers and would provide the constitutional support of a majority in the Reichstag. Reluctantly, Hugenberg allowed himself to be manoeuvred into agreeing that, if the talks with the Centre Party broke down, the Cabinet should dissolve the Reichstag and hold new elections. In return he had Hitler's solemn promise—reaffirmed at the Cabinet meeting of 30 January—that the composition of the coalition government would not be altered, whatever the results of the elections.

The next day, when Hitler saw Monsignor Kaas, he took good care that the negotiations with the Centre should fail. When Kaas submitted a list of questions and guarantees, on which the Centre would first require satisfaction—a list simply intended to serve as a basis for discussion—Hitler declared to his colleagues that his soundings had shown there was no possibility of agreement and that the only course was to dissolve at once. He gave the most convincing assurances of loyalty to his partners, and, on the advice of Papen, Hindenburg agreed once more to sign a decree dissolving the Reichstag "since the formation of a working majority has proved impossible." The Centre Party protested to the President that this was not true, that the questions they had submitted to Hitler had only been intended as preliminaries to further discussion and that the negotiations had been allowed to lapse by the Chancellor himself. But by then it was too late: the decree had been signed, the date for the new elections fixed and the first and most difficult of the obstacles to Hitler's success removed. Papen and Hugenberg had allowed themselves to be gently guided into the trap. For the last time the German nation was to go to the polls: this time, Goebbels wrote confidently in his diary, there would be no mistake. "The struggle is a light one now, since we are able to employ all the means of the State. Radio and Press are at our disposal. We shall achieve a masterpiece of propaganda. Even money is not lacking this time."

In order to leave no doubts of the expectations they had,

Goering summoned a number of Germany's leading industralists to his palace on the evening of 20 February. Among those present were Krupp von Bohlen; Voegler of the United Steel Works; Schnitzler and Basch, of I. G. Farben, Walter Funk—in all some twenty to twenty-five people, with Dr. Schacht to act as host. Hitler spoke to them on much the same lines as at Düsseldorf a year before. "Now," he told his audience, "we stand before the last election. Whatever the outcome, there will be no retreat. One way or another, if the election does not decide, the decision must be brought about by other means." Goering, who followed, was blunter. "Other circles not taking part in this political battle should at least make the financial sacrifices so necessary at this time. . . . The sacrifice asked for is easier to bear if it is realized that the elections will certainly be the last for the next ten years, probably even for the next hundred years." After a short speech of thanks by Krupp von Bohlen, at Schacht's suggestion it was agreed to raise an election fund of three million Reichsmarks from leading German firms. The fund was to be divided between the partners in the coalition, but there was little doubt that the Nazis would claim—and get—the lion's share.

Throughout the election campaign Hitler refused to outline any programme for his Government. At Munich he said: "If, today, we are asked for the programme of this movement, then we can summarize this in a few quite general sentences: programmes are of no avail, it is the human purpose which is decisive. . . . Therefore the first point in our programme is: Away with all illusions!"

At Kassel he retorted on his opponents: "They have had no programme. Now it is too late for their plans, the time for their ideas is past. . . . The period of international phrases, of promises of international solidarity, is over and its place will be taken by the solidarity of the German people. No one in the world will help us—only ourselves."

The Nazi campaign was directed against the record of the fourteen years of Party government in Germany; above all, against the Social Democratic and Centre Parties. "In fourteen years the

System which has now been overthrown has piled mistake upon mistake, illusion upon illusion." What had the Nazis to put in its place? He was no democratic politician, Hitler virtuously replied, to trick the people into voting for him by a few empty promises. "I ask of you, German people, that after you have given the others fourteen years you should give us four." "What I claim is fair and just: only four years for us and then others shall form their judgment and pass sentence. I will not flee abroad, I will not seek to escape sentence."

Hitler did not rely on the spoken word alone. Although the other parties were still allowed to function, their meetings were broken up, their speakers assaulted and beaten, their posters torn down and their papers continually suppressed. Even the official figures admitted fifty-one people killed during the election campaign and several hundreds injured. This time the Nazis were inside the gate, and they did not mean to be robbed of power by any scruples about fair play or free speech.

Papen believed he had tied Hitler down by restricting the number of Cabinet posts held by the Nazis to a bare minimum, but while Hugenberg shut himself up with his economic plans and the Foreign Office was kept in safe hands the real key to power in the State—control of the Prussian police force and of the Prussian State Administration—lay with Goering. By the curious system of dual government which existed in Germany, the Prussian Ministry of the Interior carried out the work of administering two-thirds of Germany, and was of much greater importance than the Reich Ministry of the Interior, a head without a body. In the critical period of 1933–1934, no man after Hitler played so important a role in the Nazi revolution as Goering. His energy and ruthlessness together with his control of Prussia, were indispensable to Hitler's success. The belief that Goering at the Prussian Ministry of the Interior would be restrained by Papen as Minister-President of Prussia proved ill-founded. Goering showed no intention of being restrained by anybody: he issued orders and enforced his will, as if he were already in possession of absolute power.

The moment Goering entered office he began a drastic purge of the Prussian State service, in which hundreds of officials were dismissed and replaced by men who could be relied on by the Nazis. Goering paid particular attention to the senior police officers, where he made a clean sweep in favour of his own appointments, many of them active S.A. or S.S. leaders. In the middle of February Goering issued an order to the Prussian police to the effect that "the police have at all costs to avoid anything suggestive of hostility to the S.A., S.S. and *Stahlhelm,* as these organizations contain the most important constructive national elements. . . . It is the business of the police to abet every form of national propaganda." After urging the police to show no mercy to the activities of "organizations hostile to the State"—that is to say, the Communists, and Marxists in general—Goering continued: "Police officers who make use of fire-arms in the execution of their duties will, without regard to the consequences of such use, benefit by my protection; those who, out of a misplaced regard for such consequences, fail in their duty will be punished in accordance with the regulations." In other words, when in doubt shoot. To make his intentions quite clear, Goering added: "Every official must bear in mind that failure to act will be regarded more seriously than an error due to taking action."

On 22 February Goering went a step further. He published an order establishing an auxiliary police force on the grounds that the resources of the regular police were stretched to the limit and must be reinforced. Fifty thousand men were called up, among them twenty-five thousand from the S.A. and fifteen thousand from the S.S. All they had to do was to put a white arm-band over their brown shirts or black shirts: they then represented the authority of the State. It was the equivalent of handing over police powers to the razor and cosh gangs. For the citizen to appeal to the police for protection became more dangerous than to suffer assault and robbery in silence. At best, the police turned their backs and looked the other way; more often the auxiliaries helped their S.A. comrades to beat up their victims. This was "legality" in practice. In

one of his dispatches the British Ambassador remarked that the
daily Press now contained three regular lists:

"1. A list of Government and police officials who have either been
   suspended or sent away altogether;
2. a list of papers suppressed or suspended; and
3. a list of persons who have lost their lives or been injured in political
   disturbances."

The day after Hitler became Chancellor, Goebbels noted in his
diary: "In a conference with the leader we arrange measures for
combating the Red terror. For the present we shall abstain from direct action. First the Bolshevik attempt at a revolution must burst
into flame. At the given moment we shall strike." Goebbels' require-
ment was to be literally fulfilled. On 24 February the police raided
Communist H.Q. in Berlin at the *Karl Liebknecht Haus.* An Official
communiqué reported the discovery of plans for a Communist
revolution. The publication of the captured documents was promised in the immediate future. They never appeared, but the search
for the counter-revolution was intensified, and on the night of 27
February the Reichstag building mysteriously went up in flames.

While the fire was still spreading the police arrested a young
Dutch Communist, van der Lubbe, who was found in the deserted
building in circumstances which left little doubt that he was responsible.

Goering had been looking for a pretext to smash the Communist
Party and at once declared that van der Lubbe was only a pawn
in a major Communist plot to launch a campaign of terrorism for
which the burning of the Reichstag was to be the signal. The arrest of Communist leaders, including the Bulgarian Dimitroff, followed at once, and the Reichstag Fire Trial was held in Leipzig
with all the publicity the Nazis could contrive. The publicity,
however, badly misfired. Not only did Dimitroff defend himself
with skill, but the prosecution failed completely to prove any connexion between van der Lubbe and the other defendants. The
trial ended in a fiasco with the acquittal and release of the Com-

munist leaders, leaving the unhappy van der Lubbe to be hurriedly executed.

The convenience of the pretext which Goering found for attacking the Communists led many (including the present author) to believe that the burning of the Reichstag was, in fact, planned and carried out by the Nazis themselves. A circumstantial version described how a band of Berlin S.A. men led by Karl Ernst penetrated into the deserted building by an underground tunnel and set the place ablaze. Van der Lubbe, who had been picked up by the S.A. after attempting to set fire to other buildings as a protest against the way society had treated him, was used as a dupe and allowed to climb into the Reichstag and start a fire on his own in another part of the building.

Whichever version is accepted, the part played by van der Lubbe remains a mystery, and it was this which led Herr Fritz Tobias to start an independent investigation of the evidence in 1955. Herr Tobias's conclusion (published in *Der Spiegel* in 1959) rejects both the Nazi and the anti-Nazi account in favor of van der Lubbe's own declaration, from which he never wavered, that he alone was responsible for the fire and that he carried it out as a single-handed act of protest. Herr Tobias may well be right in arguing that this, the simplest explanation of all, is the true one.

The question, Who started the fire? remains open, but there is no doubt about the answer to the question, Who profited by it? Hitler needed no prompting.

During the Reichstag Fire [he recalled later] I went in the midde of the night to the offices of the *Völkischer Beobachter*. It took half an hour before I could find anyone to let me in. Inside there were a few compositors sitting around, and eventually some sub-editor appeared heavy with sleep. . . . 'There's no one here at this time of the night; I must ask you to come back during business hours.' 'Are you mad!' I cried. 'Don't you realize that an event of incalculable importance is actually now taking place.' In the end I got hold of Goebbels, and we worked till dawn preparing the next day's edition.

The day after the fire, on 28 February, Hitler promulgated a decree signed by the President "for the protection of the People and the State." The decree was described "as a defensive measure against Communist acts of violence." It began by suspending the guarantees of individual liberty under the Weimar Constitution:

Thus, restrictions on personal liberty, on the right of free expression of opinion, including freedom of the Press; on the rights of assembly and association; violations of the privacy of postal, telegraphic and telephonic communications; warrants for house searches; orders for confiscation as well as restrictions on property, are permissible beyond the legal limits otherwise prescribed.

Article 2 authorized the Reich Government if necessary to take over full powers in any federal State. Article 5 increased the penalty for the crimes of high treason, poisoning, arson and sabotage to one of death, and instituted the death penalty, or hard labour for life, in the case of conspiracy to assassinate members of the Government, or grave breaches of the peace.

Armed with these all-embracing powers, Hitler and Goering were in a position to take any action they pleased against their opponents. They cleverly postponed the formal proscription of the Communist Party until after the elections, so that the working-class vote should continue to be divided between the rival parties of the Communists and the Social Democrats. But acts of terrorism against the leaders, the Press and organizations of the Left-wing parties were now intensified. When a British correspondent, Sefton Delmer of the *Daily Express,* asked Hitler what truth there was in rumours of a projected massacre of his political opponents, Hitler replied: "My dear Delmer, I need no St. Bartholomew's Night. By the decrees issued legally we have appointed tribunals which will try enemies of the State legally, and deal with them legally in a way which will put an end to these conspiracies."

Meanwhile, in the last week of the election campaign, the Nazi propaganda machine redoubled the force of its attack on the "Marxists," producing the most hair-raising accounts of Communist preparations for insurrection and a "bloodbath," for which the Reichstag Fire and the arrest of van der Lubbe were used to provide substantiation. Even those who regarded the official version of the Fire with scepticism were impressed and intimidated by the ruthlessness of the Nazi tactics. Hitler stormed the country in a last hurricane campaign, declaring his determination to stamp out Marxism and the parties of the Left without mercy. For the first time the radio carried his words into every corner of the country.

To leave no doubt of what they meant, Goering assured an audience at Frankfurt on 3 March:

"Fellow Germans, my measures will not be crippled by any judicial thinking. My measures will not be crippled by any bureaucracy. Here I don't have to worry about Justice, my mission is only to destroy and exterminate, nothing more. This struggle will be a struggle against chaos, and such a struggle I shall not conduct with the power of the police. A bourgeois State might have done that. Certainly, I shall use the power of the State and the police to the utmost, my dear Communists, so don't draw any false conclusions; but the struggle to the death, in which my fist will grasp your necks, I shall lead with those down there—the Brown Shirts."

The campaign reached its climax on Saturday, 4 March, the "Day of the Awakening Nation," when Hitler spoke in Koenigsberg, the ancient coronation town and capital of the separated province of East Prussia. Attacking the "November politicians," Hitler declared:

We have been asked today to define our programme. For the moment we can only say one thing: You began with a lie, and we want to make a fresh beginning with the truth. . . . And the first thought contained in this truth is this: a people must understand that its future lies only in its own strength, in its capacity, its industry, its courage. . . .

One must be able to say once again: German People, hold your heads high and proudly once more! You are no longer enslaved and in bondage, but you are free again and can justly say: We are all proud that through God's powerful aid we have once more become true Germans.

As Hitler finished speaking bonfires blazed out on the hilltops, all along the "threatened frontier" of the east. It was the culmination of a month in which the tramping columns of S.A. troops, the torchlight parades, the monster demonstrations, cheering crowds, blaring loudspeakers, and mob-oratory, the streets hung with swastika flags, the open display of brutality and violence, with the police standing by in silence—all had been used to build up the impression of an irresistible force which would sweep away every obstacle in its path.

In face of all this it is a remarkable fact that still the German people refused to give Hitler the majority he sought. With close on ninety per cent of the electorate voting, the Nazis increased their own share of votes by five and a half millions, polling 17,277,200 out of a total of 39,343,300, a percentage of 43.9. Despite the Nazi hammering, the Centre Party increased their votes from 4,230,600 to 4,424,900; the Social Democrats held steady at 7,181,600, a drop of only 66,400; while even the Communists lost little more than a million votes, still returning a figure of 4,848,100. With the help of his Nationalist allies, who polled 3,136,800 votes (a meagre gain of 180,000), Hitler had a bare majority in the new Reichstag, 288 plus 52 seats in a house of 647 deputies. Disappointing though the results were, this was just enough, and it did not escape the attention of the Nazi leaders that with the proscription of the Communist deputies they would have a clear parliamentary majority themselves, without the need of the Nationalist votes. After the experience of the past few weeks, the chances of Papen, Hugenberg and the Nationalists acting as an effective brake on their partners in the coalition appeared slight.

Hitler's dictatorship rested on the constitutional foundation of a single law. No National or Constitutional Assembly was called and the Weimar Constitution was never formally abrogated. Fresh laws were simply promulgated as they appeared necessary. What Hitler aimed at was arbitrary power. It took time to achieve this, but from the first he had no intention of having his hands tied by any constitution; there was no equivalent of the Fascist Grand Council which in the end was used to overthrow Mussolini. Long before the Second World War, even the Cabinet had ceased to meet in Germany.

The fundamental law of the Hitler régime was the so-called Enabling Law, *Gesetz zur Behebung der Not von Volk und Reich* (Law for Removing the Distress of People and Reich). As it represented an alteration of the Constitution, a majority of two-thirds of the Reichstag was necessary to pass it, and Hitler's first preoccupation after the elections was to secure this. One step was simple: the eighty-one Communist deputies could be left out of account, those who had not been arrested so far would certainly be arrested if they put in an appearance in the Reichstag. Negotiations with the Centre were resumed and, in the meantime, Hitler showed himself in his most conciliatory mood towards his Nationalist partners. Both the discussions in the Cabinet, and the negotiations with the Centre, revealed the same uneasiness at the prospect of the powers the Government was claiming. But the Nazis held the whip-hand with the decree of 28 February. If necessary, they threatened to make sufficient arrests to provide them with their majority without bothering about the votes of the Centre. The Nationalists comforted themselves with the clause in the new law which declared that the rights of the President remained unaffected. The Centre, after receiving lavish promises from Hitler, succeeded also in getting a letter from the President in which he wrote that "the Chancellor has given me his assurance that, even without being forcibly obliged by the Constitution, he will not use the power conferred on him by the Enabling Act without having first consulted me." These were more paper-dykes to hold out the flood-tide, but Hitler was prepared to promise anything at this stage to get his bill through, with the appearances of legality preserved intact.

Hitler's master-stroke of conciliation towards the President, the Army and the Nationalists was the ceremony in the Potsdam Garrison Church on 21 March, to mark the opening of the Reichstag, two days before it met to consider the Enabling Bill. At the same time Hitler established the claim of the new régime to be the heir of the military traditions of old Prussia and its Hohenzollern kings.

Potsdam, the royal town of the Hohenzollerns, and the Garrison Church, which had been founded by Frederick William I and contained the grave of Frederick the Great, stood in deliberate contrast to Weimar, the city of Goethe and Schiller, where the National Assembly of the "November Republic" had met in 1919. The date, 21 March, was that on which Bismarck had opened the first Reichstag of the German Empire in 1871, and on which Hitler was now to open the first Reichstag of the Third Reich. The guard of honour of the Army drawn up on one side, and the S.A. on the other, were the symbols of the two Germanies, the old and the new, united by the handshake of President and Chancellor.

It was a brilliant spring day in Potsdam, and the houses were hung with huge swastika banners, side by side with the black-white-red flags of the old Empire. In the church itself one whole gallery was filled with the marshals, generals and admirals of the Imperial régime, all wearing their pre-war uniforms, and headed by Field-Marshal von Mackensen in the uniform of the Death's Head Hussars. The chair reserved for the Kaiser was left empty, and immediately behind sat the former Crown Prince, in full-dress uniform. On the floor of the church were ranged the Nazi deputies, in brown shirts, flanked by the Nationalists and the Centre; not a single Social Democrat was present.

When the door was thrown open, the audience rose to its feet. The members of the Government entered the church. All eyes were on two men: the Austrian, Adolf Hitler, clad in formal morning-dress with a cut-away coat, awkward but respectful, and beside him the massive figure of the aged President, the Prussian Field-Marshal who had first stood in this church in 1866 when, as a young lieutenant of the Guards, he had returned from the Austro-Prussian War in which German unity had been forged. Slowly the old man advanced down the aisle, leaning on his cane. As he reached the centre, he turned and solemnly saluted with his Field-

Marshal's baton the empty throne of the Kaiser and the Crown Prince.

The President's address, which he read, was brief. "May the old spirit of this celebrated shrine," he ended, "permeate the generation of today, may it liberate us from selfishness and Party strife and bring us together in national self-consciousness to bless a proud and free Germany, united in herself."

Hitler's speech was framed with an eye to the representatives of the old régime who sat before him:

The revolution of November, 1918, ended a conflict into which the German nation had been drawn in the most sacred conviction that it was but protecting its liberty and its right to live. Neither the Kaiser, nor the Government nor the Nation wanted the war. It was only the collapse of our nation which compelled a weakened race to take upon itself, against its most sacred convictions, the guilt for this war. . . . By a unique upheaval, in the last few weeks our national honour has been restored and, thanks to your understanding, *Herr General-Feld-marschal,* the union between the symbols of the old greatness and the new strength has been celebrated. We pay you homage. A protective Providence places you over the new forces of our Nation.

With these words the Chancellor crossed to the old Marshal's chair and, bending low, grasped his hand: the apostolic succession had been established.

Alone, the old man descended stiffly into the crypt to the tomb of Frederick the Great. Outside, in the March sunshine, the guns roared in salute and, to the crash of trumpets and drums, the German Army, followed by the S.A. and the *Stahlhelm,* paraded before the President, the Chancellor and the Crown Prince. As night fell a torchlight procession of ten thousand S.S. troops swept through the Brandenburger Tor to the cheers of a huge crowd, while at the Opera Furtwängler conducted a brilliant performance of Wagner's *Die Meistersinger.*

As the French Ambassador later wrote: "After the dazzling pledge made by Hitler at Potsdam, how could Hindenburg and his friends fail to dismiss the apprehension with which they had begun to view the excesses and abuses of his party? Could they now hesitate to grant him their entire confidence, to concede the full powers he claimed?"

It was the other face of Nazism that was to be seen when the Reichstag assembled in the temporary quarters of the Kroll Opera House two days later. The Enabling Bill which was laid before the House contained five clauses. The first and fifth gave the Government the power for four years to enact laws without the co-operation of the Reichstag. The second and fourth specifically stated that this power should include the right to deviate from the Constitution and to conclude treaties with foreign States, the only subject reserved being the institutions of the Reichstag and Reichsrat. The third provided that laws to be enacted by the Government should be drafted by the Chancellor, and should come into effect on the day after publication.

As the deputies pushed their way in they could see behind the tribune occupied by the Cabinet and the President of the Reichstag, a huge swastika banner filling the wall. Outside, they had had to pass through a solid rank of black-shirted S.S. men encircling the building; inside, the corridors and walls were lined with brown-shirted S.A. troops.

Hitler's opening speech was restrained. He spoke of the disciplined and bloodless fashion in which the revolution had been carried out, and of the spirit of national unity which had replaced the party and class divisions of the Republic.

The Government [he declared] will only make use of these powers in so far as they are essential for carrying out vitally necessary measures. Neither the existence of the Reichstag nor that of the Reichsrat is menaced. The position and rights of the President remain unaffected. It will always be the foremost task of the Government to act in harmony with his aims. The separate existence of the federal States will not be done away with. The rights of the Churches will not be diminished, and their relationship to the State will not be modified. The number of cases in which an internal necessity exists for having recourse to such a law is in itself a limited one. All the more, however, the Government insist upon the passing of the law. They prefer a clear decision.

The Government [he concluded] offers to the parties of the Reichstag the opportunity for friendly co-operation. But it is equally prepared to go ahead in face of their refusal and of the hostilities which will result from that refusal. It is for you, gentlemen of the Reichstag, to decide between war and peace.

After a recess it was the turn of the leader of the Social Democrats, Otto Wels, to speak. There was silence as he walked to the tribune, but from outside came the baying of the Stormtroopers chanting: "We want the Bill—or fire and murder." It needed courage to stand up before this packed assembly—most of the Communists and about a dozen of the Social Democrat deputies had already been thrown into prison—and to tell Hitler and the Nazis to their faces that the Social Democratic Party would vote against the Bill. Wels spoke with moderation; to be defenceless, he added, was not to be without honour. But the very suggestion of opposition had been enough to rouse Hitler to a fury; there was not a scrap of generosity in him for a defeated opponent. Brushing aside Papen's attempt to restrain him, he mounted the tribune a second time and gave the Reichstag, the Cabinet and the Diplomatic Corps a taste of his real temper, savage, mocking and brutal. "I do not want your votes," he spat at the Social Democrats. "Germany will be free, but not through you. Do not mistake us for bourgeois. The star of Germany is in the ascendant, yours is about to disappear, your death-knell has sounded."

The rest of the speeches were an anti-climax. Monsignor Kaas, still clinging to his belief in Hitler's promises, rose to announce that the Centre Party, which had once humbled Bismarck in the *Kulturkampf,* would vote for the Bill, a fitting close to the shabby policy of compromise with the Nazis which the Centre had followed since the summer of 1932. Then came the vote, and excitement mounted. When Goering declared the figures—for the Bill, 441; against, 94—the Nazis leaped to their feet and with arms outstretched in salute sang the Horst Wessel song.

Outside in the square the huge crowd roared its approval. The Nazis had every reason to be delighted: with the passage of the Enabling Act, Hitler secured his independence, not only from the Reichstag but also from the President. The earlier Chancellors, Bruening, Papen and Schleicher, had all been dependent on the President's power to issue emergency decrees under Article 48 of the Constitution: now Hitler had that right for himself, with full power to set aside the Constitution. The street gangs had seized control of the resources of a great modern State, the gutter had come to power.

In March, 1933, however, Hitler was still not the dictator of Germany. The process of *Gleichschaltung*—"co-ordination"—by which the whole of the organized life of the nation was to be brought under the single control of the Nazi Party, had still to be carried out. To illustrate what *Gleichschaltung* meant in practice it will be best to take the three most important examples: the Federal States, the Trade Unions, and the political parties. Hitler and Frick had not waited for the passage of the Enabling Act to take steps to bring the governments of the States firmly under their control. Hitler had no intention of allowing such a conflict between Bavaria and the Reich as he had exploited in 1923 to develop again, and he knew that since 30 January there had been renewed talk of restoring the monarchy, and even of secession, in Bavaria. On the evening of 9 March von Epp, with full authority from Berlin, carried out a *coup d'état* in Munich. The Held Government was turned out, and Nazis appointed to all the principal posts. Hitler knew all the moves in the Bavarian political game. When the Prime Minister, Held, applied to the local Army C.-in-C., General von Leeb, for help against the Nazis, von Leeb telephoned to Berlin. He immediately received orders from Colonel von Reichenau at the Defence Ministry to avoid taking any part in internal politics and keep the Army off the streets. The ghost of Lossow had been laid.

Similar action was taken in the other States. Frick intervened, by virtue of the decree of 28 February, to appoint Reich Police

Commissars in Baden, Württemberg and Saxony. In each case they were Nazis, and in each case they used their powers to turn out the Government and put in Nazi-controlled ministries. Prussia was already under the control of Goering's rough hand, and the State elections held there on 5 March produced much the same results as those for the Reichstag. On 31 March Hitler and Frick issued a law dissolving the Diets of all the other States and ordered them to be re-constituted without fresh elections, "according to the number of votes which in the election to the German Reichstag were given to the electoral lists within each federal State. In this connection seats falling to the Communist Party will not be given out." A week later Hitler nominated Reich Governors (*Reichstatthälter*) in every State, and gave them the power to appoint and remove State Governments, to dissolve the Diets, to prepare and publish State laws, and to appoint and dismiss State officials. All eighteen of the new Reich Governors were Nazis, usually the local Gauleiters. In Prussia the new law afforded an opportunity to turn out Papen, who had hitherto united the offices of Vice-Chancellor and Reich Commissioner for Prussia, with Goering as his subordinate. Hitler now appointed himself *Reichstatthälter* for Prussia and promptly delegated his powers to Goering as Prussian Minister-President. Papen "asked to be relieved of his post," and the office of Reich Commissioner for Prussia, which had been instituted at the time of Papen's *coup d'état* in July, 1932, was abolished.

On the first anniversary of Hitler's accession to power, 30 January, 1934, a Law for the Reconstruction of the Reich rounded off this work of subordinating the federal States to the authority of the central Government. The State Diets were abolished; the sovereign powers of the States transferred to the Reich; and the *Reichstatthälter* and State Governments placed under the Reich Government. This was the culmination of a year of *Gleichschaltung,* in which all representative self-government from the level of the States downwards through the whole system of local government had been stamped out. Although formally the individual States were not abolished, in fact the dual system of government, divided between the Reich and States, which both the Bismarckian and the Weimar Constitutions had had to tolerate, was swept away. In March, 1934, Hitler defined the position of the *Reichstatthälter* in terms that left no doubt of his intentions. "They are not," he said, "the administrators of the separate States, they execute the Will of the supreme leadership of the Reich; their commission comes, not from the States, but from the Reich. They do not represent the States over against the Reich, but the Reich over against the States. . . . National Socialism has as its historic task to create the new Reich and not to preserve the German States."

The process of *Gleichschaltung* did not stop with the institutions of government. If Hitler meant to destroy Marxism in Germany he had obviously to break the independent power of the huge German trade-union movement, the foundation on which the Social Democratic Party rested. In March and April the S.A. broke into and looted the offices of many local trade-union branches, but the trade-union leadership still hoped that they might obtain recognition from the Government: after all, no previous German Government had ever gone so far as to touch the unions. They, too, were soon disillusioned. The Nazis cleverly camouflaged their intentions by declaring May Day a national holiday, and holding an immense workers' rally in Berlin which was addressed by Hitler. On the morning of the next day the trade-union offices all over the country were occupied by S.A. and S.S. troopers. Many union officials were arrested, beaten and thrown into concentration camps. All the unions were then merged into a new German Labour Front. "Once the Trade Unions are in our hands," Goebbels commented, "the other parties and organizations will not be able to hold out long. . . . In a year's time Germany will be entirely in our hands."

Hitler deliberately avoided placing the trade unions under the existing N.S.B.O. (National Socialist Factory Cell Organization), which was tainted with Socialist ideas and Strasserism. He gave control of the Labour Front to Robert Ley, who had been an opponent of Gregor Strasser's as long ago as 1925, and had replaced him as head of the Political Organization in December, 1932. In his initial proclamation Ley declared: "Workers! Your institutions are sacred to us National Socialists. I myself am a poor peasant's son and understand poverty, I myself was seven years in one of the biggest industries in Germany and I know the exploitation of anonymous capitalism. Workers! I swear to you we will not only keep everything which exists, we will build up the protection and rights of the worker even further."

Hitler gave similar assurances when he addressed the first Congress of German Workers on 10 May. This speech is well worth comparison with his address to the Industry Club at Düsseldorf a year before, as an example of Hitler's skill in adapting himself to the audience he was facing. But the intentions behind Hitler's talk of honouring labour and abolishing the class war were not long concealed. Before the month was out a new law ended collective bargaining and appointed Labour Trustees, under the Government's orders, to settle conditions of work.

Just as Leipart and Grassmann, the trade-union leaders, had hoped to preserve their organization intact by doing everything possible to avoid provoking the country's new rulers, the Social Democrats too attempted to carry on loyally for a time, even after the Enabling Act had been passed. Their efforts proved equally futile. On 10 May Goering ordered the occupation of the Party's buildings and newspaper offices, and the confiscation of the Party's funds. Some of the Social Democratic leaders, like Otto Wels, moved to Prague and set up a centre of opposition there; others, like Karl Severing, simply retired into the obscurity of private life. As late as 19 June a new Party committee of four was elected in Berlin, but three days later Frick put an end to their uncertainty by banning the Social Democratic Party as an enemy of people and State. Social Democratic representation on any elected or other public body, like that of the Communists, was annulled. The Communists, of course, had been virtually proscribed since the Reichstag Fire, although for tactical reasons they had been allowed to put forward a list at the Reichstag election. None of their deputies, however, had ever been allowed to take his seat, and on 26 May

Hitler and Frick promulgated a law confiscating the entire assets and property of the Party.

The remaining parties represented a more delicate problem, but this did not long delay their disappearance. After the Bavarian People's Party, the ally of the Centre, had seen their offices occupied and their leaders arrested on 22 June—on the pretext of a conspiracy with the Austrian Christian Socialists—the Party announced its own dissolution on 4 July, and was followed by the Centre Party on 5 July. The fact that a Catholic Party no longer existed in Germany was accepted by the Vatican in the Concordat which it concluded with Hitler's Government this same summer. The Democrats (*Staatspartei*) and the People's Party, which Stresemann had once led, reduced to mere shadows by the success of the Nazis in capturing the middle-class vote, had already immolated themselves. Not even Hitler's partners in the coalition, the Nationalists, were spared. Hugenberg's resistance in the Cabinet and an angry appeal to the President proved ineffectual. On 21 June the police and S.A. occupied the Party's offices in a number of German towns, and a week later the leaders, bowing to the inevitable, dissolved the Party.

On 14 July the Official Gazette contained the brief announcement:

"The German Government has enacted the following law, which is herewith promulgated:

Article I: The National Socialist German Workers' Party constitutes the only political Party in Germany.

Article II: Whoever undertakes to maintain the organizational structure of another political Party or to form a new political Party will be punished with penal servitude up to three years or with imprisonment up to three years, if the action is not subject to a greater penalty according to other regulations.

The Reich Chancellor,
Adolf Hitler.
The Reich Minister of the Interior,
Frick.
The Reich Minister of Justice,
Dr. Gürtner."

The *Stahlhelm* took a little longer to absorb. A first step was Hitler's success in persuading Seldte, the *Stahlhelm* leader and its representative in the Cabinet, to dismiss his second-in-command, Duesterberg, and to join the National Socialist Party himself. A succession of uneasy compromises with the S.A., punctuated by fights between the rival private armies, raids and arrests of *Stahlhelm* leaders, led to the incorporation of the *Stahlhelm* in the S.A. by the end of 1933, and to its formal dissolution in November, 1935.

The remnants of the old Freikorps were ceremonially dissolved at Munich on the tenth anniversary of the unsuccessful putsch of 9 November, 1923. The agitator who had then fled before the shots of the Bavarian police, now the Chancellor of Germany, laid a wreath on the tomb of the martyrs of the movement with the inscription: "Despite all, you have conquered." The roll-call of the Freikorps was called one by one—the Freikorps of the Baltic, of Silesia and the Ruhr, the Ehrhardt Brigade, Oberland, Rossbach, the Hitler Shock Troop and the rest. As each answered, "Present," their stained and tattered flags were borne forward for the last time, and solemnly laid up in the hall of the Brown House under an S.A. guard of honour. It was the closing of a strange and sinister page in the post-war history of Germany. Just as the ceremony at Potsdam in March had marked the claim of the Nazis to be the heirs of the old Prussia, so by the Munich ceremony in November they made good their claim to embody the traditions of the Freikorps.

With the suppression of the parties, the basis of the coalition which had brought Hitler into power disappeared. With the passage of the Enabling Law the need for it had gone. Hitler had never been under any illusion about the intention of Papen and Hindenburg to tie him down; but equally, he had never had any doubts of his own ability to sweep away the restrictions with which they attempted to hedge him round. "The reactionary forces," Rauschning reports Hitler saying after the Reichstag Fire, "believe they have me on the lead. I know that they hope I will achieve my own ruin by mismanagement. But we shall not wait for them to act. Our great opportunity lies in acting before they do. We have no scruples, no bourgeois hesitations. . . . They regard me as an uneducated barbarian. Yes, we are barbarians. We want to be barbarians. It is an honourable title."

As so often later in his foreign policy, Hitler resorted to his favourite tactic of surprise, of doing just the things no one believed he would dare to do, with a bland contempt for convention or tradition. In a few weeks he had banned the Communist and Social Democratic parties, dissolved the Catholic Centre and the Right-wing Nationalists and taken over the *Stahlhelm* and the Trade Unions, six of the most powerful organizations in Germany —and, contrary to all expectations, nothing had happened. The strength of these organizations, even of a revolutionary party like the Communists, was shown to be a sham. Hitler had scoffed at the tradition of making concessions to Bavarian particularist feeling, and with equal success had ridden rough-shod over the rights of the federal States. The methods of gangsterism applied to politics, the crude and uninhibited use of force in the first, not in the last, resort, produced startling results.

Any opposition in the Cabinet crumpled up before the wave of violence which was eliminating all the political landmarks in the German scene. Papen, shorn of his power as Reich Commissioner in Prussia, was a shrunken figure. Hitler no longer paid attention to the rule that the Vice-Chancellor must always be present when he saw the President; indeed, he rarely bothered to see the President at all, now that he had the power to issue decrees himself. Seldte, the *Stahlhelm* leader and Minister of Labour, was soon persuaded to hand over his organization to Hitler and surrender his independence. Hugenberg held out till the end of June, but lost his fight to preserve the Nationalist Party, and was forced to resign on 29 June. His place as Minister of Economy was taken by Dr. Schmitt. As Minister of Food and Agriculture his successor was Darré, who had already forced the once powerful Land League into a union with his own Nazi *Agrarpolitischen Apparatus,* and

ALAN BULLOCK

turned out its Junker president, Graf Kalckreuth, on a framed charge of corruption. Immediately after the elections, Goebbels had been brought into the Cabinet as head of a new Ministry of Public Enlightenment and Propaganda. Three days later, after a short conversation with Hitler, the President of the Reichsbank, Dr. Luther, suddenly resigned. His place was taken by Dr. Schacht, a former President who had written to Hitler in August, 1932, "to assure you of my unchanging sympathy—you can always count on me as your reliable assistant."

Thus by the summer of 1933 Hitler was complete master of a Government in which Papen only remained on sufferance, and which was independent alike of Reichstag, President and political allies. All Papen's calculations of January, his assurance that once the Nazi Party was harnessed to the State it would be tamed, had proved worthless. For Hitler had grasped a truth which eluded Papen, the political dilettante, that the key to power no longer lay in the parliamentary and presidential intrigues by means of which he had got his foot inside the door—and by means of which Papen still hoped to bind him—but, outside, in the masses of the German people. Papen, deceived by Hitler's tactics of legality, had never grasped that the revolutionary character of the Nazi movement would only be revealed after Hitler had come to power, and was now astonished and intimidated by the forces he had released.

For it is a mistake to suppose, as Papen did, that because Hitler came to power by the backstairs there was no genuine revolutionary force in the Nazi Party. The S.A. regarded Hitler's Chancellorship and the election victory of 5 March as the signal for that settling of accounts which they had been promised for so long. In the circumstances of Germany between 1930 and 1933, with the long-drawn-out economic depression and the accompanying political uncertainty and bitterness, the revolutionary impulse of the S.A. was bound to strike echoes in a large section of the German people. This wave of revolutionary excitement which passed across Germany in 1933 took several forms.

The Nazi Revolution

Its first and most obvious expression was violence. Violence had been common enough in Germany for many months before 1933, but the violence of the period between the Reichstag Fire and the end of the year was on a different scale from anything that had happened before. The Government itself deliberately employed violence and intimidation as a method of governing, using such agencies as the Gestapo (the Prussian Secret State Police established by Goering), and the concentration camps opened at Oranienburg, Dachau, and other places. At the same time, the open contempt for justice and order shown by the State encouraged those impulses of cruelty, envy and revenge which are normally suppressed or driven underground in society. Men were arrested, beaten and murdered for no more substantial reason than to satisfy a private grudge, to secure a man's job or his apartment, and to gratify a taste for sadism. In Berlin and other big cities local S.A. gangs established "bunkers" in disused warehouses or cellars, to which they carried off anyone to whom they took a dislike, either to maltreat them or hold them to ransom. The normal sanctions of the police and the courts were withdrawn, and common crime from robbery to murder brazenly disguised as "politics." The only measure taken by the Government was to issue amnesties for "penal acts committed in the national revolution."

This breakdown of law and order, of the ordinary security of everyday life, not from any weakness or collapse of authority, but with the connivance of the State, was a profound shock to the stability of a society already shaken by the years of depression and mass unemployment. Yet violence, if it repelled, also attracted many, especially among the younger generation. It was indeed a characteristic part of revolutionary idealism. For 1933, like other revolutionary years, produced great hopes, a sense of new possibilities, the end of frustration, the beginning of action, a feeling of exhilaration and anticipation after years of hopelessness. Hitler recognized this mood when he told the German people to hold up their heads and rediscover their old pride and self-confidence. Germany, united and strong, would end the crippling divisions which had held her back, and recover the place that was her due in the world. Many people believed this in 1933 and thought that a new era had begun. Hitler succeeded in releasing pent-up energies in the nation, and in recreating a belief in the future of the German people. It is wrong to lay stress only on the element of coercion, and to ignore the degree to which Hitler commanded a genuine popular support in Germany—so much less, as Mill once remarked, do the majority of the people prefer liberty to power. The law introducing the plebiscite is evidence of the confidence Hitler felt that he could carry a majority of the German people with him, once he had come to power and broken all organized resistance. To suppose that the huge votes which he secured in these plebiscites were solely, or even principally, due to the Gestapo and the concentration camps is to miss what Hitler knew so well, the immense attraction to the masses of force plus success.

Side by side with this—and yet another expression of the mood of 1933 in Germany—went the familiar and seamy accompaniment of all revolutionary upheavals, the rush to clamber on the band wagon and the scramble for jobs and advantages. The Germans invented a word, the *Märzgefallene,* for those opportunists who first joined the Party in March, 1933, and were eager to secure the favour of the new bosses. The purge of the civil service, the closing of the professions to Jews, the creation of new posts in government and local government service, in industry and business whetted the appetites of the unsuccessful, the ambitious and the envious. Most of the men who now held power in Germany, Hitler himself, Goering, Goebbels, and the thousands of Nazis who had become mayors of cities, Reichstag or Landtag deputies, government officials, heads of departments, chairmen of committees and directors on company boards, belonged to one or other of these classes. The *Altkämpfer,* the old Fighters, and many who claimed without justification to be Party members of long standing, now crowded their ante-chambers, clamouring for jobs. Rauschning relates how one man, who asked him for a job in Danzig, shouted at him: "I won't get down again. Perhaps you can wait. You're not sitting on a bed of glowing coals. No job, man, no job! I'll stay on top no matter what it costs me. We can't get on top twice running." The six million unemployed in Germany, who had not disappeared overnight when Hitler came to power, represented a revolutionary pressure that was not easily to be dammed.

It was by harnessing these forces of discontent and revolt that Hitler had created the Nazi movement, and as late as the middle of June, 1933, he was still prepared to tell a gathering of Nazi leaders in Berlin: "The law of the National Socialist Revolution has not yet run its course. Its dynamic force still dominates development in Germany today, a development which presses forward irresistibly to a complete remodelling of German life." A new political leadership had to be established; it was the job of the National Socialist movement to provide this new ruling class. "Just as a magnet draws from a composite mass only the steel chips, so should a movement directed exclusively towards political struggle draw to itself only those natures which are called to political leadership. . . . The German Revolution will not be complete until the whole German people has been fashioned anew, until it has been organized anew and has been reconstructed."

Hitler used the same language to the S.A. At Kiel on 7 May he told them: "You have been till now the Guard of the National Revolution; you have carried this Revolution to victory; with your name it will be associated for all time. You must be the guarantors of the victorious completion of this Revolution, and it will be victoriously completed only if through your school a new German people is educated."

In the early summer of 1933 it seemed probable that this revolutionary wave, with its curious compound of genuine radicalism and job-seeking, would not exhaust itself until every single institution in Germany had been remodelled and brought under Nazi control.

But there was a point beyond which this process could not go without seriously endangering the efficiency of the State and of the

German economy. This was a threat to which Hitler, who was now the head of the Government as well as the leader of a Party, could not remain indifferent. The two dangers to which he had to pay particular attention were the disruption of the economic organization of the country, and attempts to interfere with the inviolability of the Army.

Hitler's arrival in power had been accomplished by a recrudescence of Nazi attacks upon the big capitalists. Otto Wagener, the head of the Party's Economic Section in the Brown House, attempted to secure control of the employers' associations which had combined to form the Reich Corporation (*Reichstand*) of German Industry. Dr. Adrian von Renteln, the leader of the Combat League of Middle-Class Tradespeople, established himself as president of the German Industrial and Trade Committee (the union of German Chambers of Commerce), and declared that the Chambers of Commerce would be the cornerstone in the new Nazi edifice of Reich Corporations. The hostility of the small shopkeepers, whom Renteln represented, was especially directed against the department stores and co-operatives. Walther Darré, the new Minister of Agriculture, demanded a drastic cut in the capital value of agrarian debts and the reduction of the rate of interest to two per cent. Men like Gottfried Feder believed that the time had come to put into practice the economic clauses of the Party's original programme, with its sweeping proposals for nationalization, profit-sharing, the abolition of unearned incomes and "the abolition of the thraldom of interest." (Points 13, 14 and 11.)

Hitler had never been a Socialist; he was indifferent to economic questions. What he saw, however, was that radical economic experiments at such a time would throw the German economy into a state of confusion, and would prejudice, if not destroy, the chances of co-operation with industry and business to end the Depression and bring down the unemployment figures. Such an argument, an argument which directly touched his own power, took precedence over the economic panaceas peddled by Feder, or the importunate desires of those who believed, as Hitler told Rauschning, that Socialism meant their chance to share in the spoils. Hitler made his charged attitude perfectly clear in the course of July.

To the *Reichstatthälter,* gathered in the Reich Chancellery on 6 July, Hitler now said bluntly:

The revolution is not a permanent state of affairs, and it must not be allowed to develop into such a state. The stream of revolution released must be guided into the safe channel of evolution. . . . We must therefore not dismiss a businessman if he is a good businessman, even if he is not yet a National Socialist; and especially not if the National Socialist who is to take his place knows nothing about business. In business, ability must be the only authoritative standard. . . .

History will not judge us [Hitler continued] according to whether we have removed and imprisoned the largest number of economists, but according to whether we have succeeded in providing work. . . . The ideas of the programme do not oblige us to act like fools and upset everything, but to realize our trains of thought wisely and carefully. In the long run our political power will be all the more secure, the more we succeed in underpinning it economically. The *Reichstatthälter* must therefore see to it that no organizations or Party offices assume the functions of government, dismiss individuals and make appointments to offices, to do which the Reich Government alone—and in regard to business the Reich Minister of Economics—is competent.

A week later Hitler summoned the gauleiters to Berlin and made the same point to them: "Political power we had to conquer rapidly and with one blow; in the economic sphere other principles of development must determine our action. Here progress must be made step by step without any radical breaking up of existing conditions which would endanger the foundations of our own life. . . ."

At the end of June when Hitler replaced Hugenberg as Minister of Economy and Trade he chose as his successor Dr. Schmitt, director-general of the largest insurance company in Germany, the Allianz. Schmitt, like Schacht at the Reichsbank, was wholly opposed to the plans of economic cranks like Feder, who was only made an Under-Secretary. Wagener was dismissed and his place taken by the "reliable" Wilhelm Keppler, who now became the Fuehrer's Deputy for Economic Questions. Krupp von Bohlen remained as president of the Reich Corporation of German Industry, and Thyssen became the chairman of the two powerful Rhineland groups, the *Langnamverein* and the North-western Employers' Association. The Combat League of Middle-class Tradespeople was dissolved in August: on 7 July, Hess, the deputy leader of the Party, had issued a statement forbidding members of the Party to take any action against department stores and similar undertakings. Darré, it is true, remained as Minister of Agriculture, but no more was heard of his demand to reduce the rate of interest on rural debts to two per cent. Finally, Schmitt let it be known that there would be no further experiments in the corporate development of the national economy, and Hess banned such talk in the Party on pain of disciplinary measures.

July, 1933, in fact marked a turning point in the development of the revolution. At the end of June, about the time that the crisis over economic policy came to a head, Hitler had been summoned to Neudeck to receive a remonstrance from the President on the turmoil caused by the Nazi "German Christians" in the Protestant Churches. On his return to Berlin he knocked the Church leaders' heads together and enforced a compromise for the sake of ecclesiastical peace. In a speech which he delivered a few days later at Leipzig he spoke of the ending of the second phase of the battle for Germany: "We could with a single revolutionary onrush frame our attack to win power in the State; now before us lies the next phase of our struggle. . . . The great fighting movement of the German people enters on a new stage." The task of this new phase Hitler described as "educating the millions who do not yet in their hearts belong to us."

Hitler's own wish to bring the revolution to an end, for the time being at least, and to consolidate its gains, is plain enough. To quote another sentence of his speech to the *Reichstatthälter* on 6 July: "Many more revolutions have been successful at the outset than have, when once successful, been arrested and brought to a standstill at the right moment."

Hitler, however, was far from convincing all his followers of the necessity of his new policy. Once again opposition found its strongest expression in the S.A. Its leader was Ernst Roehm, the S.A. Chief of Staff, who spoke in the name of the hundreds of thousands of embittered Nazis who had been left out in the cold, and wanted no end to the revolution until they too had been provided for. At the beginning of August Goering, in line with the change of policy, announced the dismissal of the S.A. and S.S. auxiliary police; they were no longer needed. On 6 August, before a parade of eighty thousand S.A. men on the Tempelhof Field outside Berlin, Roehm gave his answer: "Anyone who thinks that the tasks of the S.A. have been accomplished will have to get used to the idea that we are here and intend to stay here, come what may."

From the summer of 1933 to the summer of 1934 this quarrel over the Second Revolution was to form the dominant issue in German politics.

Throughout the autumn of 1933 and the spring of 1934 for the next nine months demands to renew and extend the Revolution grew louder and more menacing. Roehm, Goebbels and many of the S.A. leaders made open attacks on *Reaktion,* that comprehensive word which covered everyone the S.A. disliked, from capitalists and Junkers, Conservative politicians and stiff-necked generals, to the respectable bourgeois citizen with a job and the civil service bureaucrats. The S.A. looked back nostalgically to the spring of the previous year, when the gates to the Promised Land had been flung open, and Germany had appeared to be theirs to loot and lord it over as they pleased. Then an official job, a Mercédès and an expenses account had appeared to be within the reach of every S.A. sub-leader. Now, they grumbled, the Nazis had gone respectable, and many who had secured a Party card only the day before were allowed to continue with their jobs while deserving *Altkaempfer* were left out on the streets. In characteristically elegant language the S.A. began to talk of clearing out the pig-sty, and driving a few of the greedy swine away from the troughs.

While the S.A., which was a genuine mass movement with strong radical and anti-capitalist leanings, became restive, and attracted to it all those dissatisfied elements who sought to perpetuate the revolution, Roehm and the S.A. leadership became involved in a quarrel with the Army. It was the old issue which Roehm had fought over with Hitler in the 1920s. On this subject Hitler's views had never wavered: he was as strongly opposed as ever to Roehm's inveterate desire to turn the S.A. into soldiers and to remodel the Army.

There were particularly strong reasons why Hitler wished to avoid alienating the Army leaders at this time. The willingness of the Army to see Hitler become Chancellor, the benevolent neutrality of the Army during the months following 30 January, in which he successfully crushed all resistance and arrogated more and more power to himself—these were decisive factors in the establishment of the Nazi régime, just as the Army's repudiation of Hitler in 1923 had been decisive for his failure. The key figure in guaranteeing the friendly attitude of the Army was General von Blomberg who took the office of Minister of Defence in Hitler's Cabinet. On 2 February, three days after he became Chancellor, Hitler visited the house of Hammerstein, the Army Commander-in-Chief, and spoke for two hours to the leading generals and admirals. He laid stress on two points which made a powerful appeal to his audience. The first was his promise to restore German military strength by rearmament, the second his assurance that the Army would not be called upon to intervene in a civil war. As an earnest of his willingness to preserve the unique position of the German Army in the state, Hitler promulgated a new Army Law on 20 July which ended the jurisdiction of the civil courts over the military and abolished the republican practice of electing representatives of the rank and file.

The Army remained loyal to its bargain, and Hitler's relations with Blomberg became closer as he began to take the first steps in rebuilding the military power of Germany. Hitler was dependent upon the generals for the technical skill necessary to plan and carry out German rearmament. Looking ahead to the time when the aged President must die, he recognized the importance of having the Army again on his side, if he was to secure the succession to Hindenburg for himself. For both reasons, Hitler was anxious that nothing should disturb the confidence of the Army leaders in the new régime.

Roehm took a different view. By the end of 1933 the S.A. numbered between two and three million men, and Roehm stood at the head of an army more than ten or twenty times the size of the regular Reichswehr. The S.A. leaders, ambitious and hungry for power, saw in their organization the revolutionary army which should provide the military power of the New Germany. Most of the S.A. leaders had come through the rough school of the Freikorps; they were contemptuous of the rigid military hierarchy of the professional Army, and resentful at the way they were treated by the Officer Corps. Like the gangsters they were, they were envious and avid for the prestige, the power and the pickings they would acquire by supplanting the generals. Their motives were as crude as their manners, but undeniably men like Roehm and Heines were tough, possessed ability and commanded powerful forces. To Rauschning, Roehm grumbled: "The basis (of the new army) must be revolutionary. You can't inflate it afterwards. You only get the opportunity once to make something big that'll help us to lift the world off its hinges. But Hitler puts me off with fair words. . . . He wants to inherit an army all ready and complete. He's going to let the 'experts' file away at it. When I hear that word, I'm ready to explode. Afterwards he'll make National Socialists of them, he says. But first he leaves them to the Prussian generals. I don't know where he's going to get his revolutionary spirit from. They're the same old clods, and they'll certainly lose the next war."

In the long run Hitler was to treat the German generals just as roughly as Roehm would have done, but in 1933–1934 he needed their support, and was not prepared to let Roehm and the S.A. spoil his plans. On their side, the generals were adamant in their refusal to accept the S.A. on an equal footing with the Army, and determined to maintain the Army's privileged position in the

State. Here was one institution which they were resolved should not be Nazified, and Roehm's pretensions were rejected with contempt.

In a number of speeches in the latter half of 1933, Hitler went out of his way to reassure the generals that he remained loyal to his compact with them. On 1 July, addressing his S.A. leaders at Bad Reichenhall, he declared: "This army of the political soldiers of the German Revolution has no wish to take the place of our Army or to enter into competition with it."

On 19 August at Bad Godesberg he repeated: "The relation of the S.A. to the Army must be the same as that of the political leadership to the Army." On 23 September, after recognizing the debt the movement owed to the Army at the time he became Chancellor he added: "We can assure the Army that we shall never forget this, that we see in them the bearers of the tradition of our glorious old Army, and that with all our heart and all our powers we will support the spirit of this Army."

But the problem of the S.A. remained. If it was not to be incorporated into the Army, as Roehm wanted, what was to become of it? The S.A. was the embarrassing legacy of the years of struggle. In it were collected the "old fighters" who had been useful enough for street brawling, but for whom the Party had no further use when it came to power and took over the State; the disillusioned radicals, resentful at Hitler's compromise with existing institutions; the ambitious, who had failed to get the jobs they wanted, and the unsuccessful, who had no jobs at all. As the revolutionary impetus slackened and more normal conditions began to return, the S.A., conscious of the unpopularity which their excesses had won for them, began to feel themselves no longer wanted. In a speech to fifteen thousand S.A. officials in the Berlin *Sportpalast* in November, 1933, Roehm gave expression to this mood of frustration in a violent attack on the "reactionaries," the respectable civil servants, the business men and the army officers, on whom Hitler now relied for co-operation. "One often hears voices from the bourgeois camp to the effect that the S.A. have lost any reason for existence," he declared. But he would tell these gentlemen that the old bureaucratic spirit must still be changed "in a gentle, or if need be, in an ungentle manner." Roehm's attack was greeted with loud applause.

Thus the particular issue of the relations between the S.A. and the Army became part of a much bigger problem. It became a test case involving the whole question of the so-called Second Revolution—the point at which the revolution was to be halted—and the classic problem of all revolutionary leaders once they have come to power, the liquidation of the Party's disreputable past.

Hitler first attempted to solve this problem by conciliation and compromise, a policy to which he clung in the face of growing difficulties, up to June, 1934. A Law to Secure the Unity of Party and State, promulgated on 1 December, made both Roehm as Chief of Staff of the S.A., and Hess, the deputy leader of the Party, members of the Reich Cabinet. So far as Roehm was concerned, this repaired an omission which had long been a grievance with the S.A.

At the beginning of the New Year Hitler addressed a letter to Roehm of unusual friendliness, employing throughout the intimate form of the second person singular:

My dear Chief of Staff,
The fight of the National Socialist movement and the National Socialist Revolution were rendered possible for me by the consistent suppression of the Red Terror by the S.A. If the Army has to guarantee the protection of the nation against the world beyond our frontiers, the task of the S.A. is to secure the victory of the National Socialist Revolution and the existence of the National Socialist State and the community of our people in the domestic sphere. When I summoned you to your present position, my dear Chief of Staff, the S.A. was passing through a serious crisis. It is primarily due to your services if after a few years this political instrument could develop that force which enabled me to face the final struggle for power and to succeed in laying low the Marxist opponent.

At the close of the year of the National Socialist Revolution, therefore, I feel compelled to thank you, my dear Ernst Roehm, for the imperishable services which you have rendered to the National Socialist movement and the German people, and to assure you how very grateful I am to Fate that I am able to call such men as you my friends and fellow combatants.

In true friendship and grateful regard,

Your Adolf Hitler.

With Roehm and Hess in the Cabinet more attention was now paid to the needs and grievances of the "old fighters," and the end of the first year of Hitler's Chancellorship was signalized by a law passed in February, 1934, "Concerning Provision for the Fighters of the National Movement." Members of the Party or S.A. who had suffered sickness or injury in the political struggle for the national movement were to receive pensions or payments from the State in the same way as those injured in the First World War.

Roehm, however, was not to be silenced by such sops. In February he proposed in the Cabinet that the S.A. should be used as the basis for the expansion of the Army, and that a single Minister should be appointed to take charge of the Armed Forces of the State, together with all para-military and veterans' organizations. The obvious candidate for such a post was Roehm himself. This was to touch the Army on its most tender spot. Hindenburg had only agreed to Hitler's Chancellorship on the express condition that he, and not Hitler, should appoint the Minister of Defence, and the Army would never agree to a Nazi, least of all to Roehm, in such a position. The Army High Command presented a unanimous opposition to such a proposal and appealed to the President, as the guardian of the Army's traditions, to put a stop to Roehm's attempted interference.

Hitler declined to take Roehm's side in the dispute, and the plan was allowed to drop for the moment. When Mr. Eden, then Lord Privy Seal, visited Berlin on 21 February, Hitler was prepared privately to offer a reduction of the S.A. by two-thirds, and to permit a scheme of supervision to see that the remainder neither possessed arms nor were given military training. These proposals were renewed in April. Not only were they a clever piece of diplomatic bargaining on Hitler's part, but they provide an illuminating sidelight on the direction in which he was moving. For, although temporarily checked, Roehm kept up his pressure on the Army, and relations between himself and General von Blomberg, the Minister of Defence, grew strained. Among the captured German documents is a letter of Blomberg's dated 2 March, 1934, in which he drew Hitler's attention to the recruitment and arming of special S.A. Staff Guards. "This would amount to six to eight thousand S.A. men permanently armed with rifles and machine-guns in the area of the VI Military District H.Q. alone." It is evident that each side in the dispute was taking every opportunity to score off the other.

At the end of March, Hitler indignantly—almost too indignantly—repudiated the suggestions of an Associated Press correspondent that there were divisions in the Party leadership. A few days later, however, the situation was transformed for Hitler when he and von Blomberg were secretly informed that President Hindenburg could not be expected to live very much longer. Within a matter of months, perhaps of weeks, the question of the succession would have to be settled.

It had long been the hope of conservative circles that Hindenburg's death would be followed by a restoration of the monarchy, and this was the President's own wish, expressed in the Political Testament which he signed secretly on 11 May, 1934. Although he had at one time found it politic to talk in vague terms of an ultimate restoration, Hitler never seriously entertained the project, and in his Reichstag speech of 30 January, 1934, he declared the times to be inopportune for such a proposal. He was equally opposed to a perpetuation of the existing situation. So long as the independent position of the President existed alongside his own, so long as the President was Commander-in-Chief of the Armed Forces and so long as the oath of allegiance was taken to the President and not to himself, Hitler's power was something less than absolute. While the old Field-Marshal remained alive Hitler had to accept this limitation, but he was determined that when Hindenburg died he and no one else should succeed to the President's position. It was to Adolf

Hitler, and not to a possible rival, that the Armed Forces should take the new oath of allegiance. The first and most important step was to make sure of the Army, whose leaders, in the tradition of General von Seeckt, claimed to represent the permanent interests of the nation independently of the rise and fall of governments and parties. This was a claim which it was virtually certain Hitler would sooner or later challenge; but he was content to bide his time and negotiate for the Army's support on the generals' own terms.

In the second week of April an opportunity presented itself. On 11 April Hitler left Kiel on the cruiser *Deutschland* to take part in naval manoeuvres. He was accompanied by General von Blomberg, the Minister of Defence; Colonel General Freiherr von Fritsch, the Commander-in-Chief of the German Army, and Admiral Raeder, the Commander-in-Chief of the German Navy. It is believed to have been during the course of this short voyage that Hitler came to terms with the generals: the succession for himself, in return for the suppression of Roehm's plans and the continued inviolability of the Army's position as the sole armed force in the State. On his return from East Prussia Hitler quietly renewed his offer to the British and French Governments to reduce the S.A. On the Army side, a conference of senior officers under Fritsch's chairmanship which met at Bad Nauheim on 16 May, to discuss the question of the succession, endorsed Blomberg's decision in favour of Hitler after—but only after—the terms of the *Deutschland* Pact had been communicated to them.

The news of Hitler's offer to cut down the numbers of the S.A., which leaked out and was published in Prague, sharpened the conflict between Roehm and the Army. Roehm had powerful enemies inside the Party as well as in the Army. Goering, who had been made a general by Hindenburg to his great delight at the end of August, 1933, once in power gravitated naturally towards the side of privilege and authority, and was on the worst of terms with the Chief of Staff of the S.A. He began to collect a powerful police force "for special service," which he kept ready under his own hand at the Lichterfelde Cadet School near Berlin. On 1 April,

1934, Himmler, already head of the Bavarian police and Reichs-fuehrer of the black-shirted S.S., was unexpectedly appointed by Goering as head of the Prussian Gestapo. With the help of Rein-hard Heydrich, Himmler was engaged in building up a police em-pire within the Nazi State, and it appears likely that Goering surrendered his authority over the Gestapo with an ill grace. But Goering found in Himmler an ally against a common enemy, for the first obstacle Himmler sought to remove from his path was Ernst Roehm. Himmler and his S.S. were still a part of the S.A. and sub-ordinate to Roehm's command, although the rivalry between the S.A. and S.S. was bitter, and Roehm's relationship with Himmler could hardly have been less cordial. When the time came the S.S. *corps d'élite* provided the firing-squads for the liquidation of the S.A. leaders, while Himmler—far more than the generals—was the ultimate beneficiary of the humbling of the rival S.A. Hess, Bormann and Major Buch (the chairman of the *Uschla*) were meanwhile diligent in collecting complaints and scandals—and there were plenty—about Roehm and the other S.A. leaders.

Roehm's only friends in the Party leadership were Goebbels and —paradoxically enough—the man who had him murdered, Hit-ler. Goebbels was by temperament a radical and more attracted by the talk of a Second Revolution than by the idea of any com-promise with the *Reaktion,* which he continued to attack in his speeches and articles. It was Goebbels who still kept in touch with Roehm and maintained a link between the Chief of Staff and Hit-ler until the middle of June. Only at the last moment did the Min-ister of Propaganda come over to the other side and turn against Roehm, in the same way that he had betrayed Strasser in 1926. As for Hitler, whatever view is taken of the conflict which was go-ing on in his mind it is clear that it was not until the latter part of June that he was persuaded to move against Roehm and the S.A., as Goering and Himmler had been urging him to do for some time past.

Roehm's strength lay in his S.A. troops, and his closest asso-ciates were all prominent S.A. leaders. But Roehm himself and other S.A. leaders, like the brutal and corrupt Heines, had acquired a bad reputation for the disorder, luxury and perversion of their way of living. Although it suited Hitler and Roehm's enemies to play this up after his murder, there is no doubt that it had seriously weakened Roehm's position, even if there were few among the other Nazi leaders who were well placed to cast reproaches. By the middle of May, Roehm so far recognized that the S.A. were on the defensive as to send out an order dated 16 May, instructing his local leaders to keep a record of all complaints and attacks directed against the S.A.

The history of the following weeks can only be reconstructed with difficulty. The outlines of the situation are clear enough, but the parts played by individuals, by Goebbels and by Strasser, for instance; the intentions of the two principal actors, Hitler and Roehm; whether there ever was a conspiracy, and if so who was involved in it—all these represent questions to which more than one answer can be given. The official accounts fail to cover all the known facts and involve obvious contradictions, while the accounts compiled from the evidence of men who survived and from hearsay necessarily contain much that is unverifiable, even where it rings true. Unfortunately, the documentary material captured in Germany at the end of the Second World War and so far published has yielded virtually nothing: perhaps this was one of the episodes in the history of the Third Reich of which no records were allowed to remain.

The situation with which Hitler had to deal was produced by the intersection of three problems, the problems of the Second Revolution, of the S.A. and the Army, and of the succession to President von Hindenburg. Neither the first nor the second of these was new, and Hitler's instinct was to attempt to ride out the crisis and avoid making an outright decision in favour of either side. It was the third problem, that of the succession, which introduced a note of urgency by making Hitler's own position vulnerable.

If Hitler was to secure their support for his succession to the Presidency, the Army and the conservative interests with which the Army leadership was identified were determined to exact in return the removal of the S.A. threat to take over the Army and renew the revolution. The only alternative to accepting their terms was that urged by Roehm—for Hitler himself to take the lead in renewing the revolution and, relying on the S.A., to destroy any opposition by force. But this was a course which would create more problems than it would remove. It would mean the risk of open conflict with the Army, avoidance of which had been a guiding principle with Hitler ever since the fiasco of 1923; it would divide and weaken the nation, wreck the chances of economic recovery and possibly produce international complications, even the threat of foreign intervention.

For weeks these were the considerations which Hitler weighed in his mind. Driven at last to decide, he chose to stand by his agreement with the Army and repudiate the revolution, but for as long as possible he sought to avoid a decision. When he had made it, he disguised it as action forced on him not by pressure from the Right, but by disloyalty and conspiracy on the Left.

On 4 June Hitler sent for Roehm and had a conversation with him which lasted for five hours. According to Hitler's later account of this talk, he warned Roehm against any attempt to start a Second Revolution—"I implored him for the last time to oppose this madness of his own accord, to use his authority to stop a development which in any event could only end in a catastrophe." At the same time as he assured Roehm that he had no intention of dissolving the S.A., Hitler reproached him with the scandal created by his own behaviour and that of his closest associates in the S.A. leadership. What else was said is not known, but it would be surprising if Hitler did not mention the succession to Hindenburg and the difficulties which Roehm was creating for him by antagonizing the Army. It would be equally surprising if Roehm did not attempt to win Hitler over to his view of the future of the S.A. as the core of a new army. Whatever was said between the two men, a day or two later Hitler ordered the S.A. to go on leave for the month of July, returning to duty on 1 August, while Roehm

announced on 7 June that he himself was about to take a period
of sick leave. During their leave the S.A. were forbidden to wear
their uniforms or to take part in any demonstrations or exercises.
This was evidently Hitler's way of relieving the tension and free-
ing himself temporarily of the embarrassment of his more im-
petuous followers. Lest there should be any misunderstanding,
however, Roehm issued his own communiqué to the S.A.

I expect, then, on 1 August that the S.A., fully rested and strengthened,
will stand ready to serve the honourable tasks which People and Fatherland may expect from them. If the foes of the S.A. are nursing the
hope that the S.A. will not return from their leave, or that a part only
will return, we are ready to let them enjoy this hope for a short time.
At the hour and in the form which appears to be necessary they will
receive the fitting answer. The S.A. is, and remains, Germany's destiny.

Roehm's statement certainly suggests that Hitler had failed to
persuade him to moderate his attitude, but Roehm left Berlin in
the belief that no decision would be taken in the near future.
Hitler indeed agreed to attend a conference of S.A. leaders to
discuss the future of the movement at Wiessee, near Munich, on
30 June. It was a rendezvous which Hitler did not fail to keep.

What then happened between 8 June and 30 June?

Hitler gave his version in his speech of 13 July. According to
this Roehm through the agency of a certain Herr von A. (identified
as Werner von Alvensleben) had renewed his old relations with
General von Schleicher. The two men, according to Hitler, agreed
on a concrete programme:

"1. The present régime in Germany could not be supported.
"2. Above all the Army and all national associations must
be united in a single band.
"3. The only man who could be considered for such a position was the Chief of Staff, Roehm.
"4. Herr von Papen must be removed, and Schleicher himself
would be ready to take the position of Vice-Chancellor,
and in addition further important changes must be made
in the Reich Cabinet."

The Nazi Revolution

Since Roehm was not sure that Hitler would agree to such a programme—and it appears that it was still proposed to retain Hitler as Chancellor—he made preparations to carry out his plan by a *coup,* the main role in which was to be played by the S.A. Staff Guards, to which, as we have already seen, Blomberg had drawn Hitler's attention. To complete the conspiracy, Hitler continued, Schleicher and General von Bredow got in touch with "a foreign Power" (later identified as France). At the same time Gregor Strasser, who had retired into private life after Hitler's Chancellorship, was brought into the plot.

After his talk with Hitler on 4 June, Roehm—still according to Hitler's version—pressed on with plans to capture the Government quarter in Berlin and take Hitler captive, hoping to use his authority to call out the S.A. and paralyse the other forces in the State. The action taken at the end of June was directed, Hitler claimed, to forestalling Roehm's *putsch* which was about to be staged in a matter of hours.

Part of this story can with some certainty be rejected as untrue from the beginning. If Roehm was preparing to make a *putsch,* his plans were certainly not ready to be put into operation at the end of June. All the evidence shows that the S.A. leaders were taken completely by surprise. On the very day he was supposed to be storming the Chancellery in Berlin, Roehm was seized in bed at the hotel in Wiessee where he was taking a cure and awaiting Hitler's arrival for the conference they had arranged. Most of the other S.A. leaders were either on their way to Wiessee or had actually arrived. Karl Ernst, the S.A. leader in Berlin (whom Hitler represented as one of the most important figures in the plot), was taken prisoner at Bremen, where he was about to leave by boat for a honeymoon in Madeira. The whole story of an imminent *coup d'état* was a lie, either invented later by Hitler as a pretext for his own action, or possibly made use of at the time by Goering and Himmler to deceive Hitler and force him to move against Roehm. Frick, the Minister of the Interior, testified after the war that it was Himmler who convinced Hitler that Roehm meant to start a *putsch*. Indeed, the view that Hitler genuinely, although mistakenly, believed that he had to deal with a conspiracy would fit very well with his own behaviour at the time. So great was Hitler's capacity for self-dramatization and duplicity, however, and so convenient the pretext, that it would be wiser, on the evidence we have, to keep an open mind.

By the time he came to make his Reichstag speech even Hitler seems to have realized that there was precious little substance in his accusation of intrigues with a foreign Power. Whatever contacts Schleicher or Roehm had with the French Ambassador, or any other foreign representative, appear to have been entirely casual, and the German Foreign Ministry later presented a note to the Quai d'Orsay in Paris officially stating that any suspicions directed against the French Ambassador in Berlin were wholly without foundation.

Stripped of its mysterious foreign complications and its melo-dramatic denouement in an S.A. march on Berlin at the end of June, there remains the double charge that Roehm discussed with Schleicher—possibly also with Strasser—the programme outlined by Hitler, and that there was talk in the S.A. leadership of forcing Hitler to take the lead in a revolutionary settlement, which would include the establishment of the S.A. as the nucleus of the new German Army. Neither charge is implausible. Roehm certainly had such ambitions for his S.A. and made no secret of them. He had been in close relations with Schleicher before 30 January, 1933—so had Gregor Strasser, who was to have been Schleicher's Vice-Chancellor. Schleicher was an able, ambitious and unscrupulous intriguer. At one time he had thought of in-corporating the S.A. as a reserve for the Army; and he had plenty of reason for seeking to revenge himself on Papen, as well as on Blomberg and the other generals who had accepted his dismissal in January, 1933, without protest. But this remains specula-tion, and the one fact that is established, namely, that Schleicher and Strasser were both shot in the same purge as Roehm, is open to a very different interpretation. For, if there were two men in Ger-many who might well have felt insecure in the event of any purge, two men whom Hitler was certain to regard as dangerous, whatever they did, they were Gregor Strasser and Kurt von Schleicher. There were many old scores levelled on the weekend of 30 June, 1934, and the murder of Schleicher and Strasser may well fall into this category.

As to the second charge, it is very likely that Roehm and those who shared his views discussed how to win Hitler over and force his hand, but there is no proof at all that such discussions had gone so far as to merit the name of a conspiracy. The conspirators of June, 1934, were not Roehm and the S.A., but Goering and Himmler, the enemies of Roehm; the treachery and disloyalty were not on Roehm's side, but on theirs and Hitler's; and if ever men died convinced—not without reason—that they had been "framed," it was the men who were shot on 30 June, 1934.

Without being dogmatic, therefore, there is good reason to regard the account which Hitler gave of these events with suspicion, as the awkward apologia of a murderer seeking to justify his crime by defaming his victims.

Throughout June, 1934, there was an ominous tension in Berlin, heightened by rumours and much speculation. At the end of May both Bruening and Schleicher were warned that, in the event of a purge, their lives were in danger. The possibility of such a purge was now widely canvassed, although there were the most divergent accounts of who was to make the purge and who was to be purged. Bruening took the advice seriously and left for Switzerland; Schleicher went no farther than the Starnbergersee, and returned in time to be shot.

On 14 June Hitler made his first foreign visit since becoming Chancellor, and flew to Venice for the first of many celebrated conversations with Mussolini. The first, as it happened, was among the least auspicious of all. Mussolini, at the height of his reputation and resplendent with uniform and dagger, patronized the worried Hitler, who appeared in a raincoat and a soft hat. Mussolini was not only pressing on the subject of Austria, where Nazi intrigues were to lead to trouble before the summer was out, but frank in his comments on the internal situation in Germany. He advised Hitler to put the Left wing of the Party under restraint, and Hitler returned from Venice depressed and irritable.

No part is more difficult to trace in this confused story than that played by Gregor Strasser—if indeed he played any part at all other than that of victim. Hitler had apparently renewed touch with Strasser earlier in the year, and, according to Gregor's brother Otto, saw him the day before he left for Venice, in order to offer him the Ministry of National Economy. Strasser, always a poor politician, made the mistake of imposing too many conditions, demanding the dismissal of both Goering and Goebbels. This was more than Hitler could agree to, and he let Strasser go.

About the same time, again according to Otto Strasser, Goebbels had been seeing Roehm secretly in a back room of the *Bratwurst-Gloeckle* tavern in Munich. Immediately on Hitler's return from Venice Goebbels reported to him on his conversations with the S.A. Chief of Staff.

These attempts to keep touch with Strasser, the one-time leader of the Left wing of the Party, and with Roehm, the leader of the S.A., in which radicalism was endemic, were evidently related to a conflict still going on in Hitler's mind. What were the terms of this conflict? Two explanations seem possible. The first is the explanation usually given, that Hitler was weighing the advantages of going with the radicals against the *Reaktion,* or with the Army and the Right against the radicals. On this view he kept in touch with Roehm and allowed Goebbels to go on with his talks, because he had still not made up his mind. The second explanation is that given by Hitler himself. In his speech of 13 July he said: "I still cherished the secret hope that I might be able to spare the movement and my S.A. the shame of such a disagreement and that it might be possible to remove the mischief without severe conflicts."

On this view Hitler was preoccupied not with the choice between the radicals and the *Reaktion,* between the S.A. and the Army, but with the possibility of postponing such a choice and patching up a compromise, at least until the question of the succession had been decided. On *a priori* grounds this seems a more plausible explanation of Hitler's hesitation than that of vacillation between the reactionary and the revolutionary course. For it is difficult to believe that Hitler ever contemplated the risk of an open clash with the Army, whereas it is very easy to believe that he was eager to avoid dealing a heavy blow to the Party, by delaying action in the hope that Hindenburg might die suddenly, or that in some other way the crisis could be solved without irrevocable decisions. At present there is not sufficient evidence to decide in favour of one view or the other.

At this stage Hitler was given a sharp reminder of the realities of the situation from an unexpected quarter. Papen had dropped into the background since the spring of 1933, but he remained Vice-Chancellor and still enjoyed the special confidence of the old President. The divisions within the Party offered him a chance of re-asserting his influence, and for the last time he made use of his credit with the President to stage a public protest against the recent course, and, even more, against the prospective course, of events in Germany. If Hitler refused to listen, or if his protest led to trouble, then Papen hoped and believed that he would have the support of Hindenburg, who was equally unhappy about the state of affairs in Germany. In case of need Papen counted on the President's ordering the Army to intervene.

Papen's protest was drafted for him by Edgar Jung, with the co-operation of a number of others who belonged to the Catholic Action group and hoped to use Papen as the mouthpiece of their ideas. Amongst them were Papen's secretaries, von Bose and von Detten, and Erich Klausener, the leader of Catholic Action. The protest was made in the course of a speech at the University of Marburg on 17 June and crystallized the anxieties and uncertainties of the whole nation. It was studded with references to Catholic and Conservative principles, but its outstanding passages were those which dealt with the talk of a Second Revolution and the short-comings of Nazi propaganda.

"It goes without saying," Papen declared, "that the supporters of the revolutionary principle will first of all occupy the positions of power. But when the revolution is completed, then the government can represent only the totality of the nation. . . . We cannot think of repeating the division of the people, on the ancient Greek model, into Spartans and Helots. . . . Selection indeed is necessary, but the principle of natural selection must not be replaced by the criterion of adherence to a special political doctrine."

The Vice-Chancellor then turned specifically to the talk of a Second Revolution.

Whoever toys irresponsibly with such ideas should not forget that a second wave of revolution might be followed by a third, and that he who threatens to employ the guillotine may be its first victim.

Nor is it clear where such a second wave is to lead. There is much talk of the coming socialization. Have we gone through the anti-Marxist revolution in order to carry out a Marxist programme? . . . Would the German people be the better for it, except perhaps those who scent booty in such a pillaging raid? . . . No people can afford to indulge in a permanent revolt from below if it would endure in history. At some time the movement must come to a stop and a solid social structure arise. . . . Germany must not embark on an adventure without a known destination, nobody knowing where it will end. History has its own clock. It is not necessary continually to urge it on.

No less outspoken were the references to the mis-handling of propaganda:

Great men [Papen remarked] are not created by propaganda, but grow until their deeds are acknowledged by history. Nor can Byzantinism cheat these laws of Nature. Whoever speaks of Prussian should first of all think of quiet, selfless service, and of reward and recognition only at the very last, or best, not at all.

In his concluding passage Papen returned to the place and purpose of propaganda:

If one desires close contact and unity with the people, one must not underestimate their understanding. One must return their confidence and not everlastingly keep them in leading strings. . . . No organization, no propaganda, however excellent, can alone maintain confidence in the long run. It is not by incitement, especially the incitement of youth, and not by threats against the helpless part of the nation, but only by talking things over with people that confidence and devotion can be maintained. . . . It is time to join together in fraternal friendship and respect for all our fellow countrymen, to avoid disturbing the labours of serious men and to silence fanatics.

The same day that Papen made his speech at Marburg, Hitler spoke at Gera and was scathing in his references to "the pygmy who imagines he can stop with a few phrases the gigantic renewal of a people's life." But Papen's protest was not so easily brushed aside. Goebbels took immediate steps to ban its publication, seizing a pamphlet version and the edition of the *Frankfurter Zeitung* in which the text had been printed, but copies were smuggled out of Germany and published abroad, creating a sensation which did not fail to penetrate to Germany. When Papen appeared in public at Hamburg on 24 June he was loudly cheered. It was evident that he had spoken for a great part of the nation.

On 20 June Papen went to see Hitler and demand the removal of the ban on publishing his speech. In a stormy interview Papen threatened his own and the resignation of the other conservative ministers in the Cabinet—von Neurath, the Foreign Minister, and Schwerin von Krosigk, the Minister of Finance. Goebbels continued to make speeches attacking the upper classes and the *Reaktion* as the enemies of National Socialism, but Hitler saw quite clearly that he was face to face with a major crisis and that action could not be deferred much longer. If he had any doubts, they were removed by his reception when he flew to Neudeck on 21 June to see the ailing President. He was met by the Minister of Defence, General von Blomberg, with an uncompromising message: either the Government must bring about a relaxation of the state of tension or the President would declare martial law and hand over power to the Army. Hitler was allowed to see the President only for a few minutes, but the interview, brief though it was, sufficed to confirm von Blomberg's message. The Army was claiming the fulfilment of its bargain, and by now Hitler must have realized that more was at stake than the succession to the Presidency: the future of the whole régime was involved.

It is impossible to penetrate Hitler's state of mind in the last week of June. Obviously he must have been aware of the preparations which were now rapidly put in hand and have agreed to them at least tacitly, yet to the very last day he seems to have hesitated to take the final step. At this stage it was not Hitler, but Goering and Himmler, who gave the orders and prepared to eliminate their rivals in the Party leadership. In the background the Army made its own arrangements. On 25 June the Commander-in-Chief, General von Fritsch, placed the Army in a state of alert, ordering all leave to be cancelled and the troops to be confined to barracks. On 28 June the German Officers' League expelled Roehm, and on 29 June the *Völkischer Beobachter* carried a signed article by General von Blomberg, the Minister of Defence, which was a plain statement of the Army's position.

"The Army's role," Blomberg wrote, "is clearly determined; it must serve the National Socialist State, which it affirms with the deepest conviction. Equally it must support those leaders who have given it back its noblest right to be not only the bearer of arms, but also the bearer, recognized by State and people, of their unlimited confidence. . . . In the closest harmony with the entire nation . . . the Army stands, loyal and disciplined, behind the rulers of the State, behind the President, Field-Marshal von Hindenburg, its Supreme Commander, and behind the leader of the Reich, Adolf Hitler, who came from its ranks and remains one of ours."

The Army leaders were quite content to leave it to Goering and Himmler to carry out the purge, but after Blomberg's article there could be no doubt that whatever was done would be done with their blessing.

On Thursday, 28 June, Hitler, who had only just returned from Bavaria, left Berlin for Essen to attend the marriage of the local Gauleiter, Terboven. It is possible, as some accounts report, that he also went to see Krupp and Thyssen; even so, his absence from the capital at so critical a time is curious and suggests that he was either deliberately trying to lull the suspicions of the watchful, or else refusing to take part in preparations to which he was was only half reconciled. While he was away, on the 28th, Goering and Himmler ordered their police commandos and S.S. to hold themselves in readiness.

Far away from the tension and rumours of Berlin, on the shores of the Tegernsee, Roehm continued to enjoy his sick leave with his usual circle of young men, and to prepare lazily for the S.A. conference at the week-end, at which Hitler was expected. So little was he aware of what was being planned that he had left his Staff Guards in Munich. His carelessness and confidence are astonishing. Yet, even in Berlin, the local S.A. leader, Karl Ernst, who was uneasily aware of something in the wind and alerted the Berlin S.A. on the afternoon of 29 June, was so far misled as to believe the danger was a *putsch* by the Right directed against Hitler. Ernst never understood what had happened, even after his arrest, and died shouting: *"Heil, Hitler."*

On the 29th Hitler, still keeping away from Berlin, made a tour of labour camps in Westphalia, and in the afternoon stopped at Godesberg on the Rhine, where in 1938 he was to receive Neville Chamberlain. At Godesberg he brought himself to take the final decision. Goebbels, who in the past few days had hurriedly dropped his radical sympathies and his contacts with Roehm, brought the news that the Berlin S.A., although due to go on leave the next day, had been suddenly ordered to report to their posts. Other alarming news of S.A. restlessness is said to have come from Munich. Whether Hitler really believed that this was the prelude to an S.A. mutiny, as he later claimed, it is impossible to say. He may have been influenced by the news that Dr. Sauerbruch, an eminent German specialist, had been suddenly summoned to the bedside of President Hindenburg. During the evening of the 29th, Viktor Lutze, one of the reliable S.A. leaders (he was later appointed to succeed Roehm as Chief of Staff), was brought hurriedly from Hanover to Godesberg to join Hitler, Goebbels and Otto Dietrich. At two o'clock in the morning Hitler took off from the Hangelar airfield, near Bonn, to fly to Munich. Before leaving he had telegraphed to Roehm to expect him at Wiessee the next day. "It was at last clear to me that only one man could oppose and must oppose the Chief of Staff."

The purge had already begun in Munich when Hitler landed at the Oberwiesenfeld airfield at four o'clock on the Saturday morning. On the evening of the 29th Major Buch, the chairman of the *Uschla,* and the Bavarian Minister of the Interior, Adolf Wagner, formed a group of men including Christian Weber, Emil Maurice and Joseph Berchthold, dim figures from Hitler's old days in Munich, and arrested the local S.A. leaders on the pretext that they were about to carry out a *coup d'état.* At the Ministry of the Interior, where the *S.A. Obergruppenfuehrer,* Schneidhuber, and his deputy were held under guard, a Hitler who had now worked himself up into a fury tore off their insignia with his own hand and cursed them for their treachery.

In the early morning of the 30th a fast-moving column of cars tore down the road from Munich to Wiessee, where Roehm and Heines were still asleep in their beds at the Hanselbauer Hotel. The accounts of what happened at Wiessee are contradictory. Heines, the *S.A. Obergruppenfuehrer* for Silesia, who was found sleeping with one of Roehm's young men, is said to have been dragged out and shot on the road. Other accounts say he was taken to Munich with Roehm and shot there.

Back in Munich, seven to eight hundred men of Sepp Dietrich's *S.S. Leibstandarte Adolf Hitler* had been brought in from their barracks—the Army providing the transport—and ordered to provide a shooting squad at the Stadelheim Prison. It was there that Roehm had been imprisoned on 9 November, 1923, after the unsuccessful Munich putsch; it was there that he was now shot by order of the man who seven months before had written to thank him for his imperishable services. Hitler ordered a revolver to be left in his cell, but Roehm refused to use it: "If I am to be killed, let Adolf do it himself." According to an eyewitness at the 1957 Munich trial of those involved, he was shot by two S.S. officers who emptied their revolvers into him at point blank range "Roehm wanted to say something, but the S.S. officers told him to shut up. Then Roehm stood at attention—he was stripped to the waist—with his face full of contempt."

In Berlin the executions, directed by Goering and Himmler, began on the night of 29–30 June and continued throughout the Saturday and Sunday. The chief place of execution was the Lichterfelde Cadet School, and once again the principal victims were the leaders of the S.A. But in Berlin the net was cast more widely. When the bell rang at General von Schleicher's villa and the general went to the door, he was shot down where he stood and his wife with him. His friend, General von Bredow, was shot on his doorstep the same evening. Gregor Strasser, arrested at noon on the Saturday, was executed in the Prinz Albrechtstrasse Prison. Goering would certainly have removed Papen too, if he had not been Vice-Chancellor and under the special protection of the President. Despite this, Papen's office was wrecked, he himself was kept under house arrest for four days, two of his advisers, Bose and Edgar Jung, were shot, and two others arrested.

Late on the Saturday, Hitler returned from Munich. Among those who waited at the Tempelhof was H. B. Gisevius, who has described the scene. Goering, Himmler, Frick and a group of police officers stood waiting for the plane. As it dived out of the sky and rolled across the field a guard of honour presented arms. The first to step out was Hitler. "A brown shirt, black bow-tie, dark-brown leather jacket, high black army boots. He wore no hat; his face was pale, unshaven, sleepless, at once gaunt and puffed. Under the forelock pasted against his forehead his eyes stared dully." Without saying a word, Hitler shook hands with the group on the airfield; the silence was broken only by the repeated click of heels. He walked slowly past the guard of honour, and not until he had started to walk towards his car did he begin to talk to Goering and Himmler. "From one of his pockets Himmler took a long, tattered list. Hitler read it through, while Goering and Himmler whispered incessantly into his ear. We could see Hitler's fingers moving slowly down the sheet of paper. Now and then it paused for a moment at one of the names. At such times the two conspirators whispered even more excitedly. Suddenly Hitler tossed his head. There was so much violent emotion, so much anger in the gesture, that everyone noticed it. . . . Undoubtedly, we thought, they were now informing him of Strasser's 'suicide'. . . . The bathos of the scene, the woebegone expressions, the combination of violent fantasy and grim reality, the gratuitously blood-red sky, like a scene out of Wagner—it was really too much for me."

The executions went on all day Sunday—while Hitler gave a tea-party in the Chancellery garden—and were not confined to Berlin. A considerable number of people, as many as fifty-four according to the *White Book* later published in Paris, were shot at Breslau, and another thirty-two in the whole of the rest of Silesia. Only on Monday morning did the shooting cease, when the German people, shaken and shocked, returned to work, and Hindenburg addressed his thanks to the Chancellor for his "determined action and gallant personal intervention, which have nipped treason in the bud." On Tuesday General von Blomberg conveyed the congratulations of the Cabinet to the Chancellor. The General had already expressed the devotion and fidelity of the Army in an Order of the Day: "The Fuehrer asks us to establish cordial relations with the new S.A. This we shall joyfully endeavour to do in the belief that we serve a common ideal." The Army was very well satisfied with the events of the week-end.

How many were killed has never been settled. According to Gisevius, Goering ordered all the documents relating to the purge to be burned. Little by little, a list of names was pieced together. Hitler in his speech to the Reichstag admitted fifty-eight executed and another nineteen who had lost their lives. In addition, he mentioned a number of acts of violence unconnected with the plot, which were to be brought before the ordinary courts. The *White Book* published in Paris gave a total of four hundred and one, and listed one hundred and sixteen of them by name.

The largest group of victims belonged to the S.A., and included, besides Roehm, three *S.A. Obergruppenfuehrer*—Heines, von Krausser, and Schneidhuber; Karl Ernst, the *S.A. Gruppenfuehrer* for Berlin, and three of the men who had been his accomplices in the burning of the Reichstag; Hans Hayn and Peter von Heydebreck, the *Gruppenfuehrer* for Saxony and Pomerania. Another group was formed by Schleicher and his wife; his former assistant in the Defence Ministry, General von Bredow; Gregor Strasser; and Papen's two assistants who served as substitutes for Papen himself, von Bose and Edgar Jung. Bose was talking to two industrialists from the Rhineland in the Vice-Chancellery when he was asked to step into the next room and see three S.S. men who had just arrived: shots rang out, and when the door was opened the S.S. men had gone and Bose was lying dead on the floor. A number of other Catholic leaders were shot, the most important being Erich Klausener, the German leader of Catholic Action.

Many of those murdered had little, if any, connection with Roehm or the S.A., and fell victims to private quarrels. Kahr, who had played a big role in 1923, but had since retired—he was now seventy-three—was found in a swamp near Dachau; his body was hacked to pieces. Father Bernhard Stempfle, who had once revised the proofs of *Mein Kampf*, was discovered in the woods outside Munich; he had been shot "while trying to escape." In Hirschberg, Silesia, a group of Jews was murdered, for no other apparent reason than to amuse the local S.S. In Munich, on the evening of 30 June, Dr. Willi Schmidt, the music critic of the *Muenchener Neueste Nachrichten,* was playing the 'cello in his flat while his wife made supper and their three children were playing. Suddenly the door bell rang and four armed S.S. men came to take him away without explanation. There never was any explanation, except that the S.S. men were looking for someone else with the same name and shot the wrong man. When Frau Schmidt got her husband's body back, she was warned under no circumstances to open the coffin: the S.S. sent her a sum of money in recognition of her loss and their mistake. When she refused to accept it, Himmler rang up and told her to take the money and keep quiet. When she still refused, Hess called and eventually, through his help, Frau Schmidt secured a pension: she should think of her husband's death, Hess told her, as the death of a martyr for a great cause.

In an effort to prevent too much becoming known, Goebbels forbade German newspapers to carry obituary notices of those who had been executed or "had committed suicide." The ban on any mention of what had happened only led to exaggerated rumours and to the intensification of the feeling of horror and fear. Not until 13 July did Hitler appear before the Reichstag and reveal a part of the story.

Hitler was very much on the defensive, at least until the end of his speech. He began with a lengthy recital of the achievements of National Socialism, in defence of his policy as Chancellor. When he came to describe the events leading up to 30 June he threw the whole blame on Roehm, who had forced him to act against his own wishes. Hitler gave great prominence to the charges of corruption, favoritism and homosexuality against Roehm's group, and went out of his way to represent them as betraying the ordinary, decent S.A. man who had been exploited by a depraved and unscrupulous leadership. Hitler did not attempt, however, to conceal the real charges against Roehm. He spoke of those who had become "uprooted and had thereby lost altogether any sympathy with any ordered human society. They became revolutionaries who favoured revolution for its own sake and desired to see revolution established as a permanent condition." But, Hitler replied, "for us the Revolution is no permanent condition. When some mortal check is imposed with violence upon the natural development of a people, then the artificially interrupted evolution can rightly by a deed of violence open up the way for itself in order to regain liberty to pursue its natural development. But there can be no such thing as a state of permanent revolution; neither can any beneficent development be secured by means of periodically recurrent revolts."

Hitler's references to the quarrel between Roehm and the Army were still clearer. After outlining Roehm's plan for a single organization to incorporate the Army and the S.A., with himself as Minister of Defence, Hitler spoke of his unalterable opposition to Roehm's ideas. "For fourteen years I have stated consistently that the fighting organizations of the Party are *political* institutions and that they have nothing to do with the Army." He recalled his promise to Hindenburg that he would keep the Army out of politics, and spoke in glowing terms of his debt to General von Blomberg, the Minister of Defence, "who reconciled the Army with those who were once revolutionaries and has linked it up with their Government today." Finally he repeated the promise, which to the Army leaders was the covenant in which they placed their faith: "In the State there is only one bearer of arms, and that is the Army; there is only one bearer of the political will, and that is the National Socialist Party."

The Officer Corps, intent only on preserving the privileged position of the Army, and indifferent to what happened in Germany so long as Nazification stopped short of the military institutions of the country, could see no further than the ends of their own noses. The menace of the S.A. was broken for good on the week-end of 30 June. Under Viktor Lutze, its new Chief of Staff, it never again played an independent, or even a prominent, role in the Third Reich. But already a new and far more dangerous challenge to the autonomy of the Army was taking shape. As a reward for their service in the Roehm purge, Himmler's S.S. were now given their independence of the S.A., and placed directly under Hitler's orders with Himmler as *S.S. Reichsfuehrer*. At last the long dispute between Hitler and Roehm was ended, and Hitler had got what he had always wanted, an absolutely dependable and unquestioning instrument of political action. When, in 1936, Himmler acquired control of all German police forces as well, the framework of Hitler's police state was complete. What the Army leaders did not foresee was that, within less than ten years of Roehm's murder, the S.S. would have succeeded, where the S.A. had failed, in establishing a Party army in open rivalry with the generals' army, daily encroaching still further on their once proud but now sadly reduced position. No group of men was to suffer so sharp a reversal of their calculations as the Army officers, who, in the summer of 1934, ostentatiously held aloof from what happened in Germany and expressed an arrogant satisfaction at the Chancellor's quickness in seeing where the real power in Germany lay.

For anyone less blind than the generals, the way in which Hitler dealt with the threat of a second revolution must have brought consternation rather than satisfaction. Never had Hitler made so patent his total indifference to any respect for law or humanity, and his determination to preserve his power at any cost. Never had he illustrated so clearly the revolutionary character of his régime as in disowning the revolution. At the close of his Reichstag speech Hitler brushed aside the suggestion that the guilty men should have been tried before execution. "If anyone reproaches me and asks why I did not resort to the regular courts of justice, then all I can say to him is this: in this hour I was responsible for the fate of the German people, and thereby I became the supreme Justiciar (oberster Gerichtsherr) of the German people." . . . Lest there should be any doubt of the moral to be drawn, Hitler added: "And everyone must know for all future time that if he raises his hand to strike the State, then certain death is his lot."

If Hitler's hesitations in the last ten days of June had led people to say that he had virtually abdicated, he triumphantly re-asserted and increased his authority in the week-end that followed. Papen's Marburg speech had its answer, but it was Hitler, not Papen and the Reaktion, the peddlers of Christian Conservatism, who emerged triumphant from the test of June, 1934.

When Rauschning called on Hitler shortly after the purge, Hitler remarked: "They underestimate me because I've risen from below; because I haven't had an education, because I haven't the manners that their sparrow brains think right. . . . But I have spoiled their plans. They thought I wouldn't dare; they thought I was afraid. They saw me already wriggling in their net. They thought I was their tool, and behind my back they laughed at me and said I had no power now, that I had lost my Party. I saw through all that long ago. I've given them a cuff on the ear that they'll long remember. What I have lost in the trial of the S.A., I shall regain by the verdict on these feudal gamblers and professional card-sharpers. . . . I stand here stronger than ever before. Forward, *meine Herren* Papen and Hugenberg! I am ready for the next round."

The easy assurances of Neurath, who had told Rauschning in the spring of 1934: "Let it run its course, in five years no one will remember it," were shown to be as worthless as Papen's confident declarations of January, 1933. Papen was glad enough to escape with his life and hurriedly accepted the offer to go to Vienna as Hitler's special envoy. A little late in the day the ex-Vice-Chancellor was beginning to learn that he who sups with the Devil needs a very long spoon.

Now that Hitler had with one blow removed the pressure on him from both the Left and the Right, he could proceed to deal with the problem of the Succession at his leisure. Having honoured his own share of the pact with the Army, he could claim the fulfillment of the Army's promise, and in General von Blomberg he had found a man he could rely on. When President von Hindenburg died on the morning of 2 August, all had been arranged. There was neither hitch nor delay. Within an hour came the announcement that the office of President would henceforth be merged with that of the Chancellor, and that Hitler would become the Head of the State—as well as Supreme Commander-in-Chief of the Armed Forces of the Reich. Among the signatures at the foot of the law announcing these changes were those of von Papen, von Neurath, Graf Schwerin von Krosigk, General von Blomberg and Schacht: the representatives of Conservatism acquiesced in their own defeat.

The same day the officers and men of the Germany Army took the oath of allegiance to their new commander-in-chief. The form of the oath was significant. The Army was called on to swear allegiance not to the Constitution, or to the Fatherland, but to Hitler personally: "I swear by God this holy oath: I will render unconditional obedience to the Fuehrer of the German Reich and People, Adolf Hitler, the Supreme Commander of the Armed Forces, and will be ready, as a brave soldier, to stake my life at any time for this oath." On 6 August, when the Reichstag assembled in the Kroll Opera House to hear Hitler's funeral oration, and on 7 August, when the old Field-Marshal was buried with the full honours of State in the monument to his victory at Tannenberg, Hitler renewed the symbolic gesture of Potsdam— but with a difference. Between March, 1933, and August, 1934, the balance of power in Germany had shifted decisively in Hitler's favour. In that year and a half he had mastered the machine of State, suppressed the opposition, dispensed with his allies, asserted his authority over the Party and S.A., and secured for himself the prerogatives of the Head of the State and Commander-in-Chief of the Armed Forces. The Nazi revolution was complete: Hitler had become the dictator of Germany.

On 19 August the German people was invited to express by a plebiscite its approval of Hitler's assumption of Hindenburg's office as Fuehrer and Reich Chancellor, the official title by which Hitler was now to be known. The Political Testament of President Hindenburg, much discussed but so far not discovered, was now conveniently produced, shorn of any reference to the restoration of the monarchy it may have contained. In it the old Field-Marshal spoke warmly of Hitler's work in creating national unity and, lest there should be any doubt, Colonel Oskar von Hindenburg was put up to broadcast on the eve of the plebiscite. "My father," he told the German people, "had himself seen in Adolf Hitler his own direct successor as Head of the German State, and I am acting according to my father's intention when I call on all German men and women to vote for the handing over of my father's office to the Fuehrer and Reich Chancellor."

On the day of the plebiscite 95.7 per cent of the forty-five and a half million voters went to the polls, and more than thirty-eight million voted "Yes," 89.93 per cent of the votes cast. Four and a quarter millions had the courage to vote "No"; another eight hundred and seventy thousand spoiled their papers.

It was an impressive majority, and when the Party Rally was held at Nuremberg in September Hitler was in a benign mood. In his proclamation he spoke a good deal about the Nazi revolution which had now, he announced, achieved its object and come to an end. "Just as the world cannot live on wars, so peoples cannot live on revolutions. . . . Revolutions," he added, "have always been rare in Germany. The Age of Nerves of the nineteenth century has found its close with us. In the next thousand years there will be no other revolution in Germany."

It was an ambitious epitaph.

Suggestions for Further Reading

MEINECKE, FRIEDRICH, *The German Catastrophe*. Cambridge, Mass.: Harvard University Press, 1950.

MOSSE, G. L., *Crisis of German Ideology: Intellectual Origins of the Third Reich*. New York: Grosset & Dunlap, 1964.

NOLTE, ERNEST, *Three Faces of Fascism: Action Française, Italian Fascism, National Socialism*. London: Weidenfeld and Nicolson, 1965.

PULZER, PETER G. J., *The Rise of Political Anti-Semitism in Germany and Austria*. New York: John Wiley and Sons, Inc., 1964.

WHEELER-BENNETT, J. W., *The Nemesis of Power: The German Army in Politics, 1918–1945*. New York: St. Martin's Press, 1954.

The Foundations of the
Cold War*

RAYMOND ARON

———————

In the nineteenth century the pace of social change was greatly accelerated and in the twentieth century the upheavals and cataclysms that represent turning points in history follow one another with bewildering speed in the historical timetable. In the past fifty years the Western world and mankind as a whole have experienced one of the great ages of revolution, with which the last decade of the eighteenth century, the first half of the sixteenth century, and the second half of the eleventh century can compare. Never before the twentieth century, however, have the upheavals taken place on such a vast scale and the cataclysms produced such a wholesale slaughter.

The social and political organization of human society is very different from what it was a half century ago, but it is highly questionable whether we live in a better world than the young men of 1914 forsook when they followed their national flags to die on

* From Raymond Aron, *The Century of Total War* (London: Derek Verschoyle, 1954), pp. 101-165.

*the battlefields of western Europe. With each upheaval and cata-
clysm, leaders of society and the wise old men have proclaimed
the justice of historical necessity and prophesied a new and better
world that would arise out of the ashes of the old. The results have
not borne out these optimistic prophecies. The dawning of a new
era of peace and common welfare seems always to lie on the far-
thest horizon and each great change has brought with it new
problems and crises and called forth yet new conflict. The unprecedented sacrifice of human life in the past fifty years has been repeatedly justified as the distressing but inevitable prologue to a
better world, but the result always seems to be only novel forms
of violence, war, and mass murder. The twentieth century has
been the era of disappointment and disillusion and has witnessed
a steady process of recession from the realization of the peace and
progress that mid-nineteenth-century liberals forecast as the future of mankind. All through the Western world and even in
eastern Europe, the new generation of the 1960's was remarkable
for its pessimism and weariness, its alienation from the state, and
its growing distrust of the leadership of the older generation and
its slogans—and no wonder!*

*The First World War was supposed to make the world safe for
democracy. It did nothing of the sort. Instead it effected the de-
moralization of European society and opened the way for the
triumph of fascism in Germany and Italy, the hegemony of Japanese militarism in Asia, and the emergence of the Communist
dictatorship in Russia. The Russian revolution was for the generation of the 1920's and 30's the great hope for a better future, for
the achievement of human freedom on a worldwide scale, and for
the overcoming of the deficiencies of nineteenth-century bourgeois
civilization. The fastening of Stalinist despotism on Russian society,
the obliteration of millions of people by the Bolshevik regime, and
the transformation of Marxist-Leninism into an instrument of Russian expansionism gave the lie to this hope.*

*The involvement of the United States in the first and second
world wars was supposed to lead to the defeat of the forces of*

despotism and to the advance of democratic liberalism throughout the world. The particular despotisms against which the Americans fought were defeated and the post-Second World War policy of containment of Communism prevented the triumph of Stalinism in western Europe. But for one reason or another the American way of life has been found to be unexportable to most of the Asian and African societies that have thrown off the yoke of European imperialism. The discovery of atomic energy was supposed to inaugurate a new era in man's control of his environment and unprecedented melioration of his material welfare. This potentiality is far from realization, because the peaceful uses of atomic energy have been scarcely exploited. This new social resource, potentially even more valuable than the discovery of steam power in the eighteenth century and electricity in the late nineteenth century, has been developed mostly for purposes of military technology and gives a dimension of unprecedented terror to the struggle between the Communist and the Western worlds.

The upshot of all the suffering and bloodshed of the twentieth century has been the armed truce and quasi-peace of the Cold War. The origins and nature of this present condition of mankind are discussed in the following essay by the French historian and political scientist Raymond Aron. In Aron's discussion we hear the authentic, impartial, and anguished voice of nineteenth-century liberalism. He bitterly condemns Bolshevik authoritarianism but neither is he lavish in his praise of American policy and achievement. Aron's study was written in 1954. Very little has happened since that time to affect the import of his argument. Stalin finally departed and there was a slight thaw in the bleak and congealed world of the Soviet autocracy, but in the mid-1960's even this momentary liberalization of the Russian regime seemed to be transitory and insignificant. In any case the Communist rulers of China took over both the ideology and mechanisms of Stalinist tyranny and Stalinism became Maoism. It is extremely disturbing, but a tribute to Aron's powers of prophecy, that in 1954 he predicted the American republic might find itself involved in an in-

conclusive and inextricable commitment in Asia and Europe that
could have the same debilitating effect on the American republic
as the involvement in Sicily during the Peloponnesian Wars had
upon the Athenian city-state.

Immediately following the First World War, Max Weber wrote that American hegemony was as inevitable as that of Rome had been after the Second Punic War. Subsequent events have brought the United States, almost involuntarily, into domination over half of the planet. The rise of the American Republic is "logical," in the sense in which Cournot used the word, i.e., predetermined by the main factors of the situation.

This American domination can be demonstrated by a few familiar statistics: In 1870 the industrial production of the United States represented 23.5 per cent of the world's total, and in 1926–29, 42 per cent. Great Britain's share dropped during the same period from 31.8 to 9.4 per cent. According to another calculation, the total annual production of the United States represented in 1925–29 about a quarter of the annual world production. After the second war the national income of the United States in international units exceeded that of the period 1925–34 by 65 to 70 per cent. At present it represents between a quarter and a third of the world total (for about six per cent of the world's population). The United States produces more steel and consumes more gasoline than all the rest of mankind. North America's share (including Canada) of the world production of fuel and energy (coal, lignite, oil, hydro-electric energy) was 54.5 per cent in 1947, compared with 41.8 per cent in 1938.

The American economy combines natural and technical advantages. It possesses an abundance of most raw materials, and it has exploited these more effectively than any other country. The capital invested per worker is at least double that of the next most advanced countries. The productivity is the highest in the world (three times that of Europe, on the average). The country has discovered the secret of combining national power and individual wealth. For the first time, an imperial nation has no need to exploit the peoples it protects or dominates. It serves its own self-interest by raising the standard of living of those whom it wishes to integrate into its system.

The transition from economic supremacy to political hegemony is normal, but it was not inevitable. The Second World War accelerated that transition and gave it a dramatic character.

Industrial potential is a necessary condition of military power, but it is not sufficient in itself. Many military critics in France and Germany doubted whether a non-military democracy would be capable of improvising a great army. From 1940 to 1945, the United States dispelled those doubts with a speed and a completeness that astonished the Germans. The managerial class quickly supplied military leaders once the country was at war. Being, moreover, less the captive of traditions and more ready to experiment than the military castes of the old countries, the American officer corps rapidly adapted itself to the requirements of scientific warfare.

Other observers doubted whether the American public would show resolution enduring enough to influence the course of history. Without the clear and present danger of a neighboring country in arms, traditionally hostile to imperialism in the European pattern, devoted by its national philosophy to peaceful industry, would the United States not remain a spectator, enjoying unequaled wealth and profiting as the result of struggles waged overseas? Here again, subsequent events gave a resounding answer. In 1917, and again in 1941, America's realization of her common destiny with Europe suppressed the temptation to isolationism. In both wars, it is true, the mistakes of the enemy were remarkably influential: the declaration of unrestricted submarine warfare and the attack on Pearl Harbor precipitated a decision which the President anticipated but which the Congress disliked or viewed with hesitation. Between the two wars the United States withdrew

from Europe, and by this abstention thereby assumed some responsibility for the outbreak of the second war.

The development of events was nonetheless unmistakable. From
1940 onward, President Roosevelt went as far as his Constitutional
powers permitted. Before December 1941, American destroyers
had received instructions to fire at sight on any German submarine.
The American Government was definitely more inclined to enter
the Second World War than the First, and at the present time it has
had no thought of withdrawing from Europe. Through the Marshall Plan and the Atlantic Pact, American presence in Europe
has been assured for a long period. Not without surprise, but with
a complete lack of enthusiasm, the American people have recognized their strength and their obligations. They are exercising a
hegemony to which they had never aspired.

The political system of the United States was created by and for
an agricultural democracy, and has been adapted in practice to the
needs of an industrial society; but can it further develop and maintain a firm and continuous diplomatic policy on a world-wide
scale? Foreigners have asked that question, some hopefully, others
with apprehension; the future alone can supply the answer. Today
it can only be said that the prospect is not discouraging.

Serious mistakes were made both during and immediately after
the war. I am afraid they are beyond repair, but they were caused
less by the American political system than by popular psychology.
They have been attributed to a man who was at the point of
death, and to his team of advisers impregnated with Left Wing
ideology. But the statesmen were not the only ones to be caught
by the illusory pictures painted by propaganda for the common
people. A whole nation, optimistic and naïve, placed its trust in
a comrade in arms.

The road to error was paved by the crusading spirit which traditionally inspires the foreign policy of the United States. Woodrow
Wilson and Franklin Roosevelt envisaged their war aims not so
much in any concrete form as in the terms of certain ideals—democracy, or the Four Freedoms, or the United Nations Organiza-

tion. Instead of recognizing the real issue at stake, and accepting as objective the establishment of international relations in a balance that would favor world peace, they tended simply to see in the enemy the incarnation of evil. In order not to admit to themselves that, like belligerents throughout history, they had accepted the co-operation even of the worst of despotisms, the Americans whitewashed their Soviet ally with all the virtues needed to allow it to fight on the side of Goodness and Truth. After the war it was decided to reconstitute the Japanese and German armies—a risk that was quite rightly accepted; but the conscience-saving delusion persists that they have been purified by democratization.

The spread of American ideas and practices was sincerely conceived as a means of promoting the conversion of the sinner. Such hopes have been bitterly disappointed. The American standard of living and the Congress were not exportable at will. Neither the Germans nor the Japanese saluted democracy as the goal either of their own aspirations or of history in general. It was not enough to expel the Europeans in order to liberate the peoples of Asia. The Americans, hostile to the age-old structure of most human societies, hated to admit that the void left by the war and the liquidation of the European empires, by the destruction of ancestral ways of living, was going to be filled by despotic instead of by free institutions.

American diplomacy tends to run, as a consequence of its very failures, from one extreme to the opposite. When there is no longer any place for the crusading spirit, the alternative seems to be force and fraud, and so as not to be duped in a world of corruption, the game of power politics is played without reserve. It is not easy to accept the strange mixture formed by human history, which never supplies irreproachable causes to defend or absolute evil to oppose; nor ever separates international or party rivalries from those of ideas. The result is that American diplomacy is alternatively threatened by cynicism and by hypocrisy.

. . . . . .

In immediate decisions the American leaders have less freedom of movement than the masters of the Kremlin. They have to convince some hundreds of congressmen and journalists and, through them, public opinion. Neither those who make the decisions nor those who form opinion have unlimited power: the governing class, in agreement on essentials but divided into competing groups, does not obey an individual word of command because it is not subject to authoritative control. Concern for election results, for individual interests, and for economic considerations is likely to obstruct the plans of the Administration. Troublesome, however, as these matters of disagreement so often are, they are not without advantages in the long run. Unity not imposed by police is often more durable in practice.

There remain the dangers which Thucydides' Pericles described to the Athenians at the outset of the Peloponnesian War. The power of the United States is great, but not unlimited. America's responsibilities in Asia and in Europe are vast. Owing to its geographical situation, it hesitates between Europe and Asia, uncertain as to the relative importance to be assigned to the two spheres. The public is inclined to attribute the nation's setbacks entirely to mistakes on the part of its leaders, as if the leaders were never faced with insurmountable obstacles. Every democracy that freely discusses the conduct of its foreign policy is likely to oscillate in the wake of public opinion and to conceive glorious plans without measuring the cost.

The American temptation to appeasement has been overcome; will expeditions to Sicily be avoided?

There is no difficulty in assembling statistics that show the extent of the material and human resources available to the Soviet Union in the near future. The experts estimate that within twenty years the Russian population will be 250 millions. Geographers and geologists are very optimistic, as a rule, in regard to its raw material resources—20 per cent of the world supplies of coal, nearly half the world's oil reserves, half the iron, 10 per cent of the copper, 11 per cent of the lead, 19 per cent of the zinc, and so on. There would be no difficulty whatsoever in showing that the known reserves of most raw materials in the United States are much less extensive.

But mineral wealth buried in the earth is no exact measure of the future potentialities of the economic system. The deposits are scattered over the immense Eurasian region, sometimes in deserts. Their exploitation would require the transport of men, the building of new towns, in many cases even food transport. The famous Urals *combinat* unites a coal basin and an iron basin 1,250 miles apart. On the political scale, or even in terms of measurable human history, any comparison between the known or probable deposits in the Soviet Union and those in the United States must remain virtually meaningless for another century. Let us admit, uncertain though it is, that the Soviet Union possesses 50 per cent of the world's oil reserves. But its annual production amounted at the end of 1950 to 35 million tons, and the United States produces without difficulty ten times as much. The development of Russian agriculture faces great difficulties, for only one third of the total land surface is arable. It can hardly be said that Russia has been blessed by nature and thereby predestined to empire.

Before the Second World War, the Soviet Union had become one of the great industrial powers of the world, with an annual production of 166 million tons of coal, 31 million tons of oil, 48,000 million KWH of electrical energy, and 18 million tons of steel. It was inferior only to Germany in the size of its industrial potential capable of being transformed into military force.

Since the war's end the five-year plans have continued to be concerned mainly with heavy industry, and at the end of the year 1950 the Soviet Union was incontestably the world's second industrial power: its annual production was 250 million tons of coal, 35 million tons of oil, more than 80,000 million KWH, 25.4 million tons of steel. These figures remain well below those of the United States, and even those of the Continent west of the Iron Curtain.

The results obtained in agriculture are less impressive. The controversies over the agricultural statistics of the Soviet Union are too complicated for us to attempt even a summary of them. It appears that on the eve of the war the grain harvest was some 15 per cent above that of 1928 (which was equivalent to that of 1913), an increase mainly attributable to the increase in area. Per head of the population the area under grain fell between 1913 and 1938 from 0.68 to 0.60 hectares; the quantity available per head of the population similarly fell, from 4.9 to 4.5 quintals.

The enormous investments in agriculture, the social upheaval, the deportations of peasants, and the suffering of millions of innocent people, have brought no noticeable increase either in the quantity of agricultural produce or in the yield per hectare. What these measures *have* done is greatly to increase the proportion of the harvest at the Government's disposal. The Government obtained less than 15 per cent of the crops in 1928 (estimated at 73 million tons); it obtained 40 per cent of a yield of 82 million tons in 1939. Collectivization, regarded as an economic measure, succeeded in its goal to free part of the farm labor for work in the factories (the urban population was 21.4 millions in 1923 and 55.9 in 1939—a movement that has continued since the war's end), and to compel the peasants to deliver the quantity of grain necessary to feed the great industrial areas. It is difficult to believe that the end secured required the terrible means that were adopted.

It is often imagined that the Revolution of 1917 transformed primitive Russia into a modern state, an agricultural nation into a great industrial power. This impression fails to take account of the continuity between Soviet industrialization and the work accomplished in the course of the last years of the Tsarist regime.

Between 1890 and 1913, the number of industrial workers doubled (from 1.5 to 3 millions), and the production of the industrial enterprises quadrupled (from 1.5 to 6 billion rubles). The extraction of coal increased from 5.3 to 29 million tons, steel production from 0.7 to 4 million tons, that of petrol from 3.2 to 9 million tons. The textile mills consumed three times as much cotton in 1913 as in 1890. During the same period, the production of sugar quadrupled. Between 1900 and 1913, more than 8,000 miles of railway lines were built. According to the calculations of S. N. Prokopowicz, the national income rose from 6.6 milliard rubles in 1900 to 11.8 milliards in 1913—an increase of 79.4 per cent. If one takes account of the increase in price, the percentage is reduced to 39.4; and if, finally, account is taken of the growth of the population, the increase in the real income per person becomes 17.1 per cent.

The average annual increase in the population was 16 per thousand, and the growth of primary, secondary, and higher educational institutions was more rapid than that of the population. From 1894 to 1914, the number of pupils in the secondary schools increased from 225,000 to 820,000, and the number of students in the universities and colleges from 15,000 to 80,000. Primary education made still more rapid strides. Among the conscripts, 21.4 per cent could read and write in 1874, 37.8 per cent in 1894, 55.5 per cent in 1904, and 67.3 per cent in 1914. Among the industrial workers in 1917, the percentage of illiterates was 22.9 among youths from 14 to 20 years of age, 35.2 among men of 30 to 35, 56.6 among those over 50. In 1880 there were 1.141 million pupils in the elementary schools; the number in 1915 was 8.147 million (21.288 million in 1938–39). The Tsarist regime was gradually "liquidating" illiteracy.

From the beginning of the five-year plans, industrial construction advanced with extraordinary rapidity. Between the two wars, coal production was multiplied by about 4.5, that of cast iron by 3.5, petrol by a little less than 4, electrical energy by 20. Industries were started for the production of tractors, automobiles, trucks, machines, and machine tools. But would this development have been more or less rapid if the Revolution of 1917 had not taken place? This question has been argued in many ways, none of them conclusive. The Russians spent ten years after the First World War rebuilding the ruins resulting not only from that war itself but from the Revolution. Between 1929 and 1939, their industrial construction exceeded all previous records. Nevertheless, there are no adequate grounds on which to compare the result finally attained by the Soviets with that which would have evolved through a non-catastrophic process under a democratic regime and with the aid of foreign capital.

There is little doubt that the nature of the industrialization would have been different. Before 1913, heavy industry represented about one third of the total production, light industry two thirds. The Soviets, under the five-year plan, reversed the proportion. Their unique contribution to the economic history of the twentieth century has been to construct a vast industrial plant without having raised the living standard of the masses. Under a semi-liberal economic regime or a parliamentary democracy, it would have been impossible to ignore working-class aspirations for better living conditions. The development of the various sections of that class itself would have been better balanced. Collectivization, the deportation of millions of kulaks, the destruction of cattle, and the famine of the 1930's would not have been conceivable.

Harvard statisticians, in submitting the Russian figures to criticism and correction, arrived at the following conclusions: Out of a national income of 44.4 billion dollars in 1940, 14.1 billion had been devoted to investment and to national defense. . . .

Whatever may be said of the future, the interpretation of past events leaves little room for doubt. The direct and sufficient cause of Russia's rise to world power is not Communism but the Second World War.

The enormous sums devoted to capital expenditure and to the Army were one of the causes of the ultimately victorious resistance to German aggression. . . .

Whatever part the Revolution played in the industrialization of Russia, and the latter in the victory of 1945, the Soviet regime contributed decisively to the political fortune of Russia not so much by its internal as by its external effects. It was Russia's good fortune (if one may regard hegemony as good fortune—though we must not judge of good fortune before the last day) that Communism found imitators among its enemies. Communism's enemies, to combat it, had to resort to the same methods of arousing their nations against Bolshevism as did the Bolshevist nations to arouse the proletariat against capitalism. They precipitated international wars in the same way that Bolshevism precipitated war between classes.

It may seem surprising that a war can develop lasting consequences. But history offers many such examples. Athens and Sparta exhausted each other in a thirty years' war, which marked the end of the age of the city states and prepared the way for the Macedonian hegemony. The outcome of a battle is capable of determining the balance of power for a long period. But in our time the validity of this general rule is questionable: as long as military force is a function of industrial potential, the vanquished will not remain enfeebled for a long time by the military defeat or the treaty terms if it can retain its industrial capacities. The war of 1914–18 is a notable example of this conception. Recent events suggest still another one.

Soviet Russia's strategic situation was radically transformed by the consequences of the last war. The German Army is eliminated in Europe as the Japanese Army is in Asia. In 1946 the world was startled to discover that there no longer existed any army that could withstand the Soviet forces. . . .

After 1945 the Anglo-Saxon democracies . . . suddenly accepted the fact that Stalin was achieving for himself the goal which they had forbidden Hitler: the domination of Eastern Europe and the Balkans. They even went so far as to accept the fact that by the Sovietization of one third of Germany Stalin had mortgaged the future of the entire country.

Germany partitioned, Japan disarmed, China turned Communist —surely Stalin in his most ambitious dreams could never have imagined that the capitalist states would carry on the war with such blind fury that the socialist state would become the sole beneficiary of such unhoped-for gains.

. . . . .

Before 1939 there was a tendency to underestimate the direct relationship between industrial potential and military power. Today there is the opposite tendency to exaggerate that relationship.

The Foundations of the Cold War

Industrial potential is the condition of military power, but military power is not the measure of industrial potential. If it had been enough to generalize from steel-production figures Germany would not have resisted for so many years a coalition which, on paper, was irresistible.

. . . . .

In wartime especially, the coefficient of industrial mobilization is decisive. Although indisputably exact figures are not available, it is known that the coefficient was lower in the United States than in the Soviet Union. In the United States only a quarter of the steel was directly employed on war production. It may be said that if necessary the United States could considerably increase that co-efficient. True, but everything depends on the privations that the nation will accept or governments can impose. Will the high stand-ard of living of the American people allow mobilization to be carried to the lengths possible in the Soviet Union? The traditional in-feriority of wealthy peoples at grips with peoples living in more primitive conditions thus reappears.

Concern for the standard of living also results in a waste of hu-man potential. For every 20,000 men in a United States division at the front there are 60,000 in the rear, according to a statement made in 1950 by General Clark. During the last war the United States mobilized 100 divisions, the Germans 300, and the Rus-sians 500.

. . . . .

When the armies actually face each other, other factors besides the quantity or quality of their matériel come into play. The intel-ligence of the commanding officers and those of the lower ranks, the discipline of the troops, individual courage and will power—in these factors lies the secret of victory in battles and of the destiny of nations, and they are not included in statistics.

Tocqueville's famous prophecy has been so often quoted since 1945 that Russia's good fortune no longer surprises anyone. We forget that during the spring and summer of 1941 the Soviet armies suffered more terrible disasters than those which crushed the ar-

165

mies of the Tsar in 1914 and 1915. We also forget that at the end of 1941 German officers were able to see through their glasses the suburbs of Moscow. It required the great spaces, the cold, the horrible, and absurd policy of the Germans in the occupied territory, it required the patient heroic resistance of the Russian people, Hitler's "intuitions," lend-lease, and the air offensive in the West, to bring the final defeat of the *Wehrmacht*.

During the first half of the nineteenth century, after the collapse of the Napoleonic empire, the conviction was already spreading that the old nations were irremediably weak. That conviction anticipated the defeatism of today. Only the Russians and the Anglo-Saxons seemed to have promising futures before them. But the events of the latter half of the nineteenth century did nothing to bear out those anticipations. On the contrary, the rise of the German empire and European expansion in Africa bore witness to the unimpaired vitality of Europe and confounded the prophets.

At the outset of the twentieth century, 200 million Europeans possessed an abnormal share of the world's wealth. But the methods of industrial civilization which European emigrants brought with them to the New World made possible an exceptional growth of material prosperity in the United States, thanks to America's vast frontiers, to its abundance of natural resources, to its lack of rigid social stratifications, and its relatively small population. In the meantime the diffusion in Asia of European liberal and nationalistic ideologies, and the introduction of firearms prepared the revolt against the West, from which Communism seems likely to benefit the most.

Neither the nature nor the rapidity of the decline of Europe had been foreseen. At the present moment Europe, or rather what remains of Europe west of the Iron Curtain, has no chance of independence. Either it will be part of a whole of which the Atlantic forms the center, just as the civilization of the ancients had the Mediterranean for its center; or else it will be incorporated in the Continental empire of which the Soviet Union is the central directing element. In that limited sense, it is not wrong to pose the alter-

native: Washington or Moscow? But it would be wrong to regard
the situation produced by the accident of the Second World War as
more durable than that created at the beginning of the century.

It is not difficult to imagine the structures that might replace the
present one—the defeat of one of the two great rivals, and a resulting universal empire; or, alternatively, the restoration of autonomous forces in Europe and Asia, and a relative loss of power by the
two existing giants. . . .

The divisions of the Red Army would arouse less anxiety if they
did not seem to be in the service of an idea. The combination of
an empire, sprung up suddenly from the ruins of the old European nations, and an apparently universal message, is spreading
terror throughout the non-Communist world.

Europe, hardly emerged from the age of bourgeois liberalism,
is unable to understand by what ruse of reason a rationally inspired doctrine has been able to revive the superstitions of the
Dark Ages.

Marxism is a Christian heresy. It is the modern form of millen-
nialism: it places the Kingdom of God on this earth, due to arrive
after an apocalypic revolution in which the old systems will be en-
gulfed. The contradictions within capitalist society will inevitably
provoke that pregnant catastrophe, and today's sufferers will triumph tomorrow. The proletariat, the witness of man's present in-
humanity to man, will achieve salvation. At a moment to be
determined by the development of the means of production, in combination with the courage of the military leaders, the proletariat
will form a universal class and take charge of human destiny.

Such an ideology, which we are considering not as a philosophical doctrine but as the subject of popular belief, combines three
sorts of themes whose historical origins may easily be traced and
whose combination has given to Marxism its explosive force.

There is, first of all, the Christian theme. All religions of salvation prophesy in one form or another the revenge of the humiliated.
They offer to the humbler classes of society compensation either in
this world or the next. Marxism makes possible a sort of belief in

the victory of the slaves. For are not the industrial workers the true creators of wealth? Is not the elimination of the parasites and monopolists, who appropriate an exorbitant share of the collective income, irresistibly demanded by an immanent logic? Thus incorporated in a materialist dialectic, the idea of the overthrow of the hierarchy dissembles its true origin: the Christian aspirations, which atheism has not extinguished, or the more or less sublimated resentments of those who are relegated to the bottom of the social scale. The positivistic camouflage deludes the faithful without diminishing the emotional sources of their belief.

Then there is the Promethean theme. Man, having discovered the secret of fire, used it to extend more and more quickly his mastery over natural forces, as, on the distant horizon, he could see an earthly paradise which Trotsky regarded as an attainable and even relatively near objective. Ancestral poverty would be pushed further and further into the past; the curse of toil would be merely a superstition current only in societies that possessed the most meager means of production. Although the establishment of socialism called for continuing efforts and privations from the common man, scientists and technicians—the demigods of our age—would eliminate the industrial purgatory, rendering inequality useless and oppression scandalous. Leisure and wealth would no longer be reserved for a few at the expense of the many, but would become, thanks to the genius of the human race, a universal possession.

Finally, the rationalist theme. Societies develop spontaneously: they need to be reconstructed rationally. Spontaneous development itself obeyed an intrinsic logic. Human progress, because at first it depends upon man's struggle with other men as well as with nature, leads inevitably to a confused society, at odds with its own best interests. But then a new phase begins: because he knows the laws of his own history, man can anticipate the future. He still cannot eliminate those inevitable disturbances that mark periods of transition, for the passage from one social structure to another, the replacement of one social class by another, does not take place without wars and revolution. But he can know the outcome beforehand

—the creation of a humane society through his own benign planning. In such a society private property and economic anarchy will give place to collective property and a planned economy.

The revolt against inequality and injustice exists in all ages. The boundless faith in science and technology nourished by the industrial achievements of Western civilization is typical of our age. It is the synthesis of that revolt and this faith that, once it is based upon a pseudo-rationalist interpretation of history, gives Marxism its popular appeal. Faith in science by itself would merely arouse a sort of messianic expectancy, a belief that in time poverty and inequality would disappear, or an acceptance of technocracy in the belief that things would be handled best by experts. Revolt by itself would only revive illusions so often proved false. (Why should new masters be any better than the old ones?) The rewards envisioned by the scientific view of man and society will come only with the victory of the proletariat.

In the last quarter of the nineteenth century, Marxism, while it had little influence in Great Britain and still less in the United States, became the official doctrine of working-class parties on the Continent. But as the proletarian parties gained strength and influence, theory and practice of social democracy drew further and further apart. Revolutionary theory was still professed, and the holding of governmental office prohibited; but reformism carried the day in practice. Ideology served to keep the militants aroused by distracting them from the prosaic, everyday demands of the movement. It convinced the members of the working class that they had a historic role to fulfill, and deterred them from fully accepting integration in the capitalist order without, however, making them permanently irreconcilable enemies of society and the state. The social legislation conceded by anti-socialist governments (that of Bismarck, for example), or wrested by trade union action, and the higher living standard made possible by economic progress had not put an end to unrest within the proletariat; but the possibility was seen that such unrest might come to an end, without either violence or revolution.

To this day nothing has proved that the autonomous development of capitalism excluded such an eventuality. The example of certain countries, like Sweden and Switzerland, spared by the two wars reveals one of the possible outcomes of the evolution which before 1914 was obscured by the ideology of the Second International. The organization of the working class into trade unions and even into socialist parties, was probably inherent in the structure of the Western democratic societies. But neither the unions nor the parties prevented the working class from acquiring a middle-class mentality under the influence of the increase in wealth and the redistribution of national income. The Communists' campaign against what they called capitalism (in which they lumped the British labor movement and the Third Reich) was not inevitable.

. . . Stalin the Terrible appeared, even in France, to millions of men of good will as the father of the poor and the redresser of wrongs, indifferent though he was to the fate of millions of human beings "condemned by history," indifferent even to the fate of the servants of the Revolution the day they ceased to be useful or violated the official discipline. One has only to penetrate the party secret or even to read the text of its doctrine or propaganda, in order to uncover radical innovations beneath the apparent continuity. The Stalinists speak the same language as the nineteenth-century Marxists, but they belong to another world.

Intellectually it is easy to explain the passage from Marxism through Leninism to Stalinism. The decisive stages were the conception of the revolutionary party and its activity, the role attributed to wars at the outset of revolutions, the doctrine of establishing socialism in a single country (or the doctrine of the "socialist bastion"), and, finally, the acceptance of the directing role of the Russian Bolshevik Party.

Originally Bolshevism was merely a single group within the social-democratic organization—a group distinguished by its extremism, its intransigence, its tendency to split up continually over controversial points of apparently secondary importance. Lenin's essential contribution today seems to us to have been neither the rather primitive materialism of his book, *Materialism and Empirio-criticism*, nor his interpretation of the general tendency of capitalism, but his theory and practice of revolutionary action. Its principal ideas are well known and may be easily summarized:

The proletarian masses, left to themselves, are in danger of satisfying themselves with trade unionism, that is to say, with the everyday, immediate struggle for improved living conditions. The intellectuals, on the other hand, seek to introduce the masses to their historic mission. They give the proletarian revolt its inspiration and its objective. The party, whose officials must include a high proportion of professional revolutionaries, is organized according to the rules of what Lenin called democratic centralism: the essentials of power are in the hands of the Central Committee, a sort of general staff to an underground army (the Bolshevik Party was generally outlawed before 1917).

At the time, this characteristic of the Bolshevik Party was insufficiently recognized by the leaders of the Second International, who considered it an aberration explainable by the conditions of the struggle against Tsarism. Democratic methods were regarded as normal, and the technique of violence and secrecy was regarded as a survival from the past. The Revolution of 1917 reversed such a view. The Bolshevik Party became the model for the other parties in the Third International.

Once they were masters of the Russian state, Lenin and his comrades sat back to wait for a European or world revolution, just as the early Christians waited for the return of Christ. When they abandoned hope for an early revolution, they adapted themselves to a situation which they had not foreseen, and which their very doctrine forbade them to anticipate: the proletariat had triumphed only in a single country; and that country—far from having arrived at the stage at which industrial development had led to the disruption of capitalism—was a country where agriculture still predominated, and whose industrial concentrations on the outskirts of the

great cities were due to Western influence and capital. It was necessary, therefore, to provide a few supplementary hypotheses to
realign theory with fact.

It was argued primarily that the conditions favorable to the
Revolution had been created less by capitalism and crises than by
wars, and that the proletariat did not necessarily win the day in the
country that was industrially most advanced, but simply in the
country in which the regime was the weakest and least well de-
fended: "the weakest link in the chain." Thereafter, instead of
waiting, as did the social democrats, for capitalism to ripen, revolutionaries must keep a continual watch for opportunities. Revolution thus ceased to be a quasi-mythological, almost undefinable
eruption, which reversed the normal course of events. It now meant
the seizure of power. All the parties in the Third International,
ambitious to imitate the Bolsheviks, had but one objective, one
obsession: the seizure of power. Trade union action, social legislation, economic reforms—all these things lost interest except as
means for attaining that one objective.

The Russian and the other parties in the Third International
work on similar principles of organization and action, and perform
various co-ordinated functions within a general plan. The first task
is to strengthen the bastion of socialism, that is to say, to speed up
the industrialization in the only country conquered by the proletariat; for the theory of "Socialism in a single country" does not
imply the abandonment of the hope of a world revolution: it im-
plies proceeding country by country. The occupied territory is
organized, and the first proletarian state is strengthened. Communist parties in other countries will be sacrificed, if necessary, to
that higher priority. Expansion will take place in a later phase.
What circumstances will make expansion possible? Once again the
sole reply is—war. The capitalist world has entered a period of
decadence, of which economic crises and especially wars are the
symptoms. A first world war made possible the Revolution of 1917.
A second would give the proletariat the opportunity for further
conquests.

The pre-eminence of the Russian party has its doctrinal justification. The Bolsheviks do not simply claim the authority rightfully conferred on them as victors, but invoke the common destiny of world revolution and of the socialist bastion. The confusion between the revolutionary cause and the national interests of the Russian state was inevitable. Leninist centralization applied to the International soon led to similar results: the Central Committee (in this case the Russian heads of the Comintern) exercises the same rigid control, the same unconditional authority over all the sections of the International as that which the Leninist, and later the Stalinist general staff exercised over the clandestine groups before 1917 and over the various activities of the party, both before and after the seizure of power.

As long as we confine ourselves to this abstract summary, it might be imagined that the change from the Second to the Third International was limited. Communism, it might be supposed, was a version of Marxism, and the most reasonable version, since it had profited by the experience of the twentieth century. In theory, its principal originality lay in the substitution of wars for crises and the decay of capitalism as an essential factor in the proletarian revolution. In practice, its originality consisted in generalizing the method of organization and action peculiar to the Bolsheviks, and in recognizing the pre-eminence of the Russian party—both because that party controls a great state and because the fate of the world revolution seems now to be bound up with that of the Soviet Union. These innovations leave intact the traditional doctrine— dialectical materialism, the class struggle, capitalist contradictions, etc. But their scope has greatly changed. Communism has introduced a foreign body into the European societies, and in thirty years they have been unable either to assimilate it or reject it.

The traditional doctrine had two basic elements: a conception of the world (or at least of human society), and an interpretation of capitalism and its natural development. The Marxist parties claimed to be acting on the strength of the idea they had formed of the inevitable future of capitalism. The Communist parties, however, . . . were not waiting for the development of the forces of production to create the objective conditions for revolution, but were adapting themselves to circumstances, one set of circumstances in nationalist China and another in the United States. In both countries their method was identical: to form a party engaged in agitation, espionage, and insurrection. In both countries the objective was identical: to undermine the existing regime and to prepare for the seizure of power. The pattern of capitalist evolution provided the link between historical materialism and the action of the socialist parties. The day that pattern disappeared there would remain on one hand revolutionary action, purely opportunist, and on the other hand an ideology justifying the former. Faith alone could unify action and ideology.

By what miracle, indeed, could the few thousand intellectuals or workers, registered members of the American Communist Party, represent the proletariat of the United States? Why should a party composed mainly of peasants represent the proletariat of China? In theory, it is easy to call the Communist Party the advance guard of the proletariat and to entrust it with guiding the masses toward the accomplishment of their mission; in practice, the party replaces the proletariat. Thenceforth it is the party, not the proletariat, that is invested with the historic mission. It is to the party that supreme value is attached. When a proletariat does not rally to the Communist Party, it is the former, not the latter, that is accused by doctrine.

The transfer of the proletariat's historic mission to the party has another and still more serious result. The only true road forward becomes that which is marked by the triumph of the Communist Party. The world is divided into two camps and two only: the countries where a Communist party is in power; and all the others, which are dubbed capitalist even if a labor party is in power, even if most of the enterprises are owned by the state, and even if the equalization of incomes is carried further than in the socialist homeland. This Manichean vision of the world follows necessarily from the role attributed to the Stalinist party. For if its conquest of power is the essential and sufficient condition of the revolution—whatever the material circumstances—then Rumania, tyrannized over by a few officials of the Kremlin, has had its revolution, and Great Britain, even under the Labor Party, remains capitalist. Here we have the irrefutable logic of schizophrenia.

In such a system, the revolutionary priority conceded to the countries described as underdeveloped becomes comprehensible. As capitalism spreads and the living standard is raised the revolutionary ardor of the masses cools. The famine-stricken masses of Asia will provide the professional agitators with a larger and more docile following than would the workers of General Motors. The Bolshevik technique that originated in Tsarist Russia proved to be naturally adapted to the societies of the Far East, which had been shaken by the advent of industrialism.

Within the Western societies, in Europe and the United States, the action of the Communist parties no longer has anything in common with that of the socialist parties. The latter described themselves as revolutionary, but they acted in accordance with democratic methods: they supported the claims of the workers, they tolerated more or less autonomous trade unions; they tried to improve the workers' lot, they secured social legislation and wage increases by fair means or foul. These activities have nothing in common with those of the Communist parties, even when the latter used the same language and put forward the same demands. According to circumstances, the Communists want to see the condition of the workers growing either worse or better, but they never interest themselves in securing reforms for their own sake. They aim to control the trade unions and the masses so as to increase their power of agitation and subversion, a power which they use according to directives from Moscow. It is a technique of propaganda and insurrection, placed in the service, theoretically, of the revolution but, actually, of a foreign state; such, for the past thirty years, has been essentially the action of the Communist parties in the West, an expansion to global dimensions of the militant enterprise started by the first Bolsheviks against the Tsarist regime.

It is not so easy to describe the passage from Leninism to Stalinism. There was no fundamental change in doctrine or language. The gap between the ideology supporting the action taken and the action itself widened and grew progressively wider. It would be difficult to say just when Marxism became no more than what Pareto called a "derivation."

Lenin himself began to believe that the proletarian cause was being confused with that of his own group. Several times before 1917 he preferred to provoke a split rather than bow to what he regarded as an erroneous opinion of the majority. He unscrupulously manipulated congresses, convinced that his judgment of the situation expressed the historical truth. He readily condemned as traitors to the Revolution those who did not accept his views. Never for a moment did he permit any doubt that the Bolshevik seizure of power must be regarded as the first step in the social revolution envisaged by Marxism. Kautsky, who objected that the dictatorship of the Bolshevik Party was in fact that of a small minority over the great mass of the proletariat and of the country, was immediately classed as a renegade.

The contempt of formal democracy does not begin with Stalin. He imposed the Soviet regime on the satellite nations against the will of their populations, but Lenin had dissolved the Constituent Assembly elected in January 1918 because it did not have a Bolshevik majority. Whatever the opinion of those intellectuals who vituperate Stalin and keep up a worship of Lenin, the decisive break with the West and with democratic socialism was made by the founder of the party, and not by his successor.

. . . . .

Stalinism is a logical development of Leninism. For the Secretary General the temptation was great to appoint reliable men to the positions of importance, and to assure in advance a majority at the Central Committee policy congresses. Lenin had exerted his ingenuity to keep hold of the organizational threads when the party was illegal, and he appointed as representatives of the local groups militants who were theoretically elected, but whom he knew to be docile followers of his directives. Democratic centralism, applied to the twin bureaucracy of party and state, ended by robbing the electoral ritual of all practical influence. Free discussion between the leaders became a discredited memory. The man who could "control" the all-powerful bureaucracy, just like the man who had formerly controlled the secret network, was in fact the supreme ruler.

The national parties in the Third International changed between the time of Zinoviev and that of "the struggle for peace and against imperialism." But these changes paralleled those in the Bolshevik Party. Free discussion of policies and ideas disappeared from the Communist parties as it had done from the Bolshevik Party. The Russian leaders of the Comintern increasingly tightened their hold on authority, manipulating the controls of those parties as they did the Soviet bureaucracy; they carried to its limit the Stalinist *Gleichschaltung* of German or French Communism, as they had done in the former Tsarist empire. They introduced throughout the world the same spirit of orthodoxy which they had imposed on the homeland of socialism. There was, however, a limit to that assimilation, a limit determined by the contrast between the conservative or reactionary work of the Russian party and the revolutionary work of the foreign parties prior to a seizure of power.

In the intellectual field, the party did not immediately claim to possess the whole truth, although the premises of the spiritual dictatorship may be traced back to Marxism itself. Historical materialism suggested a general interpretation of each epoch. The works of artists and thinkers are associated by many subtle bonds with industrial relations and with class struggles. The dominant class places its imprint on the whole society. After a fashion, the existing middle-class civilization will be carried away or transfigured by the proletarian revolution. All Marxists have declared more or less dogmatically that there is a relation between metaphysical postulates and political strategy. Most Marxists felt some inclination to regard a certain philosophical or moral orthodoxy as bound up with the revolutionary attitude.

Lenin and his comrades would have revolted against Stalinist practice. They would not have admired the official attitude toward art, they would not have agreed to the state condemnation of Mendelian theories. But they, too, had insisted on the supreme value of revolution, they had agreed to the subordination of intellectual freedom and of culture to the interest of the collectivity; they, too, had proclaimed their doctrine as absolute truth, and had regarded dialectical materialism as a rival of the transcendental religions. It only needed the coming into power of a man with no more than an elementary education for obscurantism to triumph alongside despotism.

The world as revealed by Stalinism to the faithful is peopled with some forces essentially good and others essentially bad. The Soviet Union, as such, was peaceful and democratic, even when it attacked Finland, even when it formed its alliance with Hitler, even when it reopened the concentration camps in Germany. France became imperialist from the simple fact that it accepted the Marshall Plan and received some arms from the United States. These attributes applied less to the conduct of the nations than to their essence, which was defined once and for all by the interpretation of sacred history. It matters little, in such circumstances, that the imperialist countries are or appear to be on the defensive; they are imperialist because they are capitalist, and consequently bent on expansion. Even if they were not in search of markets, they would still be imperialist because they are the incarnation of the past, as the Soviet Union is the incarnation of the future. In such an irreconcilable struggle between abstractions, such elements as current events, classes, and nations are transformed into mythical characters—capitalism, socialism, imperialism, and the like—whose ultimate end has been foreseen by the prophet.

The dialectic of purges is a simple extension of that Manichean concept. Marxists, like all men of action, have always tended to take account of acts rather than intentions, and of consequences rather than the acts themselves, and of the historical influence of ideas or procedures rather than their inspiration. Thus the non-

Marxists have more than once been affected by the application of that method: the European liberal was held responsible for colonial exploitation, and the defender of formal democracy found himself blamed for working-class poverty. But the Communists were to act with a complete lack of restraint against deviationists and oppositionists, of whom it was asked whether they were weakening the party and, consequently, whether they were adversaries of the cause. The argument is commonplace: it has justified every revolutionary terror in history. But it is no longer enough to say that the deviationist behaves like an enemy of the cause. To discredit him and to restore the unsullied prestige of the leaders it is necessary to denounce him not merely as the involuntary ally but the paid agent of the enemy. Bukharin was supposed to have prepared Lenin's assassination; Rajk was alleged to be an agent of Horthy's police or of the British Intelligence Service for more than twenty years. By this process of "linked identifications," anyone who ceases to obey the leader is deprived of life and honor.

Having come this far, the interpreter of Communism is no longer hampered by any limitation or obstacle. He can attach any meaning to anything, according to the interpretation of the world established by his sovereign decree. Since the supreme interpreter is also the head of the state, this dialectic of the purge ends by sanctifying success and power and by recognizing the master's word as the criterion of good and evil. No one can be sure of following the true path, for the paths change and the master reinterprets the past as he chooses, just as he predicts the future. Today's orthodoxy will perhaps become tomorrow's deviation.

Clearly much has changed since Lenin, who wanted to conclude peace with the Germans, waited for the course of events finally to convince his colleagues on the Central Committee. Each of the historic decisions—the November *coup d'état,* Brest-Litovsk, etc.—found the Bolshevik leaders divided. Several times Lenin found himself in the minority, but he never dreamed of taking revenge on his opponents when in the end they had to come round to his view. And he was as prompt in reconciliation as he had been in breaking with his opponent, providing that the opponent recognized his error and gave practical evidence that he was bowing to the demands of unanimity.

But Lenin did not extend his tolerance beyond the Bolshevik Party. Even during his lifetime the other parties, including the Socialist Revolutionaries of the extreme left, who had taken part in the November *coup d'état,* were expelled from politics and deprived of civil rights. The principal nonconforming militants were imprisoned, deported, or forced to emigrate. What happened next? The deviationists within the party came to be treated just as the dissidents outside had been treated, whether socialists or not. Once more it must be admitted that this development was logical, if not inevitable.

It is true that nearly fifteen years passed after the Revolution before Stalin himself decided to cross the "bloody line" and put his party comrades to death. But at a time when kulaks were being killed off by the thousands such scruples were merely a survival. In the long run it was impossible for two conflicting worlds, one based on respect for your neighbor and the other on the unlimited rights of the state over the vast mass of non-party individuals, to exist side by side. There was an intermediate phase between the Leninist phase, in which everyone in the party was free to hold his own opinion so long as he respected the rule of discipline in action, and the later phase, in which the present, past, or future, actual or potential opponents confess to crimes which have not been committed. During this phase, in order to make sure of general discipline and to break any possible resistance, the public defense of any given policy was entrusted to the very men who had opposed it in the "cells" or in the Central Committee. Such men as Zinoviev and Bukharin had renounced their own views several times before taking the supreme vows and proclaiming the justice of the judgment that condemned them to death.

The successive purges trace perhaps more clearly than any theory the actual course that the Party followed. Lenin's party was decimated; three quarters or four fifths of the militants were liqui-

dated. Many of the revolutionaries in France and Germany who had
been among the first to rally to the Third International after 1917
broke with Bolshevism in the 1920s. The general staffs of the Communist parties in exile—Polish, Yugoslav, Hungarian, Spanish—
were almost entirely destroyed. In Eastern Europe the Communist parties had scarcely come into power when, in 1949, national
leaders, such as Gomulka, Rajk, and Kostov, who had not been
trained in Moscow, or who had fought on the soil of their own
countries, or who had been in touch with the West, were succes-
sively eliminated.

Most of Lenin's colleagues were intellectuals with an international culture. They followed the Bolshevik technique in action, but
were uneasy in carrying the system to extremes. They rose against
Tsarism mainly because they were heretics by temperament and
would have nothing to do with injustice. But they were adept in
revolt, and how could they make good officials? Triumphant Stalinism no longer needed the same men as militant Stalinism.

The same mechanism was at work in all the parties outside Russia. Everywhere the revolutionaries had to be replaced by technicians, intellectuals by administrators. The incompatibility of the
two types was in fact greater among Communists abroad than at
home. One may very well ask whether Lenin's colleagues opposed
Stalin out of moral indignation, or divergence of ideas, or bitterness
over defeat. But one must remember that, on the other hand, the
Communists outside of Russia, who ended by breaking with the
party or by being executed, had rallied to an ideal Bolshevism
without being acquainted with the real thing.

Those who had been followers of Lenin thirty years earlier were
extremists, irreconcilables set against social conformity; they were
spiritual descendants of Rousseau, convinced that man is good and
that the evils from which he suffers are the fault of society. Leninism was the ultimate form of European rationalist progressivism.
On the morrow of the first war the pacifists gazed at that great Star
in the East. When the economic crisis came, the country without
unemployment became the model and the hope. The menace of

Hitler directed the sympathy of the liberals toward the champion of anti-Fascism. After 1941, the glory of the Russian soldier was appropriated by the Soviet regime, and Hitler's conqueror was hailed as the standardbearer of peace and Europe's hope.

The pacifists of 1919 discovered that the Soviet Union did not condemn war in itself, but preferred civil to international war. The anti-capitalists of the thirties discovered that they could not approve of forced labor as a means of suppressing unemployment. The anti-Fascists discovered that Stalinism had perfected the Fascist technique. The anti-Hitlerites of the forties discovered that Stalin's European unity could be as hateful as Hitler's. The renegades or victims of Stalinism are not simply idealists disappointed by reality, or revolutionaries incapable of adapting themselves to the new order, or nationalists up in arms against the Kremlin supremacy, or Occidentals weary of propaganda or unfamiliar with "eternal Russia." In thirty years the very spirit of the revolutionary movement itself has changed.

. . . . .

The Soviet society comprises social groups distinguished from each other by their occupations, their styles of living, and their incomes—*kolkhoz* workers, factory workers, skilled and unskilled workers, writers, accountants of the collective enterprises, factory managers, trust directors, *kolkhoz* managers, and trade union secretaries. But none of these groups has any power, none is able to regard itself as a historical unit with its own interests to defend. The masses are amorphous, prey to propaganda, servants of an omnipresent authority. The social and state hierarchies are identical and the considerable differences in income among the various classes are subject to official policy. The privileged hold superior offices but they are wage earners just like the non-privileged. This combination of the elements of bureaucracy and aristocracy is not so much an innovation as a return to an age-old tradition. Similarly, the managers of agricultural or industrial enterprises, the heads of trusts, and the Secretaries of Ministries, are all officials of the Soviet state.

The party is inseparable from the regime in its ideology. It regards itself as the product neither of the past nor of tradition, but of the Revolution. It finds its justification in the services it renders to socialism, but conversely it has to accept the law of orthodoxy. What socialism demands, only the chiefs, and especially the supreme chiefs, can know and proclaim. The Christian religion is not eliminated, but the supreme truth is the truth of history as it is being made. Anyone who betrays that truth is betraying the supreme value in the name of which he has exercised the right of life and death over his fellow men. The privileged class is, at one and the same time, the bureaucracy of a state that absorbs the whole community and the clergy of a militant Church.

Nothing is less Western than a society of this type. Indeed, Western societies are characterized by their rejection of unity. They distinguish between the temporal and the spiritual power, between Pope and Emperor, between national Church and Papal Church, between the nobility and the monarchy, between the bourgeoisie and the *ancien régime,* between the proletariat and the bourgeoisie: life in the West is made up precisely of such tensions, which are not repressed so much as controlled—a life that requires effort, struggle, creation. The Soviet society aims at unity: it no longer allows rivalry either between the temporal and the spiritual power, or between the social forces, or between society and the state. In uniting temporal and spiritual power it harks back to Byzantium. In forcing all persons and all resources into the service of the state, it conforms essentially with all tyrannies. The transformation of the population into an amorphous mass organized by bureaucratic and military authorities is a return to a still more ancient social system.

. . . . .

Before the First World War, the Bolsheviks represented a small part of the Russian social democratic movement, which in turn represented only one of the small revolutionary parties within the Tsarist empire. In 1917 their small sect took control of the Russian state. It soon created a new International, imposed its own techniques of organization and action upon the national groups, and established a network of espionage and subversion throughout the five continents. After the Second World War, the same Bolshevik Party, controlling one of the two great world powers, subjugated 100 million Europeans, who had been "liberated" by the Red Army. In Asia the Chinese Communist Party, repeating the exploit of the Russian party, victoriously concluded the civil war to become the master of the former Middle Empire. The Stalinist world was thereby extended from a line between Stettin and Trieste to the frontiers of Indo-China.

The extent and rapidity of those successes sowed terror everywhere. After having underestimated or despised Lenin and his companions, Europe is now inclined to admire their successors beyond all reason. Communism has even been likened to a salvationist religion and compared with Islam, whose armies overthrew the infidel and whose ideas won souls.

Bolshevism forced its way to power by violence. In Russia it began with a *coup d'état* and won the civil war that followed. In China the order of events was reversed. The Communist Party set up a civil and military organization independent of the Chinese state, and ended, after more than twenty years, by defeating the rival government of the Kuomintang. In the Eastern European countries, the Communist parties, thanks to the presence of the Red Army, set themselves up in key positions under cover of a pretended national front. After that it was child's play to seize power completely.

The technique of Sovietization in cold blood, as it was applied to the European countries of the Soviet zone, can happen anywhere. On the arrival of the Soviet troops in Rumania, the Stalinist party in that country had only a few hundred members. Polish hostility to Russia, Tsarist and Bolshevik, alike, is unquestionable. Czechoslovakia had a social structure analogous to that of the Western countries. In all these countries the Stalinists succeeded in eliminating both opponents and allies and in setting up regimes parallel to that which the Communist Party had taken twenty years to build up in Russia. They had profited by experience: imitation takes less time than creation of the prototype.

It would be absurd to seek an intrinsic affinity, such as that of the peasant majority or of the Slavic race, which might predispose the countries of Eastern Europe to follow the path of the Communists. Any country liberated by the Red Army—had it been France or Britain or even Spain—would have had the same fate. Only in Russia and in China were circumstances such that a Bolshevik revolution was possible without foreign intervention.

The two great revolutions of the twentieth century, the Russian and the Chinese, which both claimed to descend from Marxism, preceded rather than followed the spread of capitalism. They were produced in agricultural countries where the vast majority of the population lived off the land; and both countries suffered—although in different degrees—from rural overpopulation. In neither country would successful revolution have been possible without the allegiance, or at least the consent, of the peasant masses. In Russia, it is true, the workers of Petrograd and Moscow, reinforced by rebellious soldiers, played a decisive part in the *coup d'état*. But once the civil war had started, the Red Army would probably have achieved nothing had the peasants not hated the White armies so much. The Chinese Communist Party, after Chiang Kai-shek had broken with it and driven it from the cities, was even more closely associated than the Russian with the peasants. After the break with Chiang the whole party, which had originally been formed in the south, trekked all the way across China to a remote province in the northwest. There it carried out agrarian reforms that were moderate at first such as reducing the rate of interest and the landlord's share of the crops, but which later became more radical in such measures, for example, as dividing up the great estates.

In neither Russia nor China was industrial civilization indigenous. Russia was Europeanized in the eighteenth century under a succession of Tsars, with the consequent formation of a bureaucracy. In the latter half of the nineteenth century, and especially at the outset of the twentieth, industry made rapid progress, but it was financed largely by foreign capital and organized with the assistance of foreign engineers. To be sure, Russia participated heavily in the Western scientific movement, as well as in Continental literary and artistic enterprises throughout the nineteenth century and up to the explosion of 1917. But European influences were only superficial, limited in their effect to a small section of the upper class, a group aloof from the masses and divided between the desire for liberal institutions copied from the West and a more or less mystical aspiration to be faithful to the national soul.

China meanwhile has been in a state of crisis ever since European influences precipitated the collapse of its age-old civilization. For half a century it has sought to combine Western industrial techniques and administration with its own traditions. The Kuomintang having failed, the Communists have made a fresh attempt, based, apparently, on an extreme form of Westernization. Its rejection of the traditional organization of family and community and of the philosophical and religious ideologies of the past is more drastic even than that of earlier revolutionary movements. But Russia's example has inspired a certain amount of caution. Most of the intellectuals who formed the general staff of the Bolshevik Party thought that they were continuing the effort of the Russian Westernizers and not that of the Slavophils. Lenin, in 1917, thought that the Russian proletariat was sacrificing itself on the altar of the world revolution. Thirty years later, we find that the Bolshevik actuality has become exactly the reverse of its original conception.

The followers of Mao Tse-tung seem to be adopting the very latest Western fashions in political ideology and technique. Marxism enables the individual Chinese, who has suffered such humiliation in face of the material superiority of the West, to overcome his feelings of inferiority. When a country goes over to the "progressive" or the "socialist" camp, it feels that it has joined the advance guard of mankind, even if it is centuries behindhand in its equipment.

In Russia as in China, therefore, the revolutionary situation developed from a violent encounter between Western influences and the traditional society. In both cases Communism mobilized nationalism in its own interest in order to end the West's monopoly of power, to catch up industrially with the capitalist countries, and to outdistance them in terms of social structure. In this deeper sense it may be said that Leninism or Stalinism, once introduced not into established capitalistic countries but into countries humiliated, if not enslaved, by the West, has become a sort of National Socialism.

Leninism, a Western product turned against the West, does not triumph during those tranquil periods when only non-violent means are available to its adherents. In 1914, the Bolshevik section of the Russian social democrats had only a few thousand members. In 1937, when the Sino-Japanese war broke out, Chiang Kai-shek was unable to liquidate the Communists, but the Communists were even less capable of defeating the Kuomintang. Just as the war of 1914 had weakened the administration of the Russian state, so eight years of war in China helped the Communists to undermine the social and moral groupings of the old order, at least in the northern provinces, where they carried on guerrilla warfare as much against Chiang Kai-shek as against the invader.

The Communists count on war to create their opportunity to take possession of decadent states.

There is no country in which it is impossible to organize at least a minor Communist movement. Even in the United States some tens of thousands of people were won over to the cause, and, as it now appears, their network of espionage extended to the highest ranks of the Administration. It would be easy to explain these individual allegiances by one or another of the mechanisms of revolutionary or religious conversion. A list might be given of the types of the converted—idealists, cynics, misfits, or, at the other extreme, middle-class persons whose success has not satisfied their aspirations or who are disturbed by their privileges, those who are proud of belonging to a tiny minority looked down upon today and triumphant tomorrow; materialists with an unconscious nostalgia for the absolute, and Christians who are disappointed by the church-goers' cult of prosperity. But individual psychology that takes no account of the historical element misses the essence of the matter, the strength or weakness of a particular religion at a particular time or in a particular country.

In organization, tactics, and ideology, Communist parties every-where are similar if not identical. In one place they may form a clandestine group, while elsewhere they may have hundreds of thousands of adherents; here they may have sympathizers and accomplices outside their own closed circle, while there they arouse fierce hostility. . . . The effectiveness however of the party in its struggles, whether secret or open, depends on its possessing a con-siderable number of militants or sympathizers. In this respect the results obtained in the West vary considerably from region to region.

The Anglo-Saxon and Scandinavian countries have, so far, been relatively immune to the Communist virus. Not that there are no Communists in the United States or Great Britain, in Australia or Sweden, but they are few in number and are faced with the resist-ance not only of the middle class but of the great mass of the people, including the majority of the working class. The struggle against Communism is carried on by the trade union leaders, who have an accurate sense of the danger. . . .

Union leaders are too intelligent to be caught by the argument —so convincing to certain intellectuals—there there is no reason for the existence of independent trade unions after the state has be-come proletarian. They know, on the contrary, that union inde-pendence must be maintained at all costs; for whoever may be masters of the state, they naturally tend to misunderstand the claims of the governed. Whether bourgeois or proletarian, any state that has everything its own way slips into tyranny.

No doubt there are other causes that may explain the inability of a secular religion (or religions, for Fascism had little more success) to take root in these privileged countries. They all have a relatively high and still rising standard of living; and they had been spared all or most of the effects of the First World War. In spite of a rapid fall in the living standard, and in spite of the loss of Indonesia, Holland has hardly been touched by Communism. Great Britain, defeated by her victory and reduced to austerity, is little affected by the dream of the classless society. In addition to economic and social causes, a moral and historical cause is manifest. The rejection of a secular religion as such seems to be characteristic of the peoples of a genuinely democratic tradition, in the Anglo-Saxon sense of the term.

Individualist democracy, of Protestant origin and Christian inspiration, is thoroughly incompatible with the Stalinist ideal. The custom of settling affairs locally and the taste for initiative and for private enterprise are threatened by the all-powerful state. The sense of personal responsibility, and of a faith freely adopted, is opposed to the authoritarian orthodoxy of Stalinism and its extreme form of clericalism and obscurantism. The Christian faith has not always retained the full measure of its essential characteristics, but it has developed as a sort of moralism rather than renounce its heritage by turning into an anti-Church.

It is not possible to say as much of the French democratic tradition. In becoming Jacobin, it tended in the direction of an authoritarian, centralized state. The myth of the General Will justifies not the rights of individuals or of the opposition but the omnipotence of the majority. The disciples of Rousseau liked to dream of a civil religion. This line of non-Catholic thinkers envisaged substituting for traditional religion a cult of the Supreme Being and the Comtist religion of humanity, in short, a religion directly adapted to social needs—of which they considered themselves to be good judges.

In Western Europe there are only two great Communist parties. In France and Italy, Communism is the contemporary incarnation of anti-Catholicism, a Church to rival the Catholic Church. In these Catholic countries, unlike the Protestant countries, the intellectual and social movements of modern times have been, or have seemed to be, directed against the Roman Church, which in the past was bound up with the pre-revolutionary structure of society, or, in the modern world, the bourgeois structure. There was nothing of the kind across the Channel. Democracy, radicalism, and trade unionism remained impregnated with Christian ideas, which are universally held to justify the popular demands. Of what use is a violent revolution, or an orthdoxy, when there is neither an orthodoxy to replace nor a Bastille to be razed?

The Catholic populations find once more in the anti-Church the claims to universality, the dogma, and the discipline that were or are the normal form of spiritual action. But at the same time, Communism draws remarkable strength, even when temporarily beaten, from the fact that it takes its stand as a rival Church. . . . It is fair to say that transcendental religion remains the principal enemy of secular religion. But in our day transcendental religion is stronger when it is not contained within a Church and instead dedicates itself to a point of view that can be shared by both believers and non-believers.

But the spread of Communism in France and Italy is not to be explained by these generalities. Further analysis reveals other causes. Among the countries of the West, France and Italy are those in which economic progress has been abnormally retarded, and in which a pre-capitalist structure has retarded the growth of the means of production. These are the underdeveloped countries of the West.

The agricultural worker of southern Italy, without property and paid wretchedly low wages, readily becomes a rebel as soon as he stops regarding his lot as inevitable, as soon as he no longer regards his condition as ordained by God, and as soon as he perceives or is shown a glimpse of hope. Similarly the workers in the Paris suburbs in the last century, or in those of Petrograd in 1905 and 1917, ill paid, recently arrived from the villages, and remote from their normal environment, were easily accessible, as isolated units in the midst of crowds, to the appeal of a faith, either transcendental or political.

On the other hand, the industrial workers in northern Italy or in the Paris region are not normally susceptible to Stalinism; rather their rallying to reformist socialism would seem to have more in common with the general political evolution of the West. It is not difficult to see the many reasons for this situation. The wage level within a given economic unity depends largely on the average productivity of labor: the maintenance of an agricultural regime under conditions of poor productivity or overpopulation brings the wages of the workers below their natural aspirations. The French skilled worker in industry often has a living standard that is in accordance neither with the quality of his work nor with his own quality as a human being. The social conditions created by urban concentration increase his dissatisfaction. In modern industry labor conditions for certain workers in certain countries create a dissatisfaction that is vented on the capitalist system, which is held responsible for them. The tradition of the French trade unions is revolutionary rather than reformist, anarchist rather than collectivist. Stalinism aims to eliminate entirely any anarchist tendency, but so long as it remains an opposition party it keeps agitation alive and urges direct action. Thus, it is mistakenly regarded as close to revolutionary trade unionism. Outside France, the trade unions of anarchist tendency—for instance, seamen's or longshoremen's unions—are the most susceptible to the influence of Soviet agents.

Finally, it must not be forgotten that the Stalinists have not so much converted the masses as colonized the trade unions in the course of the war, the Resistance, and the liberation. The operation had several stages: a party was organized, with its militants in key positions, and from those key positions they manipulated the masses. This operation reveals the essential danger: Communism is an army as well as a Church. The number of converts matters less than the strength of the organization.

In its first phase Communism is civil war in both theory and practice; in the second phase its theory and practice become totalitarian tyranny. But the inability of Stalinism to triumph by electoral means in the West does not mean its ultimate defeat. The Stalinists know that Europe cannot be converted peacefully; but it can be conquered. By converting a minority, they pave the way for conquest. The astonishing fact is not that Europe refuses to submit to a alien Church, but that there are so many Europeans who are awaiting liberation by a despotism that would destroy age-old traditions.

In the Stalinist enterprise, the secular religion fulfills a triple function:

To begin with, it dictates the mentality of the professional revolutionary; it maintains the faith and the discipline of the parties; and, during the periods of socialist struggle and preparation, it wins enough adherents for the party to be able to paralyze the functioning of liberal societies.

Secondly, it makes its adversaries doubtful of the justice of their causes and creates an attitude of sympathy toward the party.

Thirdly, once the party has gained possession of the state, it has to create the new man to accomplish the spiritual transformation that will render the ruling elite and the masses permanently loyal to the rules, conceptions, and mode of living of the Communist society.

The first function depends mainly on the actual Leninist and Stalinist elements—the party's mission, the leaders' authority, and the dialectic of the purges; the second depends on the Marxist ideologies—the class struggle, the decomposition of capitalism, the inevitable rise of the proletariat to power, and so on. The third element is probably beyond the means of both orthodox Marxism and of Stalinism.

Stalinism is obviously out to win over the masses, but, following the example of Bolshevism, it is concerned first of all with creating a party, that is to say, a reliable political organization. The unorganized masses who do not obey the directives of a general staff render hardly any service to the Communist enterprise. A party of professional revolutionaries, even if it is separated from the masses, is at least, as it has been in the United States, an espionage organization or a cover for one. Now, it has been proved a hundred times over that the Bolshevik doctrine is highly effective when its immediate objective is to recruit a minority of militants who are ready for anything. Why is the Leninist version superior in this respect to the social-democratic version of Marxism? The explanation seems simple: It is not theory that creates unstinted devotion, but practice. The party obliges its militants to sever their relations with the world around them and to integrate themselves in the revolutionary community. This segregation and integration bind the faithful permanently and in absolute loyalty. It is not to the profundity or the truth of its ideology that Communism owes the fanaticism of those who serve it: it owes it to the effectiveness of its technique of organization and action.

For thirty years throughout Europe, those in revolt against the injustices of the bourgeois social order have been drawn to Communism as the only genuinely revolutionary movement. Men were not rallying to a particular interpretation of Marxism, but to the working-class party that had not betrayed the cause of the proletariat by making an alliance with the bourgeoisie, and that had broken with a defeatist tradition. It was by the glory of the "ten days that shook the world" that all the revolutionaries were drawn to Moscow, rather than by the doctrine of Lenin's *Materialism and Empiriocriticism* or *State and Revolution* or by Stalin's *Foundations of Leninism*. Doctrinal instruction appeared later to confirm adherence and maintain the connection between the two elements of Stalinism: on the one hand, the general philosophy of history and the description of capitalism and, on the other, the attribution of its historic mission to the party of Lenin and Stalin. At the outset, not of the century, but of the 1920s, that connection was very doubtful: Why should the proletariat of a backward country assume the leadership of the proletariat of the world? As the Soviet Union gained strength and Stalinism spread throughout the world, the connection became increasingly plausible. Proof that the cause of the Soviet Union is also that of the world revolution requires, nevertheless, the constant use of dialectics, the art of showing that any particular political line is justified by the interest of the proletariat. For this purpose the popularized Marxism of Stalin is of incomparable value: it offers an interpretation of history for the semi-educated. It gives to people with no more than an elementary

education the pleasant feeling of easily acquiring an understanding
of the world around them. It is the typical philosophy of the age of
the masses and of the popularizers.

Indoctrination of the militants enables them to accept a system
of thought, or rather a collection of phrases, that offers an explanation of any event so long as the key to the system is permanently in
the hands of the leaders of the movement. It is easy to call the social democrats at one moment Public Enemy No. 1, and at
the next the brother party. But it is also necessary for the militant
to acquire the habit of accepting the formula suited to the circumstances as dictated to him on every occasion from above. There
have been occasions—for example, the Ribbentrop-Molotov pact
—when an about-face has subjected discipline to a severe test.

Theoretical training, too, is combined with a sort of practical
training. The reflexes of the militant are cultivated like those of the
soldier; he is taught to accept orders from the responsible leader as
from an officer; he is inculcated in the conviction that the authority
of the hierarchy, from the Kremlin down to his immediate superior,
is virtually absolute. The atmosphere of solidarity and of service
becomes as indispensable to the faithful as the air he breathes.
The sense of belonging to a sect, not to be soiled by the impurities
of the corrupt world, a sect to which the future belongs, over-
comes any repugnance that might be produced by an immorality
of method. More and more it is no longer the vision of the world
and of history that inspire loyalty in the militants, but the pressure
of the organization. An army can survive long after the combative
enthusiasm of individual soldiers declines; it is necessary to believe
in the army, in honor, in the mother country in the beginning;
thereafter, organization replaces a diminished fervor.

Outside the Communist Party, however, the Marxist ideology,
viewed as a continuation of the rationalist and humanist tradition
of the West, inspires sympathy. How could we break with the
Soviet Union, one might ask, when it has created the economic
basis of a classless society through the collective ownership of the
means of production? How can we refuse to maintain contact or

alliance with the Communists when the future of the proletariat depends on it? How can we condemn the attempt to build up socialism when, for the first time, man is shouldering the tremendous task of ordering his economic environment? . . .

In order to tear away the veil of illusions, one needs direct experience of those realities. The Czech worker subjected to the system of socialist emulation and deprived of trade unions, the peasant fearing to be brought into a *kolkhoz,* the intellectual deprived of his freedom of thought, the priest required to take an oath of loyalty to the state, the independent workers, artisans, traders, industrialists, all turned into proletarians: . . . there are probably more sincere believers [in Marxism] on this side of the Iron Curtain than on the other. The Communist faith dissolves as it spreads. It destroys itself through its victories.

In all the Sovietized countries a minority comes to the support of the regime. But it seems probable that the religion finds its believers mainly among the privileged under the regime—Stakhanovists, officials, and managers—or among the young, who have known no other life. After twenty years of totalitarian propaganda, the Russian people felt no complete solidarity with their masters: it was the German atrocities that induced them to come wholeheartedly to the defense of their country and their chains. It is the Soviet myth that attracts the masses: Soviet reality disappoints them.

The disappointment is easily explained when we measure the distance between the militant ideology and the regime that is set up after victory. The land is promised to the peasants, and a beginning is made by giving it to them, but a few years later collectivization is imposed on them by force, indeed by terrorism. To this day the Russian peasants are neither converted nor resigned. . . . National feeling is roused against imperialism, and then the people's democracies are subjected to the omnipotence of Moscow. The exploitation by the homeland of socialism exceeds in brutality the worst practices of capitalism. . . .

While there is a tendency to exaggerate the moral strength of

Communism, we tend too often to fail to recognize its political and military strength. There is no need to convert the masses; it is enough to have an active minority and to keep a semi-passive majority in a state of uncertainty in order to conquer or paralyze a state or even a continent.

In Asia, where the imperial powers of Europe are being forced into an inglorious retreat, and where millions of illiterate men are being roused to revolt against hunger and the white race, a party with a small but well-organized membership, under the direction of semi-intellectuals who have become professionals in political action —a party that places itself at the head of these blind crowds—has a chance of seizing power as it did in Russia and in China. In Europe, divided by the Iron Curtain . . . , the Communist parties have an efficient machine in both France and Italy. They have won the confidence of a large section of the masses, who are tempted by the Soviet myth or simply drawn to those who seem to be the only sympathetic interpreters of their indignation and their hopes. The Communists have little chance of peacefully gaining control of the French or Italian governments, but they need only prolong the impotence of Europe in order to prevent the re-establishment of world equilibrium. And they need only set in motion a few thousand tanks to destroy an age-old civilization.

Men are ever ready to accuse statesmen of backing into the future. Determined to prevent yesterday's disaster, they bring on tomorrow's. Neville Chamberlain constantly made declarations which historians had blamed Sir Edward Grey for not having made in 1914. President Roosevelt and Prime Minister Churchill waged the war of 1939–45 as if there were nothing of which they were so afraid as the birth of a new "stab in the back" legend. Soldiers and statesmen, in avoiding the mistakes imputed to their predecessors, fall, in their turn, into the pitfalls of history.

A striking exception to that generalization may be observed today. Imagination—which was lacking to Thiers to anticipate the benefits of railways, to the French general staff in 1914 to estimate correctly the effects of firepower, and to the general staff of 1939 to foresee the potentialities of armored divisions and of mass attacks by bombers—seems now to have been conferred on everyone, from the physicist to the man in the street. The question is only who will conjure up the most frightful visions of the coming apocalypse.

For the first time, the contemporaries of an invention believe themselves to be endowed with foreknowledge. They make 1945 —the year of the explosion of the atomic bombs over Hiroshima and Nagasaki—the Year 1 of the atomic age. The so-called bold spirits do not hesitate to label as anachronisms the traditional kind of dispute between states over a frontier line or over regions that for centuries have been regarded as strategic. Actually the course of international diplomacy has not yet been radically changed by the miraculous new weapon.

Soviet Russia is even more suspicious of foreign countries than was the Russia of Nicholas I, and it continues to attribute sinister designs to them. There are many evidences of these quasi-pathological suspicions. At the time, for example, when the Soviet Union was receiving supplies valued at 10 billion dollars under lend-lease, at the time of the alliance between the bourgeois democracies and the Soviet democracy, the Soviet Ministry of Foreign Affairs insisted on having a list of the names of all the American airmen who, after a bombing raid over Germany, were to land on a Russian airdrome. Whatever importance we may attach to these feelings, the fact remains that the direction of Soviet diplomacy since 1945 cannot be attributed to the fear of any early capitalist aggression, much less to the specific fear of the atom bomb.

. . . . .

For thirty years Stalin had incessantly declared imperialist aggression to be imminent. (The threat from abroad, under the unchanging laws of tyrannies, justifies and multiplies internal terror.) But he really feared aggression only once, when Hitler had established himself in power in Germany. In a perfectly reasonable reaction, he sought security in two directions: first in agreement with the bourgeois democracies, and then in an understanding with

Hitler. Experience suggests that fear did not inspire in Stalin and his colleagues the hyper-aggressiveness characteristic of the psychology of neurotics, but rather prudent moves aimed at reducing the danger—such as rapprochement with one section or another of the camp considered to be hostile.

After 1945 Stalin was careful to avoid an explosion, but he was convinced that as long as he did not go beyond certain limits he ran no risk—and he was quite right. It may be that he did not at once recognize the military efficacy of the atom bomb. However this may be, in 1946 and 1947 the United States apparently had scarcely more than a few atom bombs; it has been said that their industrial production did not begin before 1947. The bombs then in existence could not have determined the issue of a conflict between the mighty powers of this world.

It would seem therefore that the opinion of many anti-Communists—that the atom bomb had saved Europe from Sovietization between 1945 and 1949—is just as difficult to defend, just as open to question, as the opinion of the "sympathizers" or the "impartial," who hold it responsible for the cold war and the Stalinist invective. The atom bomb gave to Washington diplomacy of 1946 and 1947, when American opinion discovered Soviet ambitions and the weakness of the democracies in conventional armaments, a confidence that was of the utmost value. But if we ask whether the fate of Europe would have been different without the atom bomb, two obvious questions arise: Even if it had not had the bomb, would the United States have tolerated the expansion of the Soviet empire as far as the Atlantic? And would Stalin have been ready to face the risk of general war?

Great Britain and the United States, who had not stinted on sacrifices in order to prevent Germany from gaining control of the whole of the Continent, could not, without committing a really inconceivable folly, have stood by to see that same unification, fatal to the metropolis of the British Commonwealth, carried out by another Continental power, and one in every respect even more formidable than the Third Reich. What Great Britain had refused, at the price of a struggle to the death, to France and to Germany—to Napoleon and to Hitler—she would not have conceded to Stalin's Russia.

Stalin, who could not have been unaware of the reactions that would have been produced by the inclusion of Germany and France within his sphere of influence, would have done everything to put off a third world war for some years, even if the United States had had no atom bombs. Probably he regarded a third war as inevitable, but meant to set the date of its outbreak himself. An immediate drive to the Atlantic would have been contrary to his constant strategy.

. . . . .

When one surveys the entire period since the Hiroshima explosion, it is difficult to resist the impression that the United States has lost rather than gained by its famous atomic monopoly. It has been of no use in the cold war. The potential and actual forces of the United States and the Soviet Union have not only not been engaged, but until 1950 had hardly figured as a means of pressure or extortion. Neither in China nor in Greece has the outcome of the civil war been influenced by the relative strength of world forces. It has been said that the stock pile of bombs was equivalent to 175 Russian divisions. But the same equivalence could have been obtained by the maintenance of aerial and naval fleets armed with conventional weapons. Furthermore, it can now be seen that the United States has been led, by its atomic superiority, to adopt military and diplomatic conceptions whose dangers are now apparent.

Confident that the stock pile of bombs would suffice to prevent the Soviet Union from employing regular armies in any part of the world, the United States reduced to a minimum its own aerial, naval, and—above all—land forces capable of immediate action. It thus allowed itself to be driven into a position where, in the event of any local aggression, it would have to choose between passivity or world war—a formidable choice for a nation aiming to avoid a world war.

The strategy of intercontinental atomic war, which the Joint Chiefs of Staff in the Pentagon seemed to have adopted, is partly responsible for European defeatism. How could the nations of the Continent have failed to be discouraged in advance when their transatlantic ally and protector relied on a weapon against which they themselves would be defenseless? On the day when the potential enemy in his turn came into possession of the miraculous weapon (and that day probably came in 1949), reprisals for the destruction of Russian cities by American bombs were likely to be aimed at the cities of Europe. Every European would be a hostage in a total war—until and unless there are enough divisions to ward off Soviet invasion at the frontier.

Paradoxically, the American stock pile became really useful when it was no longer a monopoly. In 1951 America probably had a double superiority, in the number of bombs and in the means of delivering them. But by this time its aim was to overcome Western inferiority in conventional weapons and it relied upon its atomic stock pile simply to check direct Soviet oppression. For in 1950, the atom bomb had become if not a crucial factor in any potential war, at least an indispensable factor in the balance of world forces. And it is therefore easy to understand why Russian propaganda has made the bomb the target of its attacks.

But even apart from these considerations and from the propaganda that they generate, the question remains: Even in a just cause, is the use of certain weapons in itself legitimate?

The men who took the decision to employ the first two atom bombs acted in good faith; the Americans had made their choice on the basis that a landing on the Japanese islands would cost hundreds of thousands of lives. But now, after the event, it is difficult not to conclude that the decision to use the bomb was mistaken. By renouncing the formula of unconditional surrender, or simply by replying more quickly to the repeated approaches which the Emperor had been making for several months, the war could have been ended without the atom bomb and without the Soviet intervention that mortgaged the victory.

The use of the atom bomb against urban agglomerations did not constitute a radical innovation. After all, what was euphemistically called "zone bombing" struck residential districts, historical monuments, and the ancient parts of cities much harder than it did factories. The capacity of modern weapons to distinguish between civilians and combatants is limited, and zone bombing was, in principle, an acceptance of that fact. The atom bomb completes the evolution. It consecrates the use of *any* means against the *entire* population, civil as well as military, of the enemy country. By a logic that is paradoxical only in appearance, the country least warlike in its tastes and philosophy has thus played a decisive part in the advent of unlimited war.

Those who question the wisdom and the moral legitimacy of the strategy based on the atom bomb are not few in the United States. By the very fact of its concentration, the industrial equipment of the United States will one day, according to certain experts, be more vulnerable to atomic attack than that of any other country. It is contrary to the spirit of our civilization, certain other philosophers declare, to look upon whole cities as targets to be struck by the weapons of mass destruction. The citizens of an enemy nation should continue to be regarded as fellow creatures to whom we owe certain obligations.

One would have to be fanatic or blind to disregard the weight of such objections. But what can we do once the diabolical secret is out? Should the United States proclaim its intention not to be the first to use the atom bomb? The military staffs would reply by pointing out the danger of leaving the advantage of the initiative to a predatory power. Since it would have to be prepared to take reprisals, the United Sates could not stint preparations for an atomic war. The cost of these preparations increases the temptation to use the bomb once the moment has come. Would not renunciation of scientific weapons ultimately work out in favor of the Soviet Union? It has greater human resources, and a population accustomed to a more primitive living standard, and therefore less sensitive to the rigors of conventional war. Can the United States afford to renounce the scientific weapons, to which it owes its superiority, and give battle on a field where the enemy has the advantage?

For that matter, is the atomic weapon really unique? Has not research found other means of destruction equally inhuman, equally terrifying: poisons, radioactive clouds, bacteriological weapons? In the absence of an international agreement, which seems unattainable, the only hope lies in the wisdom born of fear. . . .

The present world is situated, so to speak, at the meeting point of three processes of development. The first of these processes led to a planetary unity and a bi-polar diplomatic structure; the second to the diffusion in Asia and Europe of a secular religion of which one of the two giant powers claims to be the metropolis; and the third to the perfection of weapons of mass destruction, to a total war animated both by modern science and primitive fury, with the atom bomb and the guerrilla as the extreme manifestations of unlimited violence.

Each of these processes includes—to employ Cournot's expression—one part logic and one part chance. Diplomatic unification was not achieved until this century, but it was prepared in the previous one. Thanks to their superior military techniques, the nations of Europe had conquered Africa and part of Asia, and exercised their influence even over the still independent Asian countries. The United States, which possessed a potential force equal to that of Europe, limited itself to banning the extension of colonial empires in the direction of the two Americas. The balance of power between the European countries left Great Britain the command of the seas. Since no army of the Western type existed either in the Near or Far East, Britain's possession of bases from which she could mount naval attacks was enough to guarantee the *pax Britannica*.

Since then, the influence of military power has increased considerably. In 1945 the United States maintained tens of divisions and thousands of aircraft abroad, from the Philippines to the Elbe —that is, thousands of miles from their home bases. Similarly the Soviet Union gloried in two war industries, one in Siberia and the other in European Russia, and in two armies, one in Berlin and the other at Dairen and Mukden. In an era when heavy bombers have a combat radius of several thousand miles, when the continent-states that are the master players can mobilize populations of more than 150 million, and count on an industrial potential measured by hundreds of millions of tons of coal and by tens of millions of tons of steel, it is not surprising that the two protagonists find themselves face to face in every quarter of the globe. The amplification of the instruments of warfare and the enlargement of political units have burst the partitions between the zones of civilization. Aerial squadrons, continent-states, world-wide diplomatic unity— these three phenomena comprise a closed system; they imply one another, and no one can say which is cause and which is effect: simultaneously, they characterize the present state of affairs.

But none of these phenomena, or even their simultaneous occurrence, implied the bi-polar structure. At the beginning of the century, history seemed to be headed in a quite different direction. The rise of Japan in the Far East and of Germany in Europe led in each case to a complex configuration involving changing relations between several soverign states, none of which was strong enough to impose its will by itself—Russia, Japan, Great Britain, the United States, and China in the Far East, and Russia, Germany, France, Great Britain, Italy, and (as was twice seen) the United States in Europe. The Japanese and German attempts at expansion, the defeat of the "co-prosperity sphere" and of the Third Reich, at one stroke transformed Europe and Asia into regions of ruins, into cemeteries for empires. In the middle of the twentieth century, Russia had not yet the industrial resources of a superpower; the United States did—but, far from desiring hegemony, would have preferred to know neither the power nor the responsibilities that these resources conferred. It was the Second World War, and especially the blind fury with which it was waged, that brought the collapse of the intermediate zones and left the two giants standing alone, face to face.

It is often wondered why the United States and the Soviet Union seem to be engaged in a mortal struggle when the two peoples do not know one another, when neither lacks wealth of its own to exploit or lands to develop, and when both have plunged headlong into the adventure of technical civilization. One fair reply is to cite the ambitions, essentially limitless, of a secular religion that claims universal value; but two other causes also exist. "Glory is indivisible," and wise men dream in vain of a partition of the globe. The no man's land in Europe and Asia are, in themselves, a cause of instability. Two nations need not hate each other in order to come into collision in the four quarters of the globe. But the fact that they do collide in the four quarters of the globe is enough to make them end by hating each other.

Nor was Soviet expansion written beforehand in the book of history. Certain specific reasons for its spectacular victories can be identified easily. It is understandable that the proletariat in Western communities should have adhered to a gospel that gave promise of raising them out of their low estate and giving them dignity and hope. It is equally understandable that the semi-Westernized intellectuals of Asia, their nationalism offended by white domination, should have subscribed to a doctrine that promised them both independence and power, wrested at last from their European conquerors. In both cases the rise of the secular religion is less the cause than the effect of the decay of traditional beliefs. In both cases machines inspire, in those who handle them without understanding them, a sort of faith that they will bring an end to traditional poverty. In both cases there is a dream of equality, even though the doctrine in itself tends simply to impose a new hierarchy, technocratic, bureaucratic, military, and in part religious, in place of the ancient hierarchy, on a population reduced to an inorganic mass.

Nor is it surprising that Marxism should have been better adapted to the needs of the revolution in Asia after its passage through the Russian Revolution. The Bolshevik Party captured power through a rising of the masses against a ruling class marked by a foreign culture. It used its power not to give the people the liberties in the name of which it had preached revolt, but to accelerate technical Westernization. It borrowed from "aggressive" civilizations the tools of their material superiority. An ideology of European origin was still proclaimed, but it no longer inspired the work of construction, having been suppressed or distorted by earlier traditions. In the same way, the revolutionary intelligentsia in the Far East has borrowed its ideas—nationalism and socialism—from the civilization whose local domination it is opposing. It is seduced by a confused picture of the Soviet regime, the prospect of erecting an entirely new social order and accelerated industrialization. From this it hopes for attenuation of an age-old poverty, aggravated by the rapid increase of population. It combines an extravagant dream with effective action; it sees itself surpassing the West by rejecting it, and imagines itself lifting its people into the front rank of a history common to all peoples, while avenging the humiliations inflicted by the white man. Even in Europe, Marxism, transfigured by the Soviet experiment, continues to appeal to certain numbers of the working classes in countries weakened by war and impatient with their own decline, as well as to certain intellectuals, disappointed in democratic methods and envious of an imagined state in which the educated would take first place and power would belong not to money but to knowledge.

While the causes of these successes are apparent in retrospect, it would be wrong to forget the events that favored them—events not necessarily a part of the social structure. Only the First World War enabled the Bolshevik Party to conquer Russia. It was the determination of the bourgeois and socialist parties to continue the war, the weakness of the liberals, and the hesitations of the Mensheviks and the Social Revolutionaries that enabled the October Revolution to follow that of February 1917. Before 1914, the great majority in every socialist party rejected Lenin's political methods. But then, for four years the military leaders of the bourgeois states treated their citizens as "human material," and the Bolshevik technique of propaganda and party organization ceased to arouse indignation. Since it was a time of horrors, at least let violence have peace as its objective, and as its enemy the civilization that had made the sterile carnage possible.

And yet, neither in Europe nor in Asia was the expansion of Stalinism impressive before 1939. It was the second war that made possible the Red Army's conquests in Europe and the Communist Party's conquests in Asia. Once again, the decisive cause of Stalin's victories was the wars that created the circumstances in which a militant sect could succeed in seizing power.

The process leading to total war is highly logical, a process which, seen in retrospect, leaves little to individual initiative and unforeseeable chance. With the advent of conscription and modern industry, war automatically became hyperbolic, unless—unlikely event—statesmen had had the wisdom to renounce certain potentialities of the system. Or, perhaps, unless the victors in the first battles had shown such moderation that the losers were able to accept defeat instead of mobilizing the entire world in order to reverse it.

The experience of 1914–18 had shown the mortal peril. Philosophically inclined historians were quite aware that a new war would mark the end not only of nationalism but of Europe itself. National Socialism, which combined obscure and remote Germanic aspirations with the social and moral disintegration of the country after its military defeat and the subsequent economic crisis and with a sharp reaction against Communism, precipitated the catastrophe. The scientific barbarity of the Nazis and the aerial superiority of the Allies led ultimately to the present situation: peoples dread the ravages of the weapons of mass destruction, but they dread even more the technique of extermination which invaders are capable of employing.

It goes without saying that in spite of this logic of violence, nothing foreshadowed the gas chambers and the extermination of millions of defenseless human beings. Similarly, it could not have been foreseen that the atom bomb would be made during the second war and tried on the Japanese. In the long run, the utilization of nuclear energy for military purposes perhaps marks a revolution comparable to the invention of gunpowder. In the present crisis it merely augments factors already visible: the ubiquity of the super powers, the relative weakening of the second-class nations, especially of the overpopulated and vulnerable ones of Western Europe; the dread of war felt by the masses in all countries, victors and vanquished alike; the obvious necessity of stopping the chain reaction of violence; and the growing difficulty of establishing a stable peace, either through the traditional device of the balance of power or through a return to the more ancient tradition of imperial domination.

The meeting of these processes itself indicates a combination of logic and of chance. To some extent each begins in a common situation: the development of science, the application of science to industry, and the expansion of industrial civilization. It was industrial technique, even more than political democracy, that rendered unlimited and inexorable a war which Europe, unaware, had undertaken as a war just like any other. It is industrial technique that weakens beliefs that have justified and upheld the age-long order of human societies; that uproots the urban masses and makes them dissatisfied with their humble lot; that makes poverty, long accepted as a decree of God or nature, a sort of scandal. It is this that precipitates the anti-white revolution in Asia and the insurrection of masses ever more numerous and wretched; and this that spurs the impatience of the peoples of Europe whose standard of living rises more slowly than their aspirations. This is what has made the political structure of the Continent an anachronism, has promoted the advent of continent-states, has favored the diffusion of a secular religion—a substitute faith for souls deprived of the Gospel, and has made of Stalinism—the religion of the proletariat and the machine—a fetish for the worship of the semi-educated.

There is no justification, even after the event, for saying that things had to happen as they have in fact happened. The decisive events of this period—the 1914 explosion, the Russian Revolution, Hitler's rise to power, the coming of the second war, and the ineptitude of Anglo-American statesmanship can be explained reasonably. One can see the causes, however remote, which favored them but one cannot ignore the interval between the cause and the effect; it is man, or rather it is men, who by their action or inaction, produced this history which they did not want, and we cannot even console ourselves with the thought that in the long run the consequences of their courage or cowardice, their blindness or foresight, will be effaced, for as far as the eye can see, there loom the consequences of Russia's industrialization in the Bolshevik and not in the Western manner.

To keep to the broadest phenomena, the present crisis is not the direct and inevitable result of industrial civilization, but of its collision with certain long-standing facts of history. If the European communities have destroyed themselves, it is not because they have proved incapable of integrating their productive forces into a structure founded on private property. The eternal rivalry of nations has continued into the age of infernal machines; and nations, in their pursuit of power, have not found a way to agree either to a common law or to moderation and compromise. The techniques of modern war have made the survival of Europe incompatible with the continuance of conflicts that long antedate capitalism and that were due only in slight measure to competition between economic or social systems.

The revolt of Russia and of Asia is directed less against capitalism than against the civilization that came from the West. In Russia it began against a Westernized ruling class, in Asia against the dominance of Europeans. As a result of wars it has become an insurrection not of workers against the owners of the means of production, but of peoples of ancient civilization humiliated by the mysterious power of the creators of machines, and of wretched mobs with a vague sense of the incapacity of their traditional rulers to build a modern nation.

The recession of national states, the rise of the continent-states, the decline of Europe, the revolt against the West—all these were to a great extent foreseeable because they were implicit in industrial civilization and its material and moral repercussions. What was unforeseeable was the pace and manner of these changes. The two wars greatly hastened them and at the same time gave them a cataclysmic character. That Russia, the metropolis of a secular religion of universal dimensions, should stand at the borders of an exhausted Europe and an Asia in revolt, and should be checked in her ambition only by the far-off force of the United States, itself anxious about the future and accumulating a stock of atom bombs —such an encounter clearly was not predetermined by any historical necessity. The wars of the first half of the twentieth century have ripened a catastrophe that would be to the catastrophes of the past what the atom bomb is to Big Bertha.

Suggestions for Further Reading

BLACKETT, P. M. S., *Atomic Weapons and East-West Relations*. Cambridge, England: The University Press, 1956.

EASTON, STUART, *The Twilight of European Colonialism*. New York: Holt, Rinehart & Winston, 1960.

GATZKE, HANS W., *The Present in Perspective*. Chicago: Rand McNally, 1957.

GOLDMAN, ERIC, *The Crucial Decade—and After: America 1945–1960*. New York: Random House, Inc., 1960.

SETON-WATSON, HUGH, *Neither War nor Peace*. New York: Frederick A. Praeger, Inc., 1960.

The Change in Human Attitudes*

GEOFFREY BARRACLOUGH

After half a century of revolution, after the decline of European hegemony in the world, after the wrecking of the framework of bourgeois-liberal civilization, can we now at long last see an era of affirmation and creativity, of reconstruction and achievement coming into view? After the peoples of the West have given all their hostages to fortune, will they now be allowed to participate in that new golden age of progress, peace, and common welfare that has been prophesied several times in the twentieth century, only to be denied by yet another downturn of the historical maelstrom? Will the upheaval of the twentieth century be succeeded by the discovery of new dimensions in human thought and feeling as was the case with the medieval revolution of the eleventh century, the Protestant revolution of the sixteenth, and the French and industrial revolutions of the late eighteenth century?

In the late 1960's there was no consensus among historians of

* From Geoffrey Barraclough, *An Introduction to Contemporary History* (London: C. A. Watts & Co. Ltd., 1964), pp. 229-264.

the contemporary age in answer to these questions, asked partly out of despair and partly out of anticipation. There were those who saw nothing in the immediate future but the complete extinction of the values of liberal humanism, with nothing to replace the traditional culture of the West as a meliorative force in the world. They saw only ever widening circles of violence and disorder, the intensification of the individual's sense of alienation from society, and the further deadly triumphs of the terrible simplifiers and the disinherited minds that have already effaced the achievements of the nineteenth century.

On the other hand, there were historians who had cause to express a cautious optimism because they anticipated, from observing the current political and economic situation in the world, that the decline of the West had been arrested and that the long climb back to Western preponderance was beginning. Some observers believed that the West had learned its lesson, that during the past half century it had exorcised from its midst the power politics, capitalist exploitation of the masses, and imperialist aggression that conflicted so flagrantly with the ideals of the liberal tradition and brought on the discrediting and demoralizing of European culture. Europe, they believed, was coming out of its second dark age chastened and purified and would present to the world the model of a society that both provided for social welfare and at the same time respected the integrity and freedom of the individual. These observers, in fact, believed that the rising generation in the Communist states of eastern Europe were trying to cast off the mechanistic authoritarianism of the older bolshevism and were reaching back to find within Marxist doctrine glimmerings of a left-wing liberal-humanist tradition that was betrayed by the Russian revolution

Yet a third view of the early 1960's in history is presented in the following interpretation taken from Geoffrey Barraclough's Introduction to Contemporary History, *published in 1964. This remarkable book, fresh and original in its insight, sure and omnivorous in its learning, challenging and persuasive in its eloquence, is the work of an Oxford scholar who during the 1930's and 40's gained a richly deserved reputation as one of the leading medieval historians of his generation. In the 1950's Barraclough turned to modern and recent history and became the most powerful spokesman of a new historical interpretation, indeed a new vision and testament on the meaning of the present era.*

Barraclough believes that since 1947 we have been living in the post-European era. European hegemony came to an end after the Second World War and with it "the predominance of the old European scale of values." Liberal humanism was destroyed in the six decades after 1880 because it was undermined from within by a new insight into the individualist, irrational, and subconscious aspects of human nature and also because it failed to come to terms with the problems of industrial society and to legislate for social welfare and the emancipation of the non-European peoples. Barraclough believes we are living in a new world society to which the non-European peoples are making contributions of the greatest importance. He also believes that contemporary culture has finally turned away from the extreme individualism and irrationalism of the early twentieth century, has at last made its peace with technology and science, and has entered a new era of affirmation of the potentiality of human life in the existential circumstances of the industrial secular world. In the following selection he argues that since the mid-1950's, philosophy, art, and literature have begun to express these fundamental changes in human attitudes. We are on the threshold of a new golden age, a worldwide community free alike from the delusions of liberal humanism and the early twentieth-century nihilist reaction against it, and ready to make use of science and technology in building a universal democratic society.

Barraclough marshals some plausible evidence to support his thesis and there are some additional indices within Western culture itself of the beginning of a new era of affirmation and creativity, characteristic of previous postrevolutionary eras in Western civilization. The bankruptcy of authority and tradition and the cate-

*gorical imperative of personal commitment and private conscience
—this appears to be the faith of the new generation of the 1960's.
And this faith is being directed outward from the individual toward the reform of industrial society. The American civil rights
movement, the determination to extirpate poverty, the moderniza-
tion and revitalization of the Protestant and Catholic churches, and
the eagerness to achieve a true world community and the extinction of national privilege and racism—these movements may indeed be indications that the era which began in 1914, the age of
disappointment and disillusionment, is finally drawing to a close.
If this is the case, it represents not so much the extinction of
liberal humanism as its renaissance. But if European history
teaches us anything, it is that the forces of greed and power have
often aborted and debased movements of social reconstruction
and intellectual affirmation. As long as the Cold War continues we
have not escaped the possibility that the new philosphy Barraclough
acclaims will become only the latest in a long series of unfulfilled
expectations that have characterized the history of the twentieth
century.*

If . . . contemporary history is different in most of its basic
preconditions from what we call "modern" history, if the contemporary period marks the onset of a new epoch in the history of
mankind, it would be reasonable to expect to see this change mir-
rored not only in the social environment and in the political structure, but also in human attitudes. It is, of course, true—as Marx
was always careful to emphasize—that the relationship between
the social infrastructure and the superstructure of "sentiments,
illusions, habits of thought and conceptions of life" raised upon
it is extremely complex; and we should be foolish to expect any
direct co-ordination between them. But it would also be surprising
if the temper of literature and other forms of human self-expres-

sion had not been affected by the new social order produced by a new technological civilization. What I shall attempt to do in conclusion, therefore, is to examine some of the more outstanding changes in human attitudes in the last three-quarters of a century and see how far they indicate the emergence of a new outlook on the world and a new approach to basic human problems.

Our starting-point will be the "disintegration of the bourgeois synthesis" which stares us in the face as the nineteenth century draws to a close; the central point of our inquiry will be whether any new synthesis has yet succeeded it, or whether we can at least discern the elements of a new synthesis. Two points, in particular, will call for attention: the one is the degree to which our attitudes have been reshaped by the revolution in science and the impact of technology, the other is how far the new mass society of our times has arrived at distinctive forms of expression of its own. These are questions which have been hotly debated, often in terms of value-judgements which are subjective and largely irrelevant. We have had a surfeit of moralizing on the decadence of modern art and music, the gulf which allegedly separates them from everyday life, the spiritual erosion of western civilization, and, more recently, the shortcomings of the resurgent peoples of Asia and Africa. Such judgements cloud rather than clarify the issues, and I shall try to avoid them. The pessimism which sees all change as change for the worse is a recurrent theme of history, which history has recurrently refuted. But when all this has been said, a real question remains, which the historian cannot simply ignore on grounds of lack of technical qualifications.

In following the process of change as its affects human attitudes, we can fairly easily distinguish three main phases or periods. The first, which extends from about 1880 to the First World War, was marked above all by reaction against the tradition of the past four hundred years; the second, roughly equivalent to the inter-war years, but extending back to the decade before 1914, was a period of great experimentation in new modes of expression; in the third, which followed the Second World War, much of the experimentation of the inter-war period was left behind, but it was still not easy to perceive the crystallization of a new outlook on the world. This should not be surprising. When we consider the extent of the upheaval of the last half-century and the magnitude of the adjustments to be made, it would be unrealistic to expect the rapid emergence of a new unifying culture. In other respects—for example, in the shaping of new political terms of reference—we can say with some confidence that the transition from one era to another has been completed. In respect of our basic human attitudes we must expect slower progress. The diffusion of a new cultural pattern requires a period of stability such as we have not experienced since 1914, but which may now be beginning. Even then, there is the question whether the old liberal synthesis, which was the mark of the nineteenth century, will be succeeded by anything comparable in scope and influence.

For the historian it is easier to trace the disintegration of old attitudes and patterns than the formation of new ones. The central fact marking a break between two periods was the collapse—except in formal education, which was thereby increasingly cut off from the mainstream of social development—of the humanist tradition which had dominated European thought since the Renaissance. The attack on humanism took many forms and came from many directions; but at its heart was disillusion with humanism itself, and it was the discrepancy between its professions—namely, respect for the dignity and value of the individual—and its practice—namely, the dehumanization and depersonalization of the working classes—that initiated the revolt. What brought it to a head, after a period of growing disquiet, was the sharp deterioration of conditions in town and factory resulting from the new industrialism, and it was fostered by the new preoccupation with the maladies of poverty, unemployment and distress which marked the generation from Henry George's *Progress and Poverty* (1879) to William Beveridge's *Unemployment* (1909). It found its most eloquent expression in the best of Zola's writing, notably in his greatest novel *Germinal* (1885), with its insistent hammering on the themes of hardship, endurance, darkness, mass action and mass suffering. Something of the same quality infused Gerhart Hauptmann's greatest drama, *The Weavers* (1892).

Works such as *Germinal* exposed the hollowness of humanist professions, the implicit contradiction at the heart of liberal philosophy between human dignity and equality in theory and economic inequality and indignity in fact. At the same time Nietzsche —the mature Nietzsche of *Also sprach Zarathustra* (1883–5) and *Beyond Good and Evil* (*1885–6*)—was savagely attacking its moral pretensions, tearing away the ideological veil erected to conceal the power structure on which the social order was based, and hammering home the brutal truism of the will to power. "Seek ye a name for this world? A solution for all its puzzles? . . . This world is the will to power—and nothing else." With a directness without parallel before him Nietzsche penetrated through the optimism of his day, the facile belief in progress automatically assured by natural selection and the survival of the fittest, the assumption that man, the individual, is an infinite reservoir of possibilities and that all that is necessary is to rearrange society for these possibilities to prevail. Morality was "itself a form of immorality"; philosophy from Plato to Hegel had falsified reality and degraded life. "Nothing has been bought more dearly," Nietzsche proclaimed, "than that little bit of human reason and sense of freedom which is now the basis of our pride." It was this frontal attack on the values and assumptions on which all western culture was based that made him, after 1890, the inspired prophet of the new generation in Europe.

Nietzsche's disruptive influence on the nineteenth century's picture of intellectual man, the purposive master of his own fate, was reinforced by the work of the French philosopher, Henri Bergson, with his assertion of the superiority of intuition over intelligence. It was reinforced also by new trends in the physical sciences and by the impact of new psychological insights. Both contributed, with increasing force as time passed, to the decline of the certitudes which had sustained the commonly accepted picture of man and the universe. Science, in the first place, dissolved the old concepts both of nature and of man's place in nature. The French mathematician, Henri Poincaré, denied that science could ever know anything of reality; all it could do, he asserted, was to determine the relationship between things. In England a similar view of the world as a structure of emergent relationships was put forward in F. H. Bradley's *Appearance and Reality* (1893) and developed by Whitehead and the relativists. "Nature by itself," Bradley maintained, "has no reality"; the idea that nature was "made up of solid matter interspaced with an absolute void," which had been inherited from Greek metaphysics, was untenable and must be discarded. Space, Bradley asserted, was only "a relation between terms which can never be found." Thus nature, which from the time of Giordano Bruno had been a fixed point of reference—the totality of things and events which man encountered around and about him—began to retreat into inaccessibility; it became an intricate network of relations and functions which was beyond common experience and could only be conceptualized abstractly, until finally it dissolved into a "lost world of symbols."

The trend of modern science was to suggest that the universe is unintelligible, senseless and accidental, and that man, in Eddington's phrase, is "no more than a fortuitous concourse of atoms." Such views, as they passed into wider circulation, could not but have a dissolving effect, and the same was true of the new psychology of Pavlov and Freud. Freud, whose *Interpretation of Dreams* appeared in 1899, must be ranked with Lenin as the herald of a new age. Although his main influence was not felt until after 1917, he was a figure of formidable stature and influence, with whom, in the scientific field, only Einstein could compare. The Freudian theory of the subconscious had an immeasurable impact, above all by destroying the image of man as a co-ordinated individual responding intelligently and predictably to events. Freud's discovery that man's actions could be motivated by forces of which he knew nothing exploded the individual's illusion of autonomy, and sociology which, in Dewey's phrase, conceived "individual mind as a function of social life," worked in the same direction. If science left man groping after an elusive external reality, Freud left him seeking in vain for the reality of his inner self.

The effects of these revolutionary changes in outlook on all fields of literary and artistic expression are too obvious to need more than illustration. We know that writers like Henry James and Virginia Woolf quickly took note of the new psychological insights; we know that the early cubists, while they were living in the Bateau Lavoir on the slopes of Montmartre, learnt about the new scientific outlook from the amateur mathematician, Princet; we know that Eliot, as a student at Harvard, studied and wrote on Bradley. Such cases are, however, rare and it would be misleading to stress them. Changes in literature and art and changes in philosophy and science occurred simultaneously and largely independently, and the effect of the latter was to play upon and accentuate a process of disintegration in the former which was already under way. Confidence in the power of art to reflect the true nature of reality was already withering, and science only confirmed the existing awareness that truth does not, after all, conform to instinctive feelings or immediate perceptions. "I arrange facts in such a way," wrote Gide in 1895, "as to make them conform to truth more closely than they do in reality." "Art does not reproduce what can be seen," said Paul Klee; "it makes things visible."

From 1874, when the first impressionist exhibition was held in Paris, it was impossible to overlook the disintegration of the artistic tradition that had held sway since the Renaissance. It is true that the impressionists—Monet, Pissarro, Renoir, Degas, Sisley—were not revolutionaries breaking with the past; as Gauguin said, they "kept the shackles of representation" and remained within the tradition of realism, but now it was "a realism evaporating into the immaterial reality of air and light." It was when the problem arose of filling the void which the dissolving effects of impressionism left behind that the need for new standards and for a break with the past became explicit, and almost simultaneously painting, writing and music set off on deliberately revolutionary lines. There can be no question here of following the process step by step, from van Gogh, Cézanne and Gauguin to Kandinsky, Picasso and Jackson Pollock, from Debussy to Schönberg, Bartok and Webern, from Mallarmé and Rimbaud to Eluard and Pound. All we can do is to pick out a few trends, of which the most obvious was the rejection of accepted artistic forms.

The preoccupation with form was characteristic, for it was the bankruptcy of the old forms and the need for new ways of coming to terms with a new type of human being, the new emotions which filled him, his new relationship with the world about him, which dominated artistic expression. It led inexorably from symbolism to expressionism and cubism, and behind it was a repudiation of the preoccupation with nature—with three-dimensional space, scientific perspective, *sfumato* and *chiaroscuro*—which had dominated European art since the Renaissance. Whistler's "Nature is usually wrong!" stated the challenge of a new generation to the whole existing tradition. The central purpose of the cubists and the German expressionists was to get away from the visual, which was not real, to the essence, which was or might be. Mallarmé explicitly rejected "the claim to enclose in language the material reality of things." In the same way painters such as Paul Klee and sculptors such as Henry Moore rejected representational art, and in music Schönberg abandoned the tonal centre and introduced the technique of atonality.

Behind this experimentation with form was a conscious and resolute determination to come to grips with "the task of mastering reality afresh." It was the result of a crisis in standards and values which set in everywhere shortly after 1900. Schönberg published his revolutionary *Three Piano Pieces* (op. 11) in 1908. In Paris cubism emerged as a conscious and coherent movement in 1907. In Germany the formation of the group known as *Die Brücke* (1905), followed by the "new secession" (1910) and *Der blaue Reiter* (1911), marked the birth of expressionism. All were impelled by the collapse of the old belief that positive truth was contained in sense perception and by the problems of reality revealed by science and technical discovery and the conclusions the human mind had drawn from them. By now, the question of the nature of reality had developed into the problem whether there was a reality at all that could be grasped, and how it could be grasped. The different styles, mannerisms, techniques that followed all represented different attempts to grapple with this problem. In France the Fauves, in Germany expressionists such as Heckel, Nolde and Kandinsky used discordant colours, violent contrasts and brutal distortion to break through appearances to a truth "truer than literal truth." Stravinsky's early music employed similar methods for similar ends. But it was cubism which came closest to a new view of the world. It did so because it was more intellectual and less involved in "an augmented emotional transcription of the artist's reactions" than expressionism. For cubists the world existed, as it did not for the symbolists, but under the impact of new scientific theory it was conceived in a new way. In this they were like the artists of the Renaissance who also sought to assimilate art with the scientific discoveries of their day. Cubist painting was "a research into the emergent nature of reality," an "examination of reality in its many contingencies," "an analysis of the multiple identity of objects"; it was "painting conceived as related forms which are not determined by any reality external to those related forms." The universe the cubists depicted was one where things have no simple location, and their rejection of a single viewpoint revealed a fuller vision of reality than was possible in any art based on the artificiality of Euclidean geometry. From this point of view cubist art had the sharpness and clarity of a scientific analysis.

"The ideas behind cubist painting," it has been said, "are reflected in all the modern arts." Nevertheless, in spite of its impact, cubism was only a momentary halting place. For this there were two main reasons. The first was that the cubists themselves, by breaking up the object into its simplest elements—or, as in Picasso's famous *Man with Violin* (1911), resolving it into a series of planes —destroyed the object and opened the door for abstract art and a new wave of iconoclasm. The second was the impact of the First World War. It was no accident that dadaism and surrealism reached their peak between 1919 and 1921. The shock and disillusionment of war shook all faith in meaningful reality and gave point both to the bitter expressionist protest of Georg Grosz and Otto Dix and to the surrealist nightmares of Salvador Dali. "Had they deceived us," Eliot was later to ask—

> Or deceived themselves, the quiet-voiced elders,
> Bequeathing us merely a receipt for deceit?

For the poets and artists who flocked into the modernist movements, the slaughter between 1914 and 1918, and the mock peace which crowned it, signified the bankruptcy not only of the existing order but of the system of values of a whole civilization. Judging them by their results, they had no further use for them. Hence surrealism took shape as the "refusal of the modes of thought and feeling of traditional humanism." But throughout the experimentation of the nineteen-twenties, side by side with the deliberate attempt to shock, the struggle to discover new ways of grasping reality was never abandoned. Mondriaan, in particular, aimed in his abstract geometrical compositions at expressing "pure reality," purged of "the deadweight of the object." The life of modern man, he wrote in 1917, was "gradually being divorced from natural objects" and "becoming more and more an abstract existence," and he set himself the task of creating forms which would express this new situation. But the attempt to find a new insight into reality through abstraction did not survive the Second World War. In the post-Hitler, post-Hiroshima world Mondriaan's search for an harmonious balance was no longer acceptable. It seemed "a dishonest extenuation," and emphasis shifted from the attempt to picture reality to an existentialist attempt to express a new feeling about life. In the "tachist" painting of Pollock or Appel what the scientist calls the "field" became more important than the objects in the field. This painting expressed "a world-view where the object disappears into patterns of behaviour:" nothing, it has been said, "could more effectively dismiss the romantic belief in freedom, individualism, and the importance of the decisive act."

Cubism, dadaism and abstract painting, like the music of Bartok and Schönberg, or like Joyce's *Ulysses* and Kafka's *The Castle,* were entirely remote from the world of the nineteenth century. They are also entirely remote from the world of today. It is none of my business, even if I were competent to do so, to attempt their artistic evaluation; in the present context it is sufficient to see them as a transition from one stage of civilization to another. What happened, by the end of the transition, was the jettisoning of the inherited baggage of European culture. As Ortega wrote, the nineteenth century was bound to the past, on whose shoulders it thought it was standing; it regarded itself as the culmination of past ages. The present—he was writing in 1930—recognized in nothing that was past any possible model or standard. The Renaissance revealed itself as "a period of narrow provincialism, of futile gestures . . ."

We feel that we actual men have suddenly been left alone on the earth. . . . Any remains of the traditional spirit have evaporated. Models, norms, standards are no use to us. We have to solve our problems without any active collaboration of the past.

It was this sense of alienation, of disinheritance, of the individual's incommunicable solitude, that was the framework of art and writing in the years before and after the First World War. The plays of Ibsen and Chekhov and novels such as Thomas Mann's *Buddenbrooks* (1901) had portrayed the crisis of the old society; they were, in a sense, its requiem. Rilke, above all others, emerged as the poet of a world from which doubt had dislodged all certainties; a world in which good does no good and evil no harm, in which lovers seek separation, not union, in which the whole accepted order of correspondences had collapsed like a house of cards. Proust, seeking to perpetuate by an act of memory patterns and relationships which dissolved even as they were thought of, was its greatest novelist. Since there is no logical sequence, no causal development, since man is not a single unified person whose destiny is decided by his own actions or because the forces of nature are too overpowering for him to deal with—since he falls by the wayside because life is meaningless or because he is a purposeless bundle of atoms thrown haphazardly into the dark emptiness of space—nothing remains but to communicate, seemingly at random, whatever the writer's sensibility brings to the surface at the moment. The ultimate refinement—some would say the *reductio ad absurdum*—was the surrealistic word sequences of James Joyce, Gertrude Stein and E. E. Cummings. A not unsympathetic writer said that Gertrude Stein, in using words for pure purposes of suggestion, had "gone so far that she no longer even suggests." It was a criticism which applied more generally. Of Schönberg similarly it was said that his music had "become so abstract, so individual and so divorced from all relation to humanity as to be almost unintelligible." Some of the greatest artists, sensing that they were heading for a dead end, drew back. Stravinsky, for example, recoiled after 1923 from his early "dynamism" to neo-classicism; Picasso quickly returned from his "adventures on the borderline of the impossible" and refused to be bound by any single formula. But, in general, there was an evident tendency for art to degenerate into a mannerism, and for artists and writers to break up into coteries whose thoughts were too esoteric to strike a responsive chord.

For the most part the experimentation which was characteristic of the first half of the twentieth century failed to arrive at positive results; certainly it failed to produce a new synthesis. It would be a mistake to take this failure too tragically. Many of the writers and artists of the period were frankly destructive in purpose and had no ambition to build anew; their object was simply to clear the ground and break with the past. The result nevertheless is that much of their work has retained only historical interest. This is true in the main, for example, of the bitter social comment of the German expressionists, and of writers such as Heinrich Mann and Ernst

Toller, who were closely associated with them. For the rest, the attempts in the first thirty years of the twentieth century to make the necessary adjustments to the new world that was arising, never quite succeeded. It is an observation which has been made, for example, with specific reference to Rilke. "His attempts to adjust himself to the new world," it has been said, "have a moving helplessness in a poem like the *Sonette an Orpheus,* an alienating helplessness in the *Elegien.*" In any case, what we note about his work today is its irrelevance to the contemporary world.

In this respect Rilke was in no way a solitary exception. Symbolism and expressionism also failed to maintain their hold. As Kafka said, symbols are "of no use in daily life, which is the only life we have"; they "merely express the fact that the incomprehensible is incomprehensible, and we knew that already." As for the revolt against the machine age, against the dreary desolation of *The Waste Land,* against the whole encroaching advance of standardized civilization, which was a recurrent theme from Baudelaire to Verhaeren and García Lorca, what was it but an inverted romanticism, a failure to come to terms with inescapable facts, a futile protest, comprehensible at the time but necessarily transient? Certainly it was foreign to a generation aware that industrialism had become the basis of the only society they would ever experience.

Equally marked was the failure of the prevailing artistic and literary modes to bridge the gap to the scientific and technical revolution which was the most distinctive feature of the age. This was not contradicted by the acute consciousness of the changing connotations of reality in Eliot's later writing—in *Burnt Norton* (1935), for example, or in *The Dry Salvages* (1941)—or in cubist and abstract painting. No one would deny that here and elsewhere there are overtones of modern scientific theory. But of the positive effects of natural science in changing the face of the world and the whole condition of our lives, little was assimilated. C. P. Snow noted the slowness of novelists, in America and elsewhere, in coming to terms with the facts of modern industrial society. More fundamentally, no poet emerged capable of expressing the basic concepts of modern science, as Lucretius did with those of Democritus or Pope with Newtonian physics.

The position was summed up by a scientist writing in the early months of the Second World War, and looking back over the inter-war years. "All the cultural activities of our epoch," he wrote—

have failed in their main function. Neither painting nor literature has been able to arrive at a point of view positive and definite enough to be worth even considering as a basis for a new society. They have been very useful; they have cleared away a lot of mess which everyone wanted to see the last of; they have indicated, rather hazily, the direction in which a new outlook on the world might be found; but they have not drawn the curtains and enabled us to look through on to a promised land.

After 1945 there was a considerable shift of ground. The preoccupations of the inter-war years, remote from those of the nineteenth century, were almost equally remote from those of the post-war world. It was not so much that they were rejected as that they were left behind. The incessant speculation of Eliot and Valéry as to what constitutes poetry, what function it performs, whether there is any point in writing it, no longer aroused the same interest. Proust's introspective world of the private imagination had been so thoroughly explored and exploited that its possibilities seemed to have been exhausted. And the mood of pessimism and despair and resignation, of wandering helplessly without moorings in a world without hope, had worn thin. Perhaps its last great expression, written in 1952 under the shadow of the atom-bomb, was Beckett's *Waiting for Godot,* in which the two protagonists waited helplessly in a desolate world for the moment when "all will vanish and we'll be alone again, in the midst of nothingness."

Waiting for Godot was the end of the chapter which opened with Kafka's *The Castle.* Ten years later, when the hydrogen-bomb had become almost as familiar as the kitchen-table, people had learnt, or had begun to learn, to accept the incertitudes of the new world as a part of life. If the dominant intellectual personality of the decade after 1945 was Camus, whose message was the negative one of revolt, the typical figure in the following decade was Brecht, whose work presupposed a universe of relative values, where there were neither heroes nor saints, but in which human life had as its purpose to overcome the precarious and provisional state of human society. A similar attitude was reflected in the existentialist philosophy of Heidegger, Jaspers and Sartre, the only widely influential philosophy of the period. Here also was an attempt to break away from the negative approach characteristic of the logical positivists. Existentialism, indeed, admitted no transcendental values; the individual was alone, but he was alone among others, involved in a situation which, although he had no hand in its creation, could not be avoided by escaping, like the symbolists, into a private inner world. The adjustment of Sartre's thinking, in the short span between *Huis clos* (1944) and *Les chemins de la liberté* (1945), can be taken as the measure of a basic change in human attitudes, a shift away from the standpoint of the individual conscience to one in which the individual is absorbed in a social reality that is intensified by the accelerating rhythm of new technical processes.

Among the factors which brought about this change in point of view was the progress of sociology and the permeation of thought at all levels by notions derived from sociological investigation. Sociology taught that the group, not the individual, was the basic unit of society. It no longer started with the individual as the central concept in terms of which society must be explained, and it saw in group patterns of behaviour the norm which determined individual action. It is possible to question the social consequences of such views—they have been castigated in the United States by writers such as W. H. Whyte—but not their effectiveness. Their importance lay in the stimulus they gave to the shift, which was already taking place, from an egocentric and ultimately tedious preoccupation with the individual's personal fate and the malady of the European soul to the problems arising out of social relationships within the new, technical, industrial mass societies into which the changes of the last sixty or seventy years had plunged the world. The literature of protest and revolt—the characteristic product of an old order in decline—seemed to have shot its bolt, and a movement began away from subjectivity in the direction of objectivity. Writers of the new generation—Robbe-Grillet for example—side-stepped the old labyrinth of introspection, seeking instead to show that the world "quite simply *is*." Poets and artists who echoed Valéry's "je ne suis curieux que de ma seule essence," ceased to be typical; and people turned instead to the question whether, in spite of its complexity and the strains it imposed, it was possible to come to terms with industrial society, and whether, if this attempt failed, the existence of a few masterpieces, however refined or polished, would be sufficient to make life worth living, even for the minority in a position to enjoy them. They turned also to the question, thrust on them by social change and the spread of literacy, of the "reintegration of art with the common life of society."

The question of art and society, or of culture and civilization, was not new. It had been argued and debated ever since the Industrial Revolution. But it acquired a new dimension when the results of the introduction of universal compulsory education, as it became general in the period after 1870, began to be felt. By the beginning of the nineteen-thirties the question had become the preoccupation of a generation. It had two sides: first, whether culture could survive in the new social environment, and, secondly, whether society could survive without the binding force of a "common culture."

For anyone looking back over the subsequent controversies the main impression left is one of sterility, and for that reason little would be gained by following their course in detail. The prevailing mood was largely pessimistic. Mass civilization, it was commonly asserted, was incompatible with culture. Culture was the work of minorities, and the domination of the masses, in conjunction with "levelling," standardization and commercialization, implied the decline of civilization to the level of dull, mechanical uniformity. "Civilization and culture," F. R. Leavis wrote in 1930, "are coming

GEOFFREY BARRACLOUGH

to be antithetical terms," and Yeats foresaw "the ever increasing separation from the community as a whole of the cultivated classes." Writers and artists recoiled from the empty façade of urban life and the routine of mechanical civilization, believing with Yeats that the world of science and politics was somehow fatal to the poetic vision. Science, I. A. Richards declared, had deprived man of his spiritual heritage; a God who was subject to the theory of relativity could not be expected to provide inspiration for the poet. But the main burden of complaint, expressed with particular force by T. S. Eliot, was that "mass-culture" would always be a "substitute-culture" and that in every mass society there was a "steady influence which operates silently . . . for the depression of standards."

This cultural pessimism, which reached its peak in A. J. Toynbee's *Study of History*—particularly in the ninth volume (1954) with its gloomy lament for the ills of western civilization—was comprehensible as a reaction against the complacent assumption, common among liberal-minded intellectuals at the beginning of the century, that the spread of literacy would automatically bring about the dissemination of the existing culture through the whole of society. There was never any reason why it should. The expectation that the newly activated classes would simply absorb the literary, artistic and moral standards of the old was contrary to all historical experience. But the assumption that the breakdown of the prevailing scheme of values under the impact of social change was the same thing as the decline of all culture, was not very plausible either. It was easy to accuse the masses of indifference to serious literary and artistic activities and to blame them for the alleged gap between culture and civilization; but it was equally important to ask whether artists and writers had anything to say that was relevant to the new audience, or whether they had lost touch, in their idiom and values, with changing social realities. No one denied that there was a vast public (not necessarily of one class) devoted to trivial entertainment, commercialized art, escapist writing and cheap music; but this was not peculiar to modern society and its existence proved nothing. What was certain, on the other hand, was that the new public, which the spread of literacy had created on a world-wide scale, was different in its tastes and preoccupations from the fairly homogeneous educated *élite* to which writers and artists had hitherto addressed themselves. Its social background was far wider and the problems which attracted its attention were no longer those which had attracted attention in the minority culture of the past. When Jimmy Porter said contemptuously that he had written a poem "soaked in the theology of Dante, with a good slosh of Eliot as well," he was speaking for a generation for which the rarefied aesthetic values of the thirties were portentous bunk.

The emergence of literary and artistic forms capable of expressing the results of half a century of rapid social change was retarded —and is still in many respects retarded—by persistent attempts to salvage remnants of the old culture by grafting them on to "the new world of technological anonymity." It was held back also by the dislocation and restrictions and frustration which typified the aftermath of the Second World War. But from about 1955 a breakthrough on a wide front was apparent. It was marked in England by Osborne's *Look Back in Anger* (1956), in its way as characteristic an expression of a new social situation as *A Doll's House* had been in 1879 or *The Cherry Orchard* in 1904. It had already been expressed, almost a decade earlier, in the neo-realism of the Italian cinema. In 1958 it invaded the British cinema, which turned its back on the conventions of pre-war middle-class life and set out to investigate the social landscape of factory and public house, back-to-back cottages and Saturday nights and Sunday mornings. It was not great art, perhaps, and it degenerated too easily into clichés; but it was relevant art. It reflected a basic shift in class structure and was concerned with problems, such as the strain of human relationships in a society lacking the traditional bonds, which were identifiably "contemporary." It was, perhaps, not accidental that the media which first sought to come to terms with the new realities were the cinema, the novel and the drama. Architecture, under the inspiration of Frank Lloyd Wright and

Walter Gropius, had already discovered forms of expression which were functionally adapted to a technological age; indeed, it might be held—in spite of the rapid commercialization and debasement of the new styles—that it was architecture which took the lead. Great projects of civil engineering such as the Rockefeller Center in New York, or the vast interlacing elevated motorways of cities such as Los Angeles, expressed with precision the "spirit"—as well as the potentialities and limitations—of the new technological civilization. The classical forms of artistic expression—except perhaps music—experienced greater difficulty in bridging the gap and finding a new idiom. Poetry, in particular, with its intensely personal world, had difficulty in, reaching a new audience; in western Europe at least, it seemed by the end of the Second World War as though it had exhausted its resources. But elsewhere—in Spanish America, for example—there were signs of a new beginning, and in Russia after Stalin a new phase commenced. As Isaac Deutscher has pointed out, whatever his literary merits, Pasternak spoke for a generation which was "making its exit" and whose attitude towards life was not that of younger people: Yevtushenko represented the emergence of a new outlook on the world.

These few indications of the breakthrough of new attitudes, inadequate though they are, suggest at least the basic nature of the change—namely, from a negative to a positive reaction and from rejection of technological civilization as incompatible with culture to acceptance of its challenge. This did not imply affirmation of the new society, in the sense in which affirmation was demanded of artists in the Soviet Union—with stultifying results—in the Stalinist period, but it did imply recognition of its inescapability. In this sense it is legitimate—provided we ignore the Stalinist overtones attached to the phrase—to speak of a return to social realism. It was accompanied by a change of idiom. The reason was not merely that there was no longer a public capable of appreciating the allusive verse of T. S. Eliot, to understand which even the select and sophisticated audience to which it was addressed had to be provided with a glossary. Rather it was because the content and style of life of modern society was no longer directly related to the old poetic methods, because the new generation saw, heard and associated differently from its predecessors. How, asked Brecht, when immense innovations were being wrought on all sides, could artists hope to portray them, if they were limited to the old means of art? The result, without doubt—in this the pessimists who lamented the decline of the old values were right—was a revulsion against traditional humanism and the personality cult which lay at its core. The crisis through which society had passed, Romano Guardini pointed out, was due at least in part to the fact that "it received its historical imprint from the attitudes of a personality cult" which was no longer relevant. When the rise of a technological civilization brought new sociological types to the fore the preconditions changed. People were no longer prepared to accept unquestioningly the old assumption that "the autonomous subject is the measure of human perfection," and culture, in the sense in which it had been understood through modern history, ceased to be regarded as "a dependable rule for action."

By the end of the nineteenth century the impact of technology was changing the face of the world, but its effects on basic human attitudes were negligible. No creation of the human mind was more original than modern mathematics, but it by-passed the cultured classes and only a narrow circle of specialists troubled to learn its language. Even thirty years later European culture was still under the thrall of humanist traditions and literary values established under totally different conditions at the time of the Renaissance. Then, at last, in the decade spanning the Second World War a generation inspired by the potentialities of science and technology broke through the humanist barrier and took possession of the field. It was an irreversible victory. It implied the emergence of new criteria, linked to the great task, which science had set itself, of subduing nature and dominating the universe. Because the demands this task made on humanity were so immense, they called for a new scale of values. Atomic research, space programmes and comparable projects were far less a result of individual initiative than of overall planning and a combination of skills which could only be achieved by teamwork—that is to say, if people were ready to accept a measure of discipline and conformity formerly rejected as incompatible with human dignity. The result was a new attitude to man's place in the universe. Naturally, the old intractable problem of the individual and his relations with the world around him was not disposed of—how could it ever be?—but it was put in a new context. In Hoyle's expanding universe the underlying anthropomorphism of the humanist tradition ceased to be credible, and with it the old personality cult. People no longer imbued liberty of external action or freedom of internal judgement with the same transcendent value as in the past, or aspired in the same way to live their lives according to principles uniquely their own. They knew that, in the complex, highly articulated society in which we live, the old individualistic ethic no longer provides relevant standards and that solidarity, co-operation and comradeship are at least as important. "When all other substantial values have disintegrated," Guardini has said, "comradeship remains"; in the new society which has emerged at the end of the long transition from modern to contemporary history "it will be the supreme human value."

If we wish to measure the impact of the change in human attitudes I have attempted to sketch—a change consequential upon acceptance of the social implications of science and technology—it is important to realize that, like so much else in the contemporary world, it is not confined to Europe. Indeed, it might be true to say that the most significant aspect of the new outlook is its worldwide character. This is a consequence, in the last analysis, of the spread of industrialization, town-life, mass production and modern forms of communications, as a result of which the basic features of technological civilization, once regarded as characteristic of western Europe and North America, are rapidly becoming universal. The potential consequences of these changes, and at the same time of the spread of literacy, have as yet scarcely been grasped. Fifty years ago, the significant artistic and cultural movements radiated from Europe; today, as a result of the rapid spread of literacy and education, this has ceased to be the case. Already in the years between the First and Second World Wars, the United States had asserted a new pre-eminence in the English-speaking world, and it was American writers such as Faulkner and Hemingway who set the pace. More recently, this process of diversification has gone further, and we can see the beginnings of significant literary movements in Latin America, Africa and elsewhere. In other fields the newly rising countries are already moving ahead. The great Mexican school of painting, represented by Siqueiros, Orozco and Rivera, had already made its impact before the Second World War; Japan has won a place of distinction in the art of the cinema; and in town-planning and architecture cities such as Rio de Janeiro, São Paulo and Brasilia are unsurpassed anywhere in the world.

These developments are, of course, still at their beginning; but they are a sufficient indication that social change, however profound, may be a sign of renewal, not of collapse. As Alfred Weber has pointed out, it is simply not true, "despite all ideas to the contrary," that the industrial worker in the United States or in England has been "depersonalized," and the transformation, in barely more than a generation, of the Russian *muzhik* into a receptive, skilful, self-respecting industrial worker, with an immense appetite for literature, indicates the enormous human potentialities that lie to hand. Today we have to reckon with a similar transformation of the working classes in China, Africa, Egypt and elsewhere. What is clear is that, for none of these newly awakened peoples, is the traditional culture—either their own or that of western Europe—a sufficient answer. Even in western Europe the old literary culture, with its intensely personal preoccupations, touched the life of ordinary people at too few points; their whole scale of values was based not on individual but on group activity—on the companionship of office and workshop, the inescapable closeness of the family unit, the enjoyment of leisure in the company of others—and a social ethic which idealized individuality bore little relation to the facts of their experience. The same is even more clearly

233

true of the newly emancipated and literate workers elsewhere. Speculations and preoccupations of the type with which European writers and artists have tended to deal are alien to their experience; existentialism, with its anguish, its *néant* and its *nausée,* has little connexion, as a Mexican writer has pointed out, with American realities. On these lines it would be illusory to expect a "reintegration of art with the common life of society." But the changes outlined above indicate that a turning-point has been reached and that the gulf between cultural and social development, which had been growing wider ever since the Industrial Revolution, is again closing. With the new social awareness, the shift from the individual in isolation to the individual in society, and above all the change of viewpoint from "We" and "They" to "Us," some of the most stubborn obstacles have been removed. At the same time, they have provided the basis for a civilization which, without losing its specific national and regional modes of expression, is truly universal in its connotations.

As late as 1959 C. P. Snow could still maintain that, whereas "the scientists have the future in their bones," "the traditional culture responds by wishing the future did not exist." When we consider how recently most of the changes which distinguish the contemporary world have become plainly visible, this time-lag should not be surprising. Consciousness and interpretation cannot precede creation. Eventually we may expect that art and literature will interpret the "myth" of the contemporary age, and give expression to its beliefs and way of life. But just as their themes will be new, so also we must expect that they will reflect the change in the balance of world forces which is the clearest outcome of the events of the first half of the twentieth century. It is often argued that Europe, while losing its political hegemony, has retained and will continue to retain its cultural leadership; but this idea, though widely propagated, has little basis in fact. One of the most significant features of the contemporary age is the stimulus which the revolutions of the twentieth century, liberating them from their bonds to the past, to sterile forms and traditional themes, has given to the artistic and cultural life of other continents. Whereas by 1939 the poetry of most western countries was showing evident signs of exhaustion, new impulses were awakening in Asia, in Africa and in Latin America. This evidence of cultural renewal on a world-wide scale is one of the most significant aspects of the contemporary scene.

It is only possible to give the barest indication of the scope and impact of the new cultural movements. They were usually associated—as the birth of European literature had been associated centuries earlier—with the vernacular; and they were influenced without exception by European forms and the stimulus of European ideas. This response to European influences—often but not exclusively to those of the French symbolists—has been variously assessed and interpreted, frequently in the sense that all that has emerged is a pale, imitative version of European models, severed from native tradition. Anyone aware of the degree to which European literature at the time of the Renaissance and earlier was dependent for its forms and subject-matter on classical models will hesitate before accepting this evaluation. In reality, as Sir Hamilton Gibb has said of modern Arabic literature, "the problem has very little to do with deliberate imitation of the west." This statement may be interpreted more generally. "What the foreign examples did," an American writer has said of Japan, "was to afford the Japanese the means of expressing their new ideas and their consciousness of being men of the enlightened Meiji era"; but "unless the Japanese had felt a need to create a new literature, no amount of foreign influence would have mattered." Even so, it is undeniably true, in all the countries that came under the impact of the west, that most early writing was derivative and of small intrinsic literary merit. This applied not only to the first stirrings of new currents in Arabic literature in the nineteenth century; it was true also of Japanese writing before the great period of creativity between 1905 and 1915, and of early Anglo-Ceylonese literature which moved "with occasional pleasant detours through an imitation of English models to an inevitable dead end." But these, as

Sir Hamilton Gibb has written, were the "precursors," and their importance lies less in what they achieved than in the influence they exerted and the new currents they set in motion. Before long a new stage was reached. It occurred in South America, for example, around 1925, when the search began "for an artistic expression that should be our own and not subservient to Europe;" and in Japan the publication of Nagai Kafu's *The River Sumida* in 1909 has been picked out as marking the transition "from a period when European works were slavishly imitated to one when an awareness and receptivity to them was not permitted to blot out the native heritage."

What the new literary movements of Asia acquired from the west—including Russia—was, above all else, a model for a flexible idiom, through which to express the thoughts and ideals of modern civilization. It was here, in the liberation from obsolete images and rigid conventions, that the western impact was strongest. Everywhere in the east the old literary style—involved, periphrastic and obscure—was out of touch with present reality; it was the creation of a small *élite,* a mystery in which only the scholastically educated might participate, but above all else it lacked the resources to express the thoughts and ideals of modern society, walling them off instead in a separate compartment dividing art from life. Even the syntax required to be adjusted to meet modern methods of reasonings and feeling. The Egyptian writer, Husayn Haykal, for example, explained bitterly in 1927 his feeling of rebellion when he was unable to express in his own language what he felt in his heart and instead found the appropriate English or French expressions forming in his mind. The result everywhere was a revolt—resisted by conservatives and traditionalists—against the old literary forms and, particularly where, as in China or the Moslem world, the literary language was no longer the language of everyday speech, a deliberate use of the colloquial or vernacular idiom as the only appropriate vehicle for fresh ideas. This turning to the vernacular began early in Egypt and was continued by writers elsewhere in the Arab world, such as the Iraqi, Abd al-Malek Nouri. But it was in China that the issues were most clearly formulated. Here the Hsin ching-nien group, the "new youth" who gathered round Chen Tu-hsiu and Hu Shih in 1916 and 1917, inaugurated a cultural revolution the importance of which it would be hard to exaggerate. One writer, indeed, has gone so far as to suggest that, for the historian of the future, it may turn out to be a more significant event in Chinese history than many of the political revolutions in which historians have sought the clues to recent developments.

The literary revolution in China epitomizes the changes which underlie the cultural revival in the extra-European world. The essential point is that literary reform was part of the national awakening; indeed, it could be said that it was the most important part because, as Chen Tu-hsiu wrote, "purely political revolution" —since it brought no change in the fields of ethics, morality, literature and the fine arts—was "incapable of changing our society." Hu Shih denounced literary Chinese as a dead language because it was "no longer spoken by the people." It had decayed because of "over-emphasis on style at the expense of spirit and reality." Furthermore the theory on which classical Chinese literature was based—namely, that its purpose was "to convey the tao" (i.e. moral principles)—was too restrictive. Huang Yuan-yung had already set out that what was necessary was "to bring Chinese thought into direct contact with the contemporary thought of the world" in order to "accelerate its radical awakening"; and, he added, "we must see to it that the basic ideals of world thought must be related to the life of the average man." Hence the emphasis on the vernacular as the medium for creating a living literature, and hence also the three aims of the literary revolution which Chen formulated as follows—

1. To overthrow the painted, powdered and obsequious literature of the aristocratic few, and to create the plain, simple and expressive literature of the people.

237

GEOFFREY BARRACLOUGH

2. To overthrow the stereotyped and over-ornamental literature of classicism and to create the fresh and sincere literature of realism.

3. To overthrow the pedantic, unintelligible and obscurantist literature of the hermit and recluse, and to create the plain-speaking and popular literature of society in general.

The years 1918 and 1919, the years of revolutionary ferment which found an outlet in the Fourth of May movement, were the time when Chen's principles were put into effect. "After 1919," Hu Shih was later to write, "vernacular literature spread as though it wore seven-league boots." And with it spread a new social consciousness and a new attitude to China's problems. Its effects were reinforced after 1921 by the work of a new organization, the Society for Literary Studies, which undertook on a major scale the translation of western writing, particularly the literature of the "oppressed peoples." The result was the collapse of the archaic literary language and the old stereotyped literary forms. Henceforward creative writing in China was modelled upon the literature of the west and had little or no connexion with the Chinese classics. But the significant effects of the western impact were not literary but social. The new horizons revealed by western literature, the comparisons which it made possible, were a potent factor in opening the eyes of the new generation to the realities of the Chinese social scene. By 1925 the early tendency, which contact with western literature had stimulated, to individualism, pessimism, the expression of personal feeling and "art for art's sake" was collapsing, the social aspects of literature were in the ascendant, the prevalent mood, fostered by the new literary figure, Mao Tun (b. 1896), was against aestheticism and towards realism. The spirit of the age, Mao announced, impelled the writer to the search for social truth; the thoughts and feelings which he expressed "must be common to the masses, common to the whole of mankind, and not just to the writer himself."

In all these respects the course of development in China was representative of what was happening elsewhere. European influ-

238

ences provided the original literary stimulus; but very soon the impact of national, social and religious movements in the countries concerned transformed the new literature from a derivative literary mode into a vehicle for expressing a new social situation. This was the case, for example, with the Tamil novel in Ceylon. What western models provided was not content but "vigour of thought and congruence with the present." In India, as Pannikar has said, it was "not Europe" but "the New Life" that was echoed in the new writing—in "poetry and prose in which the conditions of our existence are constantly related to the extreme limit of possibilities." A similar development had already occurred in Spanish America. Here the *modernistas,* disciples of the French symbolists, who withdrew from politics and devoted themselves to "pure" literature, were superseded between 1918 and 1922 by writers and painters who strove to relate their art to the social movements of their countries. With poets such as the Chilean, Pablo Neruda (b. 1904), and the Mexican, Octavio Paz (b. 1914), Spanish-American writing asserted its independent status. From about 1920 it was occupied with specifically Spanish-American problems, the fight with the jungle, the stresses and clashes of conditions unknown in Europe, and particularly the social problems of the negro and the Indian—"Indio que labras con fatiga tierras que de otros dueños son," in the words of the Peruvian poet, José Santos Chocano. From around 1925 a poetry of negro life, destined to have echoes in Africa, appeared in Puerto Rico and Cuba, a poetry of immense beauty which—for example, in the works of Nicolás Guillén—expressed the dilemma of the black man condemned to a permanent state of exile, lacking a tribal name, lacking a tolerated religion, lacking a recognized culture of his own and without power or influence in the new mixed societies that had been built upon his labour.

It was not only Spanish-American literature which was remarkable, as it threw off its dependence on European models, for its social realism, its intense concern with the desperate problems of society. We find the same characteristic, utterly distinct from the prevalent mood of western writing in the 1930s, at the same period in China and Japan, and in India it became dominant through the influence of the Progressive Writers' Association, founded in 1935. In the Arab world the Egyptian modernists were inspired by the conviction that "a literary revival, reflecting a revolution in the ideas and outlook of the people, is a necessary preliminary to a full revival of national life." Their aim, in the words of Abbas Mahmud al-Aqqad, was not to create an intellectual culture, "a culture of decadence and mere words," but a natural culture, "a culture of progress." And, finally, the same profound social and political commitment was a potent element in the poetry of Africa—in Sartre's estimation "the true revolutionary poetry of our time"—as it awakened under the impact of the West Indians, Aimé Césaire and Léon Damas, and found full expression in Léopold Senghor's epoch-making volume of 1948, the *Anthologie de la nouvelle poésie nègre et malgache*.

Here also, particularly in French Africa, we are brought face to face with the pattern already familiar in Asia and north of the Sahara—the use of forms and images of European origin to express ideas and sentiments profoundly un-European and often anti-European in content. Technically writers like Senghor or the Madagascan poet Rabéarivelo stand in the tradition of French symbolism, just as Césaire makes superb use of the surrealist idiom; but behind a similarity of form was a different experience—the great experience of an historic awakening at a time when European poetry was haunted by the disintegration of the old way of life. The themes of Senghor and his fellows were "the bitter taste of liberty," "the beating of the dark pulse of Africa in the mist of lost villages." The European cultural revolution, in short, was met by an African cultural counter-revolution, a rediscovery and reassertion of African values, expressed by poets such as David Diop in the theme of *négritude*—

> Souffre, pauvre Nègre,
> Nègre noir comme la Misère,

The Change in Human Attitudes

—and its contempt for the white world—

Listen to the white world
how it resents its great efforts
how their protest is broken under the rigid stars
how their steel blue speed is paralysed in the mystery of the flesh.
Listen how their defeats sound from their victories.
Listen to the lamentable stumbling in the great alibis.
Mercy! mercy for our omniscient naïve conquerors.
Hurrah for those who never invented anything
hurrah for those who never explored anything
hurrah for those who never conquered anything
hurrah for joy
hurrah for love
hurrah for the pain of incarnate tears.

The themes of *négritude* and protest are not, of course, the sole content of African writing. The problem of Africa, as the Ghanaian poet, Michael Dei-Aneng, has pointed out, is that of a continent "poised between two civilizations," and admits of no simple answer. But its impact is such that writers and artists of every category—"believers and atheists, Christians, Moslems and Communists alike," as Alioun Diop once expressed it—"are all more or less committed." This is the distinctive feature of the resurgent literature of Asia and South America, as well as of Africa; their writers and artists are engaged in bringing out all that they can contribute to the building up of a new civilization. They know that what they are expressing is not the feeling of the people as a whole, but the views of a minority who are striving to interpret the events of the present for the people; but it is precisely in this that they see their contribution to the future.

Taken as a whole, the literary evidence shows remarkable consistency. In the Far East and the Middle East, north of the Sahara and south of the Sahara, on the Amazon and the Rio de la Plata and in the lands of the Andes, it brings before us new peoples arising, new energies seeking expression, a definite view of life set in conscious counterpoint to that of Europe. African poetry is strikingly free from the element of *Kulturmüdigkeit,* or weary disillusion, which settled like a blight in the previous generation on European writing. Is that phase now a thing of the past in Europe also? If, as I have suggested, European literature and art have also made their peace with the new civilization of machinery and technology and the "common man," if the mood of rejection and resignation has been followed by a mood of affirmation and the exploration of the new potentialities which science has opened up, then it may not be illusory to look forward to the synthesis which still eludes us—the "development of a common culture" and "the reintegration of art with the common life of society." But its basis, and the experience it reflects, will be far wider than ever before; the answers will be given "by humanity as a whole—not one country or one city, as in the past." Here the literary and artistic evidence is unequivocal. The European age—the age which extended from 1492 to 1947—is over, and with it the predominance of the old European scale of values. Literature, like politics, has broken through its European bonds, and the civilization of the future . . . is taking shape as a world civilization in which all the continents will play their part.

Suggestions for Further Reading

DAICHES, DAVID, *The Novel and the Modern World,* rev. ed. Chicago: University of Chicago Press, 1960.

GUARDINI, ROMANO. *The End of the Modern World.* London: Sheed and Ward, 1957.

HELLER, ERIC, *The Disinherited Mind: Essays in Modern German Literature and Thought.* Cambridge, England: Bowes and Bowes, 1952.

SNOW, C. P., *The Two Cultures and the Scientific Revolution.* Cambridge, England: The University Press, 1959.

The Change in Human Attitudes

SYPHER, WYLIE, *Rococo to Cubism in Art and Literature.* New
York: Random House, Inc., 1960.

WEBER, ALFRED, *Farewell to European History.* London: Kegan
Paul, Trench, and Trubner, 1948.